Margaret

PRINCESS WITHOUT A CAUSE

Also by Willi Frischauer

Margaret

PRINCESS WITHOUT A CAUSE

Willi Frischauer

London
MICHAEL JOSEPH

First published in Great Britain by Michael Joseph Ltd
52 Bedford Square, London WC1B 3EF
1977

ISBN 0 7181 1611 9

Set and printed in Great Britain by
Tonbridge Printers Ltd, Peach Hall Works, Tonbridge, Kent
in Baskerville eleven on twelve point on paper supplied by
P. F. Bingham Ltd, and bound by Redwood Burn
at Esher, Surrey

LIST OF ILLUSTRATIONS

All pictures by permission of Popperfoto except
the last, which is from Keystone Press Agency.

INTRODUCTION

Almost everything written about a royal person on any level perpetuates some myth or avoids inconvenient aspects, however significant. This need not be so. One can combine a deep appreciation of the British monarchy as a stable political factor in an unsettled world (and a very high regard for the Queen) with a rational, critical and frank approach to members of the royal family. This is the spirit in which I have dealt extensively with the break-up of Princess Margaret's marriage – this sort of thing is not often done in royal circles – and the strange settings and characters on which it has thrown the limelight. They tell something about the Princess. My aim was to be searching without being offensive or intrusive although I have set my own permissible limits rather than accept the outdated standards of the hyper-sensitive.

I was determined to keep my head above the deluge of loyal sludge that threatened to swamp my judgment and to keep a sharp ear for informed whispers which accompany the Princess's every step. I have talked to a great many people, some very close to her – at one point I was up against the old problem that those who talk don't know and those who know don't talk, but, in the event, both, friends and foes, were very forthcoming if equally anxious to preserve their anonymity.

To sail a middle course between the sycophancy of courtiers and the back-biting of detractors – Princess Margaret has stepped on too many toes to be lacking in those – was the task I have set myself. I understand her a good deal better than I did before I started in search of her, and *tout comprendre c'est tout pardonner* – well, almost all.

Willi Frischauer, London 1977

7

CHAPTER ONE

In her young days she was 'P2' at the Palace, she is 'Yvonne' in 'Private Eye', 'Ma'am' to all but her closest friends whom she tells: 'Call me "M"!' To her husband she used to be 'Ducky', Germans refer to her as 'Margaret Rose' and Americans as 'Meg' except for Danny Kaye who calls her 'Honey'. When her nephew was born she wondered whether she would become known as 'Charley's Aunt'. She is Her Royal Highness, Princess Margaret, Countess of Snowdon, only sister of the Queen.

Not only is she the most intelligent of the royals but highly intelligent by any standard. With a sharp tongue, a sensitive antenna for a comic situation, she is a great, often malicious, mimic and a fine musician. She sings and plays the piano well but hearing her you wonder whether the late Noel Coward was not over-generous in saying that she could have earned her living on the stage. Her friends at any rate would have been enthusiastic paying customers.

Reactions to her vary widely. She has been rudely criticised and venerated in turn. In Portugal some youthful Walter Raleighs trailed their coats in the mud before her – such homage leaves a psychological imprint which never fades. But when the quality of the British monarchy was discussed *à propos* the scandal around Prince Bernhard of the Netherlands, *Die Welt* of Hamburg wondered how much damage Margaret's 'fatal extravaganzas' had done to the prestige of the British crown. She had pursued her erratic course irrespective of public reaction, a stickler for etiquette one day ('You mean, His Majesty the King,' she rebuked an associate who rashly referred

9

to 'your father'), a rebel the next: 'Disobedience is my joy!' she confided to Jean Cocteau.

She is temperamental and does not suffer fools gladly which makes life difficult for her (and others) since many of the people she meets in the line of duty are foolish or pompous or both. Margaret is a romantic and earthy at the same time: 'If she were Miss Smith,' one of her friends says, 'she would be a very sexy lady.' She is, she is, although traditionalists would rather bite off their tongues than talk of a royal princess and sex in the same breath. She is also what the French call *journalière* which means she can look most attractive on one occasion and dreadful on another. Those who know her best believe her appearance reflects her mood.

'Some people think we are not human...' said the delightful Queen Mum. Margaret's trouble is that she has always been too human. She has had a tumultuous private life but at the same time has demanded respect for her royal status – sometimes difficult to reconcile. She can be surprisingly flexible – strait-laced and relaxed within a few minutes. A good illustration is an incident a few years back when she danced with a young man who made a jocular remark about her whale-boned corsetry. She excused herself and returned a few minutes later: 'Try now!' she demanded and smiled as his hand came to rest on her unenclosed waist.

Attractive as she is, she is also crushingly overpowering and demanding of her companions, and as colourful and unpredictable as her uncle, Edward VIII, in his Prince of Wales days. There is no knowing what she will do next. At least one of her official guards took to drink (off-duty, of course) because of the strain of keeping up with her erratic habits: 'Only fifteen minutes' notice of a dinner outing in a, shall we say, unorthodox restaurant – fifteen minutes to check and make security arrangements!' If Margaret stands out among the royals, it is because the Queen, though more readily amused than her great-great-grandmother, imposes greater restraints on herself, and an all-consuming preoccupation with horses makes Princess Anne a celebrated sportswoman but hardly the world's most scintillating personality.

Margaret's interests are much wider and include her evident love of the theatre, ballet, opera, pop, and the stars of the performing arts many of whom she allows to greet her with a kiss on the cheek. One so honoured was Mick Jagger but when she went backstage to see him after the Rolling Stones' 1976 Earl's Court concert, the group's fans denounced their idols as social climbers fraternising with an ageing establishment figure. Margaret's critics saw it as another attempt at trendiness unbecoming to a princess of her age.

Such excursions into the contemporary sub-culture to which she was originally introduced by Lord Snowdon are only partly motivated by her quest for titillation in non-conventional areas; they stem as much from her natural, inquisitive curiosity which prompts her to ask many blunt questions, the answers to which she adds to her considerable store of knowledge. On her travels, official or holiday, she keeps her eyes open, records each day's events in her diary and quizzes companions about details or names which may have escaped her.

She has met most of the world's outstanding people and impressed many. One of her friends told me that she was rather proud when President Giscard d'Estaing let it be known how enchanted he was with her during his state visit to Britain. Not an unusual reaction among dignitaries of a certain age when confronted with her strident femininity.

Only a princess, albeit one no higher than five foot nothing, could walk tall among the gorgeous women in their *haute couture* gowns who had come from the four corners of the world to the château in the Ile St Louis, Paris, to attend the spectacular wedding reception of Prince Karim Aga Khan, the Ismaili leader, and his ravishing English bride Sarah, formerly Lady James Crichton-Stuart.

The wedding took place in October 1968 soon after I had completed Prince Karim's biography. It was on this occasion that I first encountered Princess Margaret who had flown in earlier in the day in the Aga Khan's jet, sent to London to bring her to Paris. She had brought along, not her husband, but two friends who had hitched a ride, the young Earl of Lichfield and Jocelyn Stevens. Patrick Lichfield, a cousin (on the Bowes-Lyon side), a 'royal' photographer like Tony Snowdon – they are rivals and not at ease with each other – was one of Margaret's regular 'escorts' : not long ago I saw her striding regally, actressy, aggressively, as she usually does, into an exhibition of Patrick's photographs as if to cock a snook at her husband.

The tall, personable, wealthy Jocelyn Stevens, now managing director of Beaverbrook Newspapers, used to publish *Queen* magazine which carried many of Tony's early fashion and stage photographs. Jocelyn was with the Princess when I came across her three years later at one of the grand parties his uncle and aunt, Sir Edward and Lady Hulton, give for their friends. Wherever she went, at home and abroad, Jocelyn became a regular fixture in Margaret's entourage. She is greatly attached to him because he is at once cleverer and more amusing than many of her friends, some of them grown-up 'Sloane Rangers' of both sexes, although she seeks out men and women (mostly men) of excellence. She frequently asks his advice but does not always follow it.

Jocelyn Stevens's wife, Jane, is one of Margaret's very charming ladies-in-waiting – that she chooses such pleasant people as companions reflects favourably on her. Much of her free time is spent with Jocelyn's sister, Prudence, and her husband, Sir Eric Penn, a member of the Queen's Household. Since Jocelyn's association with Tony was his badge of entry into the tight little group around Margaret, it testifies to his social dexterity that, with a few ups and downs, he has remained friends with both beyond their parting in 1976. He speaks of her with feeling which only thinly disguises a little awe.

But if the Stevens family enjoys the affections of the Princess, the Tennants are, if anything, fractionally closer to her. Colin Tennant, scion of an old Scottish clan, was a member of the 'Margaret Set' of the fifties and, like many other eligible young men around her, regarded as a hopeful suitor. Ever since, he has hovered unobtrusively in the background whenever she was grappling with emotional problems. His wife, Lady Anne Tennant, daughter of the Earl of Leicester, is another of Margaret's ladies-in-waiting.

Mostly, though, the Stevens and the Tennants are kept in separate compartments. Though Jocelyn and Jane Stevens have travelled with the Princess far and wide they have never been with her to her retreat on the Caribbean island of Mustique where she is more woman than princess. But while the final act of Margaret's marriage crisis was played out in Tennant's

Mustique (following the publication of some 'compromising' photographs of her from the island), the man the royal family called in and consulted on the official statement about the separation from her husband was Jocelyn Stevens.

Whether Roddy Llewellyn of the vegetable commune, sixteen years younger than Margaret, was cause or catalyst in the royal separation which threw up his name or just happened to be around at the time, he was but one of the many young men who have been linked with Margaret over the years. With the possible exception of Italian-born Princess Paola of Belgium, no royal princess has been credited, fairly or unfairly, with such a busy love life as Margaret; and every kind of circumlocution has been employed to paint her as a scarlet woman.

Her decision, in 1955, 'not to marry Group Captain Peter Townsend', a courtier and divorced man, as many years older than Margaret as Roddy is younger, was seen as the sad end of a passionate love affair. Ever since, observers of the royal scene have argued that her frustration and bitterness towards the intriguing events leading up to her renunciation of the man she loved were the things that launched her on the frantic quest for happiness which involved her in so many trials and errors.

It seems a plausible theory until one remembers that it leaves out of account the platoon of ex-Guards officers and aristocratic 'chinless wonders' (as they were called at the time) who 'escorted' her in the late forties and early fifties, many of them publicly exhibited by her as covers for Peter Townsend. In the words of the German poet – 'Who counts the numbers, names the names?' They included Lord Dalkeith, the (then) Marquess of Blandford, the Reverend Simon Phipps, Robin Douglas-Home and, running through her early life and loves like the proverbial red thread, the charming, wealthy but not healthy Billy Wallace, Tom Egerton and, of course, Colin Tennant. On the fringe of the noble suitors dwelt the clowns and acrobats – Danny Kaye, Rudolph Nureyev, Peter Sellers to whom fellow comic Spike Milligan publicly and in Margaret's presence addressed the warning : 'Wherever you are, whoever you be, please take your hands off the Princess's knee !'

Marriage to Antony Armstrong-Jones, a highly unlikely addition to the royal family, was, after a brief stab at respectability, like no other royal marriage before, and did not deter a new wave of close friends – Dominic Elliot, an earl's son, Patrick Lichfield, an earl in his own right, Derek Hart, the TV producer and associate of her husband, and later, the way-out vegetable-growing Roddy Llewellyn whom she continued to cultivate in defiance of public criticism. By doing so she proved, if proof was needed, that she truly belonged to the permissive age, a rebel princess without a cause but her own, an extraordinary phenomenon.

'All that gossip, the scandal, the lovers, and now messing around on the farm...' Simon Head, son of a former Tory Minister of War, was quoted as saying about Margaret's much-publicised visit to the Wiltshire commune where Llewellyn worked. Someone else speculated that the Queen may well loathe her brother-in-law for 'driving Margaret into the arms of other men'. It all culminated in the rather sweeping conclusion that throughout Margaret has been fatally fascinated by all the wrong people all her life.

Margaret was born where Macbeth lived (at Glamis Castle). Perhaps that is why I have often thought there was something Shakespearean about her.

As a rumbling thunder follows a flash of lightning, every royal crisis comes down to somebody or other growling that the state allowance for the Queen and her family be drastically cut or altogether abolished. Royal duties are scrutinised and related to the rate for the job. The matter is raised in the House of Commons, in the Press, in pubs and wine bars before the storm blows itself out and interest dies down – until the next time.

As a 'performing' member of the royal troupe, Princess Margaret receives an annual allowance of £50,000. What she does to earn or deserve it can best be judged by a glimpse at her official programme over a certain period, say in the months following the separation from her husband (and criticism of her royal role). The list includes a number of visits to places of entertainment some of which were highly enjoyable while others were almost unbearably tedious. Many fell into the same category ('good for business') as a pop star's opening a delicatessen for a goodly sum of under-the-counter tax-free cash, gave people pleasure or at least something to talk about or were vaguely 'good for morale' as, for instance, where the hosts were local authorities or military units. Margaret is bored by provincial worthies regaling her with loyal addresses – as who would not be – but enjoys lunching with a crowd of handsome officers in their mess.

Each visit required approval of extensive arrangements, briefing on subjects and personalities involved, preparations of little speeches on strange topics or answers to an official welcome. It needed some social contortions to squeeze private pursuits into the gaps although most trips around the country were made in aircraft of the Queen's Flight, and official functions on Fridays were often combined with weekend visits to friends in the area. Last-minute changes of plan were frowned upon – no lying in late when it suited her.

On the whole, the never-ending round has become second nature to Margaret. That she sometimes regards it as a burden emerged from the outburst of one of her friends who told me : 'If she misses a single appointment there is Hell to pay, reports in the papers, questions, complaints . . . Nobody cares whether she is indisposed. If she turns up dutifully, it is seldom mentioned except in the court circular.'

When the Queen resumed her official functions after her return from the Olympics in Montreal in 1976, Margaret took a short rest. After a week's absence from the public scene, she reappeared on the Queen Mother's seventy-sixth birthday on August 4th. High summer brought relief from the routine. While her children spent a fortnight with their father at his country cottage, Margaret went to unfashionable Majorca with her detective as her only companion but it so happened that Jocelyn and Jane Stevens also flew in that direction. The Princess lunched with the King and Queen of Spain but suffered another one of those social accidents to which she seems prone when the son of her Spanish hostess was involved in a tragic accident. The ensuing police investigation drove her away a week earlier than planned.

The Queen with Prince Philip and their four children went on a cruise to the Western Isles. Balmoral beckoned with the annual royal family reunion. For Margaret's children who were joining their mother for the rest of the school holidays it was good to renew their sense of belonging. For Margaret it was a time to mend fences and tighten up loose ends, prepare herself, at the end of a phase in her life, for a new beginning. Above all it was a return to the place of her Scottish origin.

CHAPTER TWO

Constantinople was renamed Istanbul,
Ras Tafari became Emperor of Abysinnia,
the R101 crashed, Mussolini demanded a
revision of the Versailles Treaty, Pilsudski
formed a government in Poland and there was
a revolt in Peru. Keynes's Treatise on
Money *was published, Harold Laski wrote*
Liberty and the Modern State, *Nazi*
philosopher Alfred Rosenberg The Myth
of the Twentieth Century, *Trotsky his*
autobiography, Evelyn Waugh Vile Bodies
and Erich Maria Remarque All Quiet on the
Western Front. *D. H. Lawrence died, Max*
Schmeling became world champion and
Amy Johnson flew solo from London to Australia.
Noel Coward's Private Lives *was staged and*
Marlene Dietrich became a star in The Blue
Angel. *Alfred Hitchcock made* Murder *and*
Don Bradman 334 runs for Australia in the
Leeds Test. The photo-flashbulb was
invented and Princess Margaret was born.
The year was 1930.

Scotland was a good place for Margaret to take stock. In
Scotland she felt at once more secure and more animated as if
these hills and glens still echoed with the elation which greeted
her birth at Glamis Castle, the ancestral seat of the Bowes-Lyons.

The splendid residence of the Earl of Strathmore, parts of it dated back to the tenth century, boasted a hairy-armed ghost, a history of monsters, gruesome family secrets (confided to heirs on their twenty-first birthday), a hangman's room in which two ancestors had committed suicide and the chamber where Macbeth murdered Duncan

The Earl's daughter, the diminutive Duchess of York (formerly Lady Elizabeth Bowes-Lyon) had been spending the summer at Glamis with 'Bertie', as the family called the Duke of York, and their daughter, four-year-old Elizabeth (Lilibet), when her second child demanded admittance to this world, a little awkwardly, it seems, since Sir Henry Simpson, an expert in Caesarian operations, was standing by.

A howling hurricane and driving rain did not dampen the enthusiasm of the locals when the arrival of the baby was announced late on Thursday, August 21st, 1930. The skirl of bagpipes sounded to celebrate the first royal birth in Scotland for three hundred years, and when the storm subsided old folks and young lads and lassies, as a contemporary report put it, gave themselves up to song and dance in the village square. But the pyre on Hunters Hill overlooking the castle was soaked with rain and it took a day before it could be lit and flames rose a hundred feet into the air to carry the message abroad. It was a right royal occasion for Scotland.

Dating back to an ancient attempt to present a 'strange' child as a royal baby, tradition and the law demanded the presence of an officer of the Crown at the birth of an infant in line of succession to the throne. Home Secretary J. R. Clynes, a Scot, greeted the little princess before Nurse Beevans took her back to her mother's bedside. Stuttering with excitement, Bertie called his father King George V at Sandringham to tell him the news. Queen Mary graciously welcomed her new grandchild. Little Lilibet, when told the following morning, clapped her hands with joy and demanded to see her sister. The shy, mild-mannered Duke was disappointed that his wife had not borne him a son the second time round but immediately took the baby to heart.

Having prepared to greet a future sailor prince, the Navy ordered gun salutes to be fired from naval vessels just the same but there was disappointment among Scots who had been hoping for another Bonnie Prince – Charlie or otherwise; others were angry when they found that the little princess would not be christened in Scotland but they were promised a name that would be popular north of the Border. The Yorks whisked the baby to their London town house at 145 Piccadilly, a residence modest by royal standards. The christening took place early in November at the Royal Chapel in Buckingham Palace. Performing the ceremony, Cosmo Gordon Lang, Archbishop of Canterbury, dipped his fingers into the lily-shaped, solid-gold font and sprinkled the infant's head with water from the River Jordan : 'Margaret Rose', he addressed the baby swathed in Queen Victoria's rich satin and lace christening robe, 'I baptise thee in the name . . .'

The Prince of Wales was the only member of the royal family not present but, a royal rebel he rarely was where he was supposed to be or did what he was expected to do. He must have been there in spirit because Margaret grew up to be more like him in outlook and temperament than any other member of the family. Presently, a new controversy flared up around her, this time about her ranking in the succession stakes. One suggestion – another Scottish ploy? – was that she should rank equal with her elder sister Elizabeth, the King's favourite grandchild. He would have none of it. Shortly after the christening, George V announced the order of succession. Heir to the throne – the Prince of Wales, followed (subject to change if he should have children) by the Duke of York. Next in line was Princess Elizabeth while Margaret Rose occupied fourth place ahead of the King's two younger sons, the Duke of Gloucester and Prince George, later Duke of Kent. If, however, Bertie and Elizabeth of York should have a third child, a son, that would again alter the pattern . . .

Succession seemed a long way away as the Yorks settled down to an almost bourgeois existence under the royal umbrella. The two girls occupied a nursery on the top floor where they kept their toys including a large collection of wooden horses of all shapes and sizes. Margaret's Scottish timbre was polished to a fine southern hue but a Scottish governess, Marion Crawford, the legendary 'Crawfie', who took charge of the children's education (after six p.m. a nurse and a couple of nursery maids took over), helped the little Duchess to keep the Scottish heritage alive. Every year Lilibet and Margaret – the 'Rose' was dropped before long – spent a holiday in Scotland, first at Birkhall, a little lodge the Duke was given in 1931, then at Balmoral. Whatever the girls did, they referred to it as 'before' or 'after' Scotland.

Whenever Margaret refuses to conform to accepted, if outdated, royal standards, which is often, her relationship with the Queen and the Queen Mother is sorely tested. Although one loyalist in the royal camp claims poetically that the three principal ladies operate in adversity like Alexandre Dumas's three musketeers – one for all and all for one – there are others as well informed if perhaps less loyal who speak of the latent tension between Margaret and the Queen (not to mention Philip). They say it dates back to Margaret's younger sister complex in childhood which developed into intense jealousy of the elder sister's position (common talk among Margaret's friends who cite chapter and verse) and was aggravated by the Townsend affair. These people point to the royal news coverage at certain periods (for instance during the royal tour of India) when Margaret stole the headlines as if she had deliberately set out to upstage the Queen.

On other occasions, the royal ranks are closed for the benefit of the public, and evidence suggests that the Queen takes a much more relaxed attitude to Margaret than vice versa. When stories about Margaret's house guest on the Caribbean island of Mustique reached Clarence House in 1976 and newspapers published photographs of her and young Roddy Llewellyn in unmistakable togetherness, one courtier described the Queen Mother's reaction in these words : 'All she was concerned about was to save Margaret's marriage'. But, taking the business of being royal very seriously, the 'sweet old lady's' mood changed when the scandal threatened to draw wider circles. 'She can be as tough as old boots', one of her admirers said, 'when it comes to the prestige of the monarchy!' She was very angry with Margaret.

The Queen no longer raised her eyes to the ceiling, as she used to do in mock despair, half-smiling, half-sighing. She regarded Margaret's parting from Tony as a blow to everything she stood for. She blamed her sister and could not forgive her, and the break between them was not likely to be healed for a long time. Once upon a time, when courtiers felt that Margaret was embarrassing the Queen, they had to admit ruefully that the Queen refused to be embarrassed. That was no longer true, yet, even when advised to put her foot down – though it was difficult to see what she could do without aggravating the damage to the monarchy – she would not allow herself in the presence of courtiers to react other than with the standard phrase : 'What are we going to do with Margaret ! ?'

It rings a bell, takes the Queen back to her and Margaret's childhood. When the family reminisce, they return inevitably to some of the highlights – or low points – in their young lives which are no longer private because they became widely known via Crawfie's account of 'the little princesses' in *Woman's Own* in the early fifties. Sophisticates have scoffed at the unctious, gushing, naive tales from the nursery; the principal characters have winced at the public laundering of their nappies, and accounts of intimate, silly, little happenings. They are embarrassing but they still provide a remarkable insight into the making of a Queen and a Princess.

The anecdotes about Lilibet are tempered by hindsight respect for the girl who became Queen, a role for which, from an early age, she seemed so admirably suited. Stories about Margaret are less restrained. With a pinch of bitchiness flavouring the treacle, they bring out early symptoms of characteristics which have since become apparent. Margaret is shown to be obstreperous, less disciplined than the elder sister (who, eventually, as heiress to the throne, was indeed subjected to stricter discipline). The girls seemed fond of each other but there were also some fearful rows. Neither was above taking a whack at the other, Lilibet quick with a left hook, Margaret more of a close-in fighter. More than once their little hands bore deep teeth marks. There were shrill cries : 'You brute ! You beast !' Margaret, but never Lilibet, was naughty, defied orders, made a scene, then kissed and was friends again. Lilibet, all agree, always had more dignity.

Child psychology was not a factor in the girls' old-fashioned upbringing. Margaret was coquettish – it needs the outmoded word to convey her manner – using her charm to score over Elizabeth, her way of compensating for privileges the elder sister enjoyed but were denied to her. She could be mute with rage and jealousy, so much so that a rumour went round (probably linked to the Duke's speech defect) that the Yorks' younger daughter was deaf and dumb. Nothing was further from the truth as was noisily revealed when Margaret could be heard in Hyde Park – across the garden fence of 145 Piccadilly – shouting after Lilibet: 'Wait for me! Wait for me!' Margaret mute? The family claims that she could hum the Merry Widow Waltz before she could talk. (She started singing lessons with the Countess of Cavan when she was seven.)

Charades and dressing-up were the children's main entertainments – Margaret never really grew out of them. She was an imaginative child especially when it came to making excuses. At one stage she invented a 'Cousin Halifax' whom she blamed for everything, being late, forgetting things, failing to learn her lessons. There were hints of future turbulence when sleep did not bring peace to her lively mind. She had appalling dreams of green horses, stampeding wild elephants, talking cats . . . While Lilibet read 'Black Beauty' and 'Lamb's Tales from Shakespeare', Margaret's favourite was a thumbed and tattered penny-dreadful with tales of blood and pirates.

The elder-younger sister conflict erupted at the slightest provocation: 'Margaret always wants what I want!' Lilibet grumbled ('including the throne . . .' it was said in later years). Margaret, as Lilibet did before her, bit her nails furiously, often evidence of mental disturbance. The girls were overjoyed to see the Prime Minister (Neville Chamberlain) gnawing away at his. If *he* could . . . ! Margaret was rather plump and Lilibet's harping on it did not make things easier. Seeing the little one wobbling about on a bench when taught swimming movements, the elder sister taunted her: 'You look like an aeroplane about to conk out.'

For people who live in palaces, doing what 'ordinary folk' do is as much a thrill as life in a palace for ordinary people. Margaret's first titillating excursion into the exciting humdrum world beyond 145 Piccadilly was a trip on the London underground from Hyde Park Corner to Tottenham Court Road to visit a Y.M.C.A. but the rare pleasure of travelling by public transport could not be fully indulged because crowds gathered and the return journey, rather than on top of a bus as planned, had to be made in a royal car.

For two girls who were nearly four years apart, it was not really ideal to be taught together by the same governess. The situation became even more complex by 1936, the year of royal traumas. The death of King George V, Uncle Davis's succession to the throne, and the mounting tensions brought by his brief reign as Edward VIII unsettled the staid Yorks and infected the children – anything might happen. The problem of Mrs Simpson was moving to a climax but, though they realised that the King's determination to marry the twice-divorced lady from Baltimore would create a constitutional crisis, Bertie and Elizabeth did not for a moment expect it to lead to the sensational abdication and their translation to Buckingham Palace.

When this was exactly what happened, Margaret was upset because she had only just learned to write her name – Margaret Rose of York. That was no longer much good. Papa (pronounced Puppa), also a little bewilderingly, changed his name to George – George VI – but remained 'Bertie' at home. Another problem name was that of Uncle David whose abrupt departure confused the girls. Margaret suspected that he had done something evil: 'Are they going to chop off his head?' she asked. She was told that he was now the Duke of Windsor but he was not mentioned again. When Papa and Mummy returned for the first time as King and Queen, the children asked whether they had to curtsey ... The answer was: 'In public, yes!' But even so, a problem of identity troubled little Margaret: 'Now that Papa is King,' she said gravely, 'I am nothing.'

Then came the move to the family's new residence, the vast cavernous, impersonal Buckingham Palace with its show pieces and treasures – 'like camping in a museum'. For the principal characters, the superbly conducted coronation ceremony was, to change the metaphor, like performing in a shop window. Not a hint of the problems, big and small, or tribulations such as Margaret's tantrums when she was denied a train to her dress as long as Lilibet's. In the end she had her way and, in spite of some doubts on the part of Lilibet, behaved throughout the ceremony with admirable dignity, an early hint of her ability to redeem herself or switch from unorthodoxy to tradition.

The new status widened the gap between the sisters. The

old pram had been stored away a long time ago. Elizabeth was the undoubted heiress to the throne while Margaret – there was not really a role for her except in the wake of big sister. When Margaret heard the prayer for her sister in church after her father became king, she said : 'Why don't they pray for me too? I'm just as naughty as Lilibet!' There seemed to be no place for her in the hierarchy; she was literally in everybody's way, a stoutish, clumsy little girl rushing through the corridors and getting under the feet of the Prime Minister and other notables on the way to an audience with the King. She could be a terror. Time and again, Lilibet shook her head gravely : 'I don't know what we are going to do with Margaret!'

She could not even join the new Girl Guide Company because she was too young but Lilibet pleaded for her : 'She's very strong,' she insisted. 'Pull up your skirt, Margaret! Doesn't she have a very fine pair of hiking legs!' (Margaret's legs are still strong and she has a stance which enables her to remain on her feet when all around her are wilting – in the same way as Hitler could hold his arm outstretched in the Nazi salute longer than any other man.)

Margaret had to be content with joining the Brownies instead but the age-lag remained a bugbear. She was allowed to look in at a Royal Garden Party but not to attend Court at the Palace. 'Never mind,' Lilibet comforted her, 'one day you'll be down there sharing the fun . . .' One day! 'When I'm grown up,' Margaret said admiring the ladies' fineries from afar (the top of the stairs), 'I shall dress like Aunt Marina' – the elegant, Greek-born Duchess of Kent. She made up her mind to have fun when her time came, down there and everywhere.

Then Balmoral, the Dee Valley, grouse moors, Scottish firs – and another tiresome discrimination. Unlike Lilibet, Margaret was not allowed to go to the Ghillies' Ball, held every year at Balmoral. At least she was not subjected to the extra lessons a future Queen had to endure and swot up on constitutional history like Lilibet. In the south, weekends were spent at Windsor where the King, in an old pair of flannels and rolled-up shirtsleeves, hacked and sawed away and burned dead wood, communing with nature and communicating his love of open-air life to his daughters.

A rare parting from the parents when King and Queen went

to Canada, and the first trip on a destroyer to meet them in mid-Channel on their return. A happy reunion. 'Look Mummy,' said Margaret who had lost a few ounces here and there, 'I'm no longer like the football I used to be.' The weight problem troubled her, shape of things to come. Another naval interlude, a voyage in the royal yacht *Victoria and Albert*, the girls learning the Lambeth Walk ('Any time you're Lambeth way, any evening, any day...' Margaret intoned) and the Palais Glide. Next a visit to Dartmouth with the King and Queen for an inspection of the Royal Naval College where Papa had been a cadet.

When the Queen was told that two college boys had mumps, she gave instructions for the girls to be taken to the Captain's house – Captain Sir Frederick Dalrymple-Hamilton was a relative through his kinsman the Earl of Stair whose mother was a Bowes-Lyon. He took the princesses to the tennis court to join a fair-haired young cadet who was showing off and jumping over the net: 'How good he is, how high he can jump!' Lilibet remarked.

The youngster teased plump little Margaret about her size. The villain! 'Who is that boy?' she asked. 'That is Prince Philip of Greece.' Next day at lunch, the acquaintance was renewed by which time the young Greek who was as English in speech and manner as makes no difference (his mother was a sister of Lord (Louis) Mountbatten), seemed to have discovered the attractions of the elder sister. 'Lilibet was a bit pink-faced,' Crawfie recalled. Philip was eating platefuls of shrimps, and to Margaret anyone who could eat that many shrimps was a hero. Hero or villain? The question weighed on her mind until it was answered with a shattering verdict.

The villain of the day was the Nazi leader of Germany: 'Who is this Hitler spoiling everything?' Margaret asked when their trip to Balmoral was delayed. Travelling to Scotland at long last in the first week of August 1939, their routine was again upset when Mummy and Papa had to go back to London almost at once. Three weeks later the girls listened to the voice of the Prime Minister coming over the radio: '...We are at war with Germany.'

'Do you think the Germans will come and get us?' Margaret asked.

In the Highlands all was peace. 'People should not talk about the war and battles and things in front of Margaret,' Lilibet said. 'We don't want to upset her.' Out of harm's way like other evacuated children, the princesses followed the war news. They threw books at the wireless when the voice of Lord Haw Haw tried to spread gloom and despondency. The gramophone brought light relief with the voice of Gigli rendering 'Your tiny hand is frozen'. Margaret giggled and joined in – it was indeed very chilly, water in jugs frozen hard, no central heating. (Margaret looks sybaritic but has been hardened by the austerities of her early Scottish holidays.)

She was a strange child. She was not yet ten but already had a curious effect on some people. Old men were frightened of her, according to her governess who made a few observations which have remained valid. Margaret had too witty a tongue, she thought, too sharp a way. People worried lest they were next on her repertoire of lampoons. Her kind of fun and frolics was bound to get her into trouble. She could be very awkward: 'Margaret went through a phase when she could be extremely tiresome,' Crawfie notes. 'She would dawdle over her dressing pleased to know she kept us waiting. I cured her by going off with Lilibet . . . and leaving her behind.' Cured her? She has been exasperating aides and friends ever since. Margaret's pranks made paragraphs in the newspapers, an early start.

The royal family spent the first war Christmas at Sandringham, then it was Royal Lodge, Windsor, long hikes, chats with cockney evacuees, messengers arriving with war news for the King, mostly bad. Looking down from the ramparts of Windsor Castle into the courtyard, Margaret said: 'Boiling lead was a pretty good idea!' (She still feels that way about harbingers of unwelcome tidings or, for that matter, critical columnists.) She was growing up, grown up enough for dancing lessons. 'Girls only' classes, the governess decided. 'The princesses did not understand the antics of little boys – and this did not seem the time to teach them.'

Another lesson Margaret learned early was how to keep cool under fire. The stiff upper lip was much in evidence in Windsor. She recalled her first bomb alert early in 1940, enemy aircraft overhead, and her rushing down to the old dungeons which served as air-raid shelters. It did not stop Sir Hill Child, Master of the Royal Household, laying down the rule for etiquette at table: 'We dress!' Dinner jackets were de rigueur.

Lunch was more casual, enabling the adolescent girls to be – well – girls. They took their mid-day meals with the staff and the young officers of the local units who were the chief attraction: 'Margaret becomes a real personality when the male element is about,' someone remarked in the peculiar language of the time and place. Lilibet was the perfect little lady, Margaret the inveterate flirt. Away from the social whirl she resumed her supporting role. Lilibet making her first radio speech, an address to the country's children, ended by saying: 'Come, Margaret, and say goodnight!' 'Goodnight, children!' Margaret chimed in.

Once rehearsals for a Christmas show started, Margaret's craze for dressing up dominated proceedings. The man in charge was a teacher from Windsor with acting experience. The parts which attracted Margaret were those demanding the most elaborate get-ups – her passion for theatrical effects has remained strong and she has, over the years, startled many of her weekend hosts by making a grand appearance at the top of the stairs in some extraordinary costume or other.

At the 1940 Christmas show, she played a little child in the Shepherd's Hut in a white dress with turquoise beads, and sang 'Gentle Jesus, Meek and Mild...' In a pantomime to be performed before invited guests, she was given the part of Cinderella – crinoline, white wig, beauty spot. Should they be charged an entrance fee? 'No one will pay to see us,' Lilibet worried. 'Nonsense,' Margaret countered, 'they'll pay anything to see us!'

Lilibet who blushed easily was red in the face as she asked Margaret to guess who was coming to see them act. 'Philip,' she answered her own question. She was in the clouds when he arrived on leave from the Navy, solemn, weatherbeaten, very handsome. Margaret, without a boy-friend of her own, threw herself into parties and games with duty officers as the 'male element'. She already practised the provocative stare which has since unnerved platoons of strong men. Come-on and freeze, as the mood took her. It was no longer innocent and childish.

Both girls were in the Sea Rangers, their unit based on a boathouse. Lilibet would not spend the night with the others, would not undress in front of strangers. The younger Margaret had no such qualms. She made the most of the occasions. From her sleeping bag came giggles, a voice aping her superiors and laughter until late into the night.

The gap between the sisters widened again when Lilibet moved into her first 'private apartment' where she busied herself with her studies and with correspondence, mostly letters to Philip whose photograph decorated her shelf. On reaching her sixteenth year, she registered at the local labour exchange, was allowed to join the A.T.S. as a subaltern, learned to drive, jack up a car and take the engine apart. Margaret was intensely jealous and angry to see her sister doing things she could not do.

Instinctively, she discovered a way to deal with painful situations, a very sour grapes device. When Lilibet's uniform arrived, Margaret was desolate but heaved a sigh of relief when she saw it did not look very becoming. If it was that ugly, she was not sorry she was not entitled to a uniform of her own. She simply rejected what she could not have. Lilibet, for instance, became a fine shot but Margaret was too young to take up shooting and therefore decided that it was not feminine – it was something she would never do. Later, wanting to be different, she took up cigarettes, (Lilibet did not smoke.) She became a heavy smoker and her spectacular long holders, one tortoiseshell, the other ivory, became her trademark.

For the time being, though, she simply suffered frustration. While big sister drove herself to London, Margaret had to stay at Windsor doing her lessons and be satisfied with Lilibet's account of her thrilling foray into the blackout. She was fourteen, very mature for her age but not really happy. Resentful at being left behind, she was, as Crawfie saw her, '. . . a girl at a most awkward age, neither child nor grown-up, taking the interlude much harder than Lilibet.' In other words, an unsettled puberty. But her spirit was not easily dampened, not while she could put her hand on a bottle of champagne. She was found tasting some in the company of a young officer. (More recently, though, she drinks gin or whisky instead.) Around this time she had a windfall, £20,000 left to her by Dame Margaret Helen Greville, an M.P.'s widow who used to be known as 'the friend of three kings' – Margaret was not yet as materialistic as she became in later years after inheriting a considerable amount from

Princess Margaret Rose, aged three, and (*below*) at her father's coronation on the balcony of Buckingham Palace, 1937.

A study in concentration: with Elizabeth at the National Pony Show, 1939.

'Grandma England', as the children called Queen Mary.

It was certainly in a very grown-up manner that she cast a searching look over the slim, elegant R.A.F. officer, high in rank for his age, who was with the King when he came on one of his weekend visits to Windsor. The finely sculpted features, strong, steady eyes, as blue as her own, the feline grace of his movements appealed to the impressionable teenager. She could hardly wait for father to introduce them : 'This is Group Captain Townsend,' the King said and, turning to his new equerry : 'This is my daughter Margaret.' (Legend has transferred time and place of the encounter to the year 1943 and Buckingham Palace when the airman left the King's study after their first meeting. But Margaret was not in London at this stage of the war.)

Townsend had joined the royal household as a result of the King's decision to take one of the 'Few' who had defended Britain against the Luftwaffe in 1940 onto his staff. Some of the older courtiers doubted whether it was wise to depart from tradition and to give such a job to a man who did not come from a great aristocratic family. Only when the King insisted did they produce a list of candidates of whom Group Captain Peter Townsend was easily the most distinguished.

Closer acquaintance confirmed Margaret's first impression. Her father's new equerry, soon promoted to Deputy Master of the Royal Household, was a pleasant, personable man to have around. It was evident how much the King liked the tactful, discreet, reliable new courtier. Margaret remembers her father saying on one occasion : 'I'd have liked a boy like Townsend!' There could be no higher praise. But, while he was much in evidence, there was as yet no hint of the emotional turmoil into which the King's well-intentioned choice of an aide would throw his younger daughter.

The war was drawing to a close at least in Europe, yet the prospect of peace was puzzling to a girl who could only dimly recall a time when the country was not at war, when there were no restrictions, no air-raid shelters, when she did not have to wear Lilibet's hand-me-down clothes (because it would not do for a royal princess to demand extra clothes coupons), when an extra egg was not pointed out as a luxury, and London was not a theatre of war out of bounds to young girls.

In what may well have been a subconscious attempt to cope with her own infatuation with the handsome new courtier (what was then called a crush), Margaret occupied herself with Lilibet's romantic attachment to the fair-haired sailor prince whose photograph, amidst much twittering by the younger sister, was presently replaced by a new one in which the familiar face was hidden behind a bushy beard and almost totally unrecognisable. Almost but not quite. A newspaper came out with a story about the photograph and named the young man as Prince Philip of Greece. Elizabeth was furious, Margaret commiserated with her, but the older members of the royal family were resigned to intimate details about them leaking out by one means or another.

Return from distant Windsor to the heart of London should have been liberating, but Margaret felt like the proverbial bird in the gilded cage. At Buckingham Palace, much more so than at Windsor, there were eyes and ears everywhere. The place literally swarmed with servants, high and low – footmen, butlers, pages, porters, vermin men, table-deckers, clock-winders, dressers (as the parlourmaids were called), valets, housemaids, chefs, cooks, kitchen maids, clerks, secretaries, governesses, tutors and courtiers, a huge cast with Margaret playing one of the star roles.

No girl could have been treated with greater indulgence by the family. Margaret only needed to throw her arms around his neck for the King to dissolve with tender love and ill-disguised embarrassment at such uninhibited show of feelings. She was as affectionate with the Queen but relations with Elizabeth were not as simple. Inadvertently and totally unaware, big sister added to Margaret's frustration with every week, every month. There she was, Princess Elizabeth – no longer Lilibet – getting her own flag, her own coat of arms, her own lady-in-waiting, her own secretary. Winston Churchill discussing matters of state with her, the King calling her to show her secret documents. Elizabeth opening bazaars, visiting factories, learning about every facet of the country. The heiress to the throne.

Where did this leave Margaret? Disgruntled, missing out, she thought, on the good things. What was there for her to do? She played some outrageous pranks on members of the staff who could not complain even when they recognised the culprit behind the studiedly angelic expression of 'P2' as the princess number two was called behind her back. Another way of making life tolerable was to escape into a world of fantasy. Margaret read a lot, if indiscriminately, classics, comics, whatever came to hand.

In the process she acquired a rich vocabulary and a feeling for the value and deeper meaning of words. That is how she learned to express herself without effort, if often with a sharp edge and an aggressive irony, quickly latching on to people's weaknesses and exploiting them cruelly. A mimic and a gifted imitator of strange accents, it was no coincidence that of all the showmen who crossed her path Peter Sellers became her favourite. From practical jokes she graduated to mockery which caused much offence. It was the performance of a typical younger sister with a chip on her shoulder and a flair for farce, satire, verbal combat. At the same time she was untidy, unpunctual, inconsiderate, the exact opposite of the future Queen. It was as if she was at war most of the time – she only relaxed when she was at the piano, playing, singing, play-acting, preferably with an audience.

Once Japan had been battered by two H-bombs, it only remained for her formal surrender to end the war in the Far East. VJ-Day on August 15th, 1945 found a vast crowd converging on Buckingham Palace and clamouring for King and Queen. Flanked by Elizabeth and Margaret, the royal couple appeared on the balcony to respond to the huge wave of patriotic fervour welling up from below. Infected by the popular enthusiasm, the two girls hardly waited for their parents' permission before rushing downstairs and out of the gate with a few young guards officers in tow to mingle with the crowds. To be caught up in the general jubilations was an exhilarating experience. After half an hour, the girls, a little out of breath and eyes shining, returned to the Palace.

Soldiers, (and sailors) from the wars returning included Lieutenant Prince Philip of Greece. His arrival on the scene had a remarkable, though not quite unexpected, effect on Elizabeth who devoted more time than ever to her appearance. Margaret teased her mercilessly and pursued her with giggles which Elizabeth brushed aside good-naturedly. Irritating Margaret may be, but it did not stop Elizabeth working the gramophone to death pounding out the 'Oklahoma' hit 'People will say we're in love . . .' It was not long before Margaret, in turn, was hooked on a popular song. Hers was 'Folks I know where I come from . . .' ('Annie Get Your Gun!') which she rendered with words of her own lampooning the old palace guard. With lines and names brought up to date again and again it remained a royal favourite for years . . .

At the time, however, Elizabeth was the principal target as Margaret watched her going off to shows and parties with Philip. When Philip spent an afternoon at the Palace, she – Margaret – could at least share in the pleasure of his company or, in other words, make a nuisance of herself. As Crawfie put it: 'The constant presence of the little sister who was far from understanding and liked a good deal of attention herself was not helping the (Elizabeth's) romance.'

The nuisance did not stop until Elizabeth was married and Margaret herself in the throes of a romance which all but shattered the tranquillity and harmony of the family, and struck wounds which had not healed even thirty years later.

CHAPTER THREE

Margaret was sixteen and looked carefree and content but at close quarters her romantic inclinations were seen to be crystallising slowly. Horses, dogs, clothes, not necessarily in that order, commanded most of her attention. Favourite horse – 'Gipsy'; favourite dog (Corgi) – 'Sue'. Favourite clothes? Margaret was inspired by Elizabeth's early grown-up frocks to draw some imaginative fashion sketches which showed talent. These were the kind of clothes she did not mind having second-hand, not until observant reporters noticed and commented, and she adopted Dior's New Look which was all the rage.

While Elizabeth went out dancing to restaurants and night-clubs, Margaret took Madrigal lessons at the Palace – no great excitement but a chance to meet people. One girl she came to like was Jennifer Bevan, charming, petite like herself, lively if not quite as lively as she. When, at long last, Margaret became entitled to a lady-in-waiting, her immediate choice was Jennifer, first in a long line of devoted official companions. The younger princess learned to drive but, unlike Elizabeth, did not yet get a car of her own and had to make do with one of the royal Daimlers.

Parties were still in the junior league but invitations came by the score and littered the round table in Margaret's room (colour scheme: salmon pink). Her dressing-table was covered with a chaotic assortment of manicure utensils, scent bottles, cream and make-up jars, combs, brushes, the adolescent girl's armoury for what was still referred to as the battle of the sexes.

Who would have expected this battle to be fought with passion and intrigue in the palace of George VI with its low-key domesticity? Who would have suspected an undercurrent of emotion when Margaret leaving her room ran into Peter Townsend in the corridor and stopped to talk, or put her head round Elizabeth's door and was asked in to join her and Philip for tea?

Yet when Peter and Philip brushed against each other it was like ice floes passing in the arctic. Difficult to say how these things start but perceptive, experienced palace staff could already discern a clash of temperaments of two men who, as often in small circles or within one family, though equally worthy and with much in common, were yet incompatible and jousting in a narrow space big enough only for one. They were both attractive, one looming on the family horizon, the other a cog in the royal machinery. One, in a manner of speaking, belonged to the elder sister while the other would be claimed by the younger – these things augured ill for the future. No less deadly for being fought with subtle moves over a long period and with strict observance of court etiquette, the battle between Philip and Peter – Prince Philip of Greece, Lieutenant, R.N., and Peter Townsend, Group Captain, R.A.F. – altered the course of Margaret's life.

Peter was deeply involved in the affairs of his royal master's family. Margaret looked on him as the man in residence, an attentive listener to her girlish chatter and, perhaps, with all due deference, a bit of a flirt. His appointment to the Royal Household entitled him to a grace and favour cottage in the Windsor grounds into which he moved with his attractive wife Rosemary, daughter of Brigadier Timothy Pawle.

The King became godfather to their second son, and Margaret dropped in occasionally at the cottage but before long the marriage deteriorated as the glitter of palace life for Peter caused Rosemary to be more and more seriously neglected. Rosemary was not so much in evidence as to put a damper on Margaret's growing infatuation with her father' favourite courtier. By contrast, all things considered, Philip, inevitably widening the distance between her and her sister, was the intruder. Across thirty years she still remembers him as he first appeared on the royal scene, an impecunious, if well-connected young foreigner, and Germanic (after a few years in a liberal German school) though 'Greek' is what his passport said.

He was, in truth, impossible to tell from an Englishman as one would expect from a nephew and protégé of 'Uncle Dickie', Lord Mountbatten, the glamorous naval hero who was soon to commune with history in India and acquire the patina of an elder statesman. Philip's nationality would not have mattered a whit had he not cast a covetous eye on the brightest jewel in the British crown, the King's elder daughter and heiress to the throne, and had she not been so completely in love with him. (Such a minor matter could, of course, be adjusted with the stroke of a pen – and was.)

With Philip so much around, Margaret could not help comparing him with Peter. One the tough sailor with an arrogant approach, the other the perfect courtier with the delicately smooth touch. Compared with Philip's rugged manliness, Peter appeared almost effeminate in spite of his superb war record. That, perhaps, was the source of the trouble.

Royal Air Force and Royal Navy did not mix. Two separate worlds, they produced separate breeds of men. At a time when war records were much in people's minds, more so in the Palace, Philip's was proud enough. Before moving to the Pacific where Uncle Dickie ruled supreme, he had been a midshipman in H.M.S. *Valiant* in the Eastern Mediterranean and received his baptism of fire in the Battle of Matapan in which the Navy, supported by Malta-based R.A.F. squadrons, fought a major Italian naval force protected by the German Luftwaffe. The *Valiant*'s searchlights under Philip's command were battered by the Luftwaffe, many were extinguished but Philip did not flinch and, miraculously, escaped unscathed – no, not escaped: triumphed with an important share in a naval victory which wrecked the Italian Navy – four cruisers, three destroyers sunk, several battleships damaged.

Impressive though it sounded, Philip's contribution could not compete with the kind of individual exploit in the air which the R.A.F. recognised as heroism. Matapan could not hold a candle to the Battle of Britain; directing searchlights was not in the same class as shooting down Nazi aircraft in a dogfight. As a war hero, Townsend was inclined to look down on Philip, as a pukka Englishman he did not particularly care for 'foreigners'.

By this time, Margaret knew enough about Peter to admire, to hero-worship him. He had been so eager to join up – instead of going from Haileybury College into the Indian Civil Service as most of the successful boys did, he had opted for the R.A.F. and, as a fighter pilot in the early days of the war which were still vividly alive in Margaret's memory, had helped to guard Britain's coastal approaches. In February 1940, the squadron under his command had shot down the first enemy bomber over English soil . . .

Time and again in conversation, the King returned to Peter's well-documented war record and his legendary courage in combat. Margaret had heard him talk of Peter's exuberant aerial pirouettes in rumba rhythm as he and his comrades shouted to each other over their Spitfire's intercom. But Peter himself confessed that, returning from combat, he used to fly over his home village whenever he could, rolling his aircraft in salute.

However much the young princess quizzed the ex-fighter ace she could not guess that this quiet and gentle man – so quiet some people still describe him as 'weak' – had been as hard as steel, almost venomous, as soon as he had an enemy aircraft in his gunsight; that it was his killer instinct which made him such a formidable opponent. It seemed more in character to show compassion as he did when, after shooting down an enemy aircraft over England, he visited the wounded Luftwaffe pilot in hospital. Peter made light of his own brushes with death – he had to bale out twice – and joked about the only injury he had suffered, the loss of the big toe of his left foot.

He was, for all that, no less sure-footed as he paced the polished palace parquet grappling with a problem which demanded tact and diplomacy, and would, though he did not know it at the time, have far-reaching repercussions on his future – and Margaret's. The problem, Elizabeth's involvement with Philip, was agitating the King and the Queen who were discussing it constantly. Margaret, as was everybody in the

Palace, was sure it was the principal topic when the King and Peter Townsend chatted together for hours on end, as they frequently did, but nobody knew for certain what was said or not said on these occasions. Townsend has never spoken about it nor, by all accounts, intended to touch on the subject in the book he was preparing in 1976. Margaret's reaction was ambiguous: she envied her sister the romance but was still anxious to help Elizabeth as best she could over the hurdles on the road to ... marriage. For marriage was the issue.

The Palace grapevine hummed and buzzed with rumours and conjectures. Did Peter Townsend, as Philip came to suspect, advise the King to insist on tests and safeguards before giving his daughter permission to marry? 'What infernal cheek', Philip was supposed to have exploded in the presence of a friend when the matter cropped up around 1950 (that is, long after it had been settled in his favour) 'for a man who was already heading for a break-up with his wife to set himself up as a marriage counsellor ...!'

In 1946 the King's closest adviser still called the tune. He was regarded as the inspirer of the plan which would enable the King to observe Philip over a time at close quarters before deciding whether he could become a member of the royal family. 'Why not take him along to Balmoral?' Townsend is said to have suggested. Yes, it was the weak Townsend taking the initiative and strong Philip at the receiving end. If there was any question about who started the unpleasantness, Townsend did not seem to mind being regarded as the culprit (though this may no longer be the correct assessment) because he was only doing his duty by the sovereign. The King adopted the idea with the result that the normally most pleasurable summer holiday in Balmoral turned into an ordeal for the royal family.

Philip would have been prouder of the invitation had he not been so acutely aware that he was being watched and judged, and that the judges might include the ubiquitous Deputy Master of the Royal Household. Margaret, observing the scene from an entirely different angle, was largely interested in the young lovers' reactions, gestures, words ... The King kept his eyes open but the Queen would much rather have opened the door to Elizabeth's happiness without such painful preliminaries. After a brief holiday with his family, Townsend joined the uneasy gathering adding another pair of eyes firmly focused on the hapless suitor. Unhappy and feeling as much under observation as Philip and, in turn, watching him with anguish was Elizabeth, the girl whom it was all about.

It was an ordeal for all of them but, whether it was Townsend's doing or not and though the whole family was now deeply involved, Philip blamed the King's aide for the awkward situation. But if Townsend was gambling on the Greek Prince not making it, the odds were heavily against him although Philip, under severe strain, made a mistake. In his anxiety to prove himself, he outstayed his welcome. He continued to go out riding with Elizabeth, Margaret and Peter trotting behind as chaperons, and joined in the other holiday activities. However Townsend saw the outcome, Margaret firmly believed in a happy ending and thought that her sister's formal engagement was imminent. But the King was still uncertain and could obviously not make up his mind. Philip's presence, if anything, made things only more difficult for him. 'The boy ought to go south!' he said at long last.

Elizabeth's distress was evident. Margaret counselled patience – it was surely only a matter of time before Papa would give his consent, she insisted. She and Townsend passed the time playing games – they were not close enough for the expression to suggest anything but its literal meaning. Philip left and the holiday fizzled out in general gloom. From the gloom, with Townsend once more suspected of being the originator, emerged yet another device, a final safeguard against 'a hasty marriage' and 'a disastrous mistake' – not that Elizabeth had the slightest doubt that she had made the right choice.

What happened was – and it may have been purely accidental – that, at the end of another long consultation with Townsend, the King emerged from his study to talk to the Queen at some length before announcing his conclusion. It was a simple, straightforward decision in line with a long-established precedent. Part the couple and see whether their love was strong enough to survive a long separation; find out whether absence would make their hearts grow fonder or whether time would wither their feelings for each other. A ready-made opportunity would come early in the new year (1947). All that was needed was to take up Smuts's long-standing invitation to visit South Africa which no previous monarch had done – and take the girls along on the trip.

Back in London, reporters suspecting that there had been a secret engagement in Balmoral clamoured for news. There was no engagement, they were told firmly. Furthermore, it was announced, the whole royal family, King, Queen, Elizabeth and Margaret, was going on an extended tour of South Africa and would be away for over three months. For the young lovers it sounded like an eternity. Although he was told that a marriage was possible if he and Elizabeth still felt the same way by the time the tour was over, the prospect predictably did not commend itself to Philip who once more, rightly or wrongly, blamed Townsend.

Margaret would have sympathised more with Elizabeth who was as distressed about the enforced separation as Philip, if she had not looked forward to the tour with irrepressible excitement, even more so since one of the aides joining the party would be Peter Townsend. What has become known over the years in dribs and drabs of deliberate indiscretions or unguarded remarks, provides an inside view of an extraordinary juxtaposition – an utterly miserable Elizabeth being torn away from the man she wanted to marry and the jubilant Margaret being thrown together on a romantic voyage with the man she was already quite sure she loved

A post-puberty crush, a teenager's passing infatuation, a young girl's romantic notions about a married man – it was, as it turned out, more serious than that. To Margaret, the South Africa trip sounded like a honeymoon – without, of course, the sexual connotation – a voyage together to an exciting new territory. Experiences and impressions shared, confidences exchanged, a great adventure. Margaret wanted to look her best for him, for her hosts, for the world to see, and here, after years of austerity, was a chance to forget about those ghastly clothing coupons. Let a Palace spokesman pay pious lip service to the restrictions which were still in force as long as they did not limit her choice!

As Elizabeth who dreaded the trip went a little sluggishly about her own selections, Margaret dived enthusiastically into clouds of silk and linen and tulle and ribbon and straw...At

39

some stage in the proceedings, a warning note came from above – from the Queen – that her outfits ought to be on a lower key than her sister's : simpler lines, less adult styles – Elizabeth, after all, would be celebrating her twenty-first birthday before the end of the tour. Margaret battled for every bow, every pleat, every flourish. Consulting with Elizabeth to avoid duplications or clashes of colour, she opted for several shirt dresses.

Her *pièce de résistance* was the big ball gown, some sixty yards of tulle decorated with coloured paillettes in a flower motif, but public imagination fastened on another item, a shocking pink wool coat which was later widely copied by teenagers. That Margaret was already wearing Schiaparelli's 'Shocking' perfume was still a well-kept secret. Both girls included sailor suits in their wardrobe for the voyage in H.M.S. *Vanguard*.

Elizabeth had launched the ship and inspected her at the time but the first she and Margaret saw of their state rooms were colour photographs which showed rather small cabins with simple furniture, blue bedspreads, dressing-tables and a telephone by the bedside. The girls studied maps of South Africa with the royal route marked out and read up on the sights they would see and the people they would meet. A first trip abroad is a heady prospect, and no less so for being a royal tour. For Margaret it was a great event. Only much later did she come to resent the inevitable drawbacks, the crowds, the stares, the strangers, the formalities : 'Would it not be nice', she said with charming unanswerable disregard for logic, 'if we could travel when there's no royalty about.'

Everybody in the Palace, and Margaret more acutely than most, was aware that the trip promised to be a watershed for Elizabeth – and an ordeal. The press speculated about the puzzling state of play between her and Prince Philip. Why no engagement? Anxious to take his daughter's mind off the man she was forced to leave behind, the King tried to involve her, much more than Margaret, in his preparations for the tour, composing short addresses, studying the finer political points, but her heart was not in it. It was increasingly difficult to disguise the delicate and embarrassing situation in which the heiress to the throne found herself and, though the public was unaware of it, the atmosphere in the Palace was oppressive. Long after the event, official chroniclers despaired of providing rational explanations for the on-off, off-on engagement and the official denials that there would be an engagement. Then this trip . . .

According to Stanley Clark's *Palace Diary*, for instance, the King had only just realised that Princess Elizabeth had arrived at full womanhood as if that had not been the root of the trouble in the first place. Almost in the same breath, Clark asserted that the announcement of her engagement had only been delayed until Prince Philip's naturalisation papers were completed – how long would that take? One day, two days? – and Elizabeth had reached her majority and 'taken her full place in the life of the Commonwealth' whatever that was supposed to mean. Crawfie was more honest with her reaction: 'No mention of Prince Philip,' she noted. 'So that was that, said some.' But those who knew Elizabeth better, she added, were certain that that was not that at all.

Margaret was also cast in a dubious light. Irked at being excluded from the jamboree, Crawfie took a jaundiced view of the effect the tour would have on Margaret and was gloomy with evil foreboding for the 'spoilt, disorganised girl'. The Queen would find it hard to cope with her once this trip had transported her into an adult world. The Princess would surely not be in the mood to revert to a demure schoolgirl! This, Crawfie suggested to the Queen, might be a good time for her to make a break, leave the royal service – and Margaret to her own devices. If this was a ploy to book herself a trip to South Africa after all, it failed. The Queen was sweet and diplomatic and told her that neither she nor Margaret could do without her. The governess agreed to stay on. According to her there were tears in Margaret's eyes when they said farewell. Crocodile tears?

More realistically, there were doubts whether the tour might not prove too strenuous for Margaret. How would this slender girl who was not yet seventeen stand up to the strain of travelling some ten thousand miles by car or train in two months (not adding the sea voyage) or an average of two-hundred miles for every day of the tour, and a succession of receptions, inspections, official dinners, parties – rest days would be few and far between. Margaret herself had no qualms. She would have Peter Townsend to lean on. It was all cut and dried, anyway. The day of departure, February 1st, 1947, was at hand.

After weeks and months of wearying preparations, after the worrying anticipation, after a formal farewell party at the Palace, it was a relief – for all but Elizabeth who was inconsolable – to get on the train to Portsmouth and embark in *Vanguard* for the seventeen days' voyage and relax in the intimate atmosphere of a family excursion. Once the *Vanguard* had weighed anchor, the royal party settled in quickly. Peter looked solicitously after Margaret and helped as she leafed through the volume of notes covering every aspect of the tour savouring the pleasures in store. Elizabeth spent much time with her father discussing the major speech she would be making on her birthday, still almost three months away. Now and then she shed her misery and joined Margaret on deck and even had fun as a delightfully dated photograph of the princesses in their sailor suits suggests.

Having been brought up to exercise self-control – Margaret's would slip before long, Elizabeth never once let the side down – only intimates could guess at the two girls' real feelings. As in Richard Tauber's *Land of Smiles*, they managed to look cheerful most of the time – and how they felt deep inside was nobody's business. Behind the scenes, Elizabeth's misery rubbed off on Margaret to add to the emotional problem with which the younger sister was already trying to cope. Like most teenagers in love, Margaret was exultantly jubilant one moment and down in the dumps the next.

Whether it was Elizabeth's depression or Margaret's changing moods they were not 'noticed' or touched upon. As if the (current) Queen's marriage had not so splendidly triumphed over these early complications, it has remained normal to cover her ordeal at the time with oblivion. With Margaret, too, because it was not seemly for a girl of seventeen to be involved – and with a married man twice her age – the beginning of her love story has been post-dated like a dubious cheque and the period of her affair with Townsend put with skilful obfuscation at a much later date when Townsend's marriage was about to be officially dissolved and Margaret grown up to a respectable age (like Elizabeth and her majority), say twenty-two, twenty-three or twenty-four when everything was presumably all right.

Had I not the testimony of some of Margaret's early confidants, I needed only study photographs of her and Peter together in South Africa, he looking at her in his boyish manner, she almost transfixed, lowering her eyes and blushing (even in black and white). Yes, it was all happening on this tour – not the ripe joy of adult passion but the enticing, bitter-sweet taste of young love.

Although subject to changing moods, as she still is, Margaret went through the crowded programme in a state of euphoria. That Townsend might have anything to do with Philip's predicament and Elizabeth's did not occur to her or to Elizabeth for that matter. And for a long while yet there was still so much harmony between Philip and Margaret that she could be credibly quoted as saying (I could not find out within whose hearing) that 'Philip was the big brother I needed when I was younger to keep me in order'. It does not sound in character.

The tour was demanding of mind and limb. So much to see, so much to do to give as many people as possible an opportunity to participate. Crowds lining the streets in their thousands when they arrived at Cape Town gave the royal visitors an inkling of their popularity and a foretaste of the whole tour. Rousing cheers greeted the King, the Queen, Elizabeth – with Margaret, looking very fetching and sexy, getting more than her share of the applause. As heiress to the throne, Elizabeth took precedence but even when Margaret kept modestly back a step or two her glow shone through strong and bright. Starting on a high note, the royal party was pitchforked into a ceremonial ball arranged by the Mayor of Cape Town, Mr Abe Bloomberg, and his wife the day after their arrival.

Dancing on this occasion, and many that followed, was not an undiluted joy because the young men from the services and leading families selected as partners had been rigorously briefed in the correct procedure – approach Margaret, or Elizabeth, make your bow, get on with the dance, don't speak unless spoken to, step back as soon as the band stops, bow again and depart. It was not exactly a riot. Somehow, though, and not only in South Africa where Elizabeth was less than exuberant, Margaret often stole the show. All

43

over South Africa she was hailed as 'Britain's Dresden China Princess'.

As a host, the aged Field-Marshal Jan Christian Smuts exerted a grandfatherly charm on the two girls. He took them for walks, climbed up the Table Mountain with them, collected bunches of wild flowers and talked knowledgeably and amusingly about them: 'I'm actually an expert on grass,' he explained, 'but you may find flowers more interesting.' He was a first-class all-round botanist. From hereon, whether with their parents or on their own, the tour was one long succession of functions for the two princesses, meetings with tribes and their chiefs, inspections of military units, visits to national shrines and natural beauty spots. On free days, they went riding and swimming. Margaret did not realise what complicated arrangements were necessary to provide horses in the right place and at the right time. Local farmers lent their animals but not all of them owned horses and police mounts were pressed into service. The girls cooled down in pleasant, picturesque lakes.

Margaret, it was later said, was visibly maturing, growing up in the course of the tour. She was also sometimes getting a bit beyond herself. She liked a glass of sherry – and another one. It is impossible to put a date to one of her celebrated remarks which has been associated with the tour but does not fit in well with the proceedings. Denied a second sherry by the King, Margaret was supposed to have exclaimed petulantly: 'If you won't let me have another glass of sherry, I won't launch your old ships for you!' In other versions there are variations on the word 'old'. Although it is not on record whether Margaret did get that other sherry, she probably did because her threat was not carried out and, a year later, she launched her first ship.

As the weeks went by and the royal party covered wide distances, royal duties kept Elizabeth too busy to mope – or to enjoy all her free days. Mindful of an engagement to open a new graving yard the following day, she did not join Margaret swimming in the sea, and worked on the speech instead. Later in the royal train she rehearsed it with Margaret as her 'audience'. Margaret commiserated with her sister who was valiantly trying to keep her mind on the job when the tabu was broken and the delicate subject of her relationship with Philip raised at a barbecue reception in Orange Free State. In the relaxed atmosphere, a member of the Provincial Council approached Elizabeth and asked her whether it was true that she would soon announce her engagement. She smiled wanly and said nothing. When the man was out of sight she turned to Margaret with a pained expression, and Margaret squeezed her arm to comfort her.

On and on the tour went. In the heat and dust of an African reservation, the royal party found themselves getting up and down like yo-yos when a loyal band completed the first verse of the National Anthem, paused, struck up again for another verse and, after a further pause, for another until everybody was almost overcome with exhaustion. Was the tour not getting too strenuous for a tender young thing like Margaret? She was losing weight, quite true, but welcomed that and was in high spirits. No need to worry about her. Manfully – if that's the word – she trotted behind Elizabeth up the quarter-mile, steep, rough path to the burial place of Cecil Rhodes in the Matopo Hills near Bulawayo (in Southern Rhodesia, as it was then) finishing up barefoot. If the heat was an ordeal, at least Margaret escaped what, by all accounts, was the worst winter England had experienced in a hundred years.

For Margaret there were presents to be inspected before they were packed up – they included a diamond bracelet, very valuable if not as precious as the casket of diamonds Elizabeth garnered – and the final entries on the tour to be made in her diary. Those straining to get a peek at the diary expecting to find secret thoughts committed to paper would have been disappointed – the notes are less trenchant or revealing than some of Margaret's open remarks.

Elizabeth was getting more animated the nearer the end of the tour approached. Once more she roped in Margaret to listen to a run-down of her speech which she finally delivered on April 21st, her twenty-first birthday. With it the older sister moved another step ahead of the younger one. A big Government House birthday ball brought the tour to an end on the note on which it had started. Three days later it was farewell to South Africa and, more important – after just over two final, agonising weeks at sea – hello to Britain. Elizabeth would be reunited with Philip, and Margaret briefly parted from Peter who was going on leave to his home and to his wife.

CHAPTER FOUR

Once the adrenalin stopped flowing as freely as throughout the South African tour, Margaret looked tired and worn out, much more so than her parents and her sister. That her state was due to psychological and emotional rather than physical strain did not occur to the family. That – a problem troubling teenagers even in our permissive days – she was suffering the pangs of an infatuation which, while not yet amounting to physical desire, seemed incapable of consummation, was too sophisticated a thought to be hazarded at the Palace. To make matters worse, all around Margaret minds were concentrated on love and marriage. Even Crawfie was getting married and was still on about Margaret not needing her any more whereupon the Queen who could be very firm put her little foot down and said that at this stage a change for Margaret was not at all desirable.

Elizabeth, of course, could not think of much but marriage. She was more in love than ever and confided in her sister more than in anyone else. Naturally, the Queen was preoccupied with the subject, and so was the King who, however, kept his own counsel and no longer seemed to share his thoughts with Peter Townsend. His daughters suspected that he was still wrestling with the problem but Lord Mountbatten's support – though he was at his post in India – was bound to weigh strongly in favour of Elizabeth's handsome young suitor. Margaret who was taking a growing interest in religion was surprised to hear that Philip's mother – Mountbatten's sister – was the Abbess of a small religious order on the Greek island of Tinos. At the same time some amusing whispers reached her ears that Philip's late

47

father had been (what was later called) 'a bit of a lad'. Philip himself was full of tales about his years at Salem School in South Germany (whose head, Dr Hahn, opened a similar school in Gordonstoun when the Nazis closed down Salem) and some ripe stories about life in the Navy. His streak of irreverence appealed to Margaret.

Such distractions did not relieve the tension of waiting, despairing, hoping, which showed in Elizabeth and infected Margaret, superseding her own amorous feelings. She was more even-tempered and resumed her studies without the fuss Crawfie had expected. Her curriculum of general reading, plays, poetry, history, literature, appealed to her and she kept it up even when social engagements – read : parties – began to interfere seriously with organised lessons which became shorter and shorter and eventually fizzled out completely. She was making new friends and amused them with her stories about South Africa. For the first time she became aware – awareness later turning into a kind of intellectual snobbery – that she could dominate a gathering without 'pulling rank' as a princess. She knew she could impress. It was not long before she tried to go further, seek conversational challenges and pit her wits against those of older and more erudite partners. Because none of them would rudely tell a princess to her face that she was talking rubbish, even when she did, she came to take a rather lofty view of herself. She was good but not as good as she thought she was. Modesty was not her scene.

Once Peter returned to duty, Margaret sought him out as often as was decently possible to go over photographs of the tour, many snapped with their own cameras, others from photographic agencies. He helped to annotate them and together they relived highlights of the tour which they had shared. They never discussed the Philip situation. As emerged later, Townsend had already given up his campaign as guardian of the royal family's well-being, at least with regard to Philip – not that Philip would forget, as became dramatically evident before many years went by. It was obvious that the King had come down in favour of Philip as a most desirable consort for his daughter. So had everybody else with the exception of a few fuddy-duddies who shivered in the fresh air sweeping through the Palace in the wake of the independent-minded young sailor.

Early in July, Elizabeth drew Margaret aside, brought her left hand forward from behind her back where she had kept it hidden and told her the big secret. Yes, it was all settled. Margaret cried out with surprise and excitement when she saw the engagement ring. Not much later, when Elizabeth received the traditional gift of a nugget of Welsh gold to be made into a wedding ring, there was enough for another one which went to Margaret. One of the thousands of gifts reaching Elizabeth was a good luck piece of rock from Snowdon . . . Increasingly, the big event cast its glow ahead and the Palace reverberated with the bustle of preparations. Margaret shared in the anticipation but not without a secret reservation. As she let slip to a friend years later – and he repeated to others until it was no longer a secret – she was oppressed by the thought that life had condemned her to play second fiddle for ever and ever after. It went against the grain, it hurt. She did not hold it against Elizabeth but the rebellion against fate threatened to break through the veneer of a loving sister and a dutiful princess.

On July 10th, 1947, the Court Circular carried the formal announcement that 'The King is graciously pleased to give his consent to the betrothal of his beloved daughter . . .' Philip was taking the family name of his guardian, Lord Mountbatten . . . Margaret embraced Elizabeth, offered her cheek to Philip who kissed her. They were moved and there was, at this moment, no hint of ill-feeling. The engagement was celebrated with a big garden party in the grounds of the Palace with Margaret managing to attract a good deal of attention.

They were still juggling with the royal and political programme to pick the best day for the wedding, when Crawfie scooped the pool and fixed her own marriage to a gentleman by the name of George Buthlay for mid-September ('GOVERNESS BEATS LIZ TO ALTAR' – U.S. headline). Another event which momentarily occupied Margaret more than the sound of wedding bells was her first 'solo' royal assignment. Accompanied only by Jennifer Bevan and a detective, she flew to Belfast to launch a new liner, the *Edinburgh Castle*, from the Harland and Wolf shipyards. Performing the christening ceremony with poise and self-assurance beyond her age, she named this ship . . . A young sailor presented her with a bouquet and blushed as he felt her enormous, eloquent, smiling eyes boldly fixed on him.

His colour darkened still further when Margaret puckishly picked out one of the roses and presented it to him.

She was the centre of a swirling mass of people, some coming forward to be presented, others trying to explain technical details as the ship glided down the slipway. Margaret was surveying the scene until her face lit up with a sign of recognition. She leaned over and whispered into Jennifer's ear: 'Look, over there, are Mr and Mrs Bloomberg – the Mayor of Cape Town and his wife who were our hosts. Bring them to me.' Greeting the Bloombergs like old friends, she invited them to tea at Buckingham Palace. She took them to the theatre and gave them seats in the royal box for a concert at the Albert Hall.

The forthcoming wedding took precedence over all other royal business. Palace staff were working on the elaborate schedule setting out every stage of the proceedings. Details were slowly emerging. Margaret would be Matron of Honour – she only just recalled being a bridesmaid at the age of five at Uncle Harry's (the Duke of Gloucester) wedding to Lady Alice Montagu-Scott. Best man would be David, the Marquess of Milford Haven, Philip's closest friend. The honeymoon – a secret for the time being – was to be at 'Broadlands', the Mountbatten estate in Hampshire.

It was all Elizabeth . . . And Margaret? She could not really visualise life without her sister except that, once Elizabeth had set up an establishment of her own, 'P2' would become 'P1' at least at home and – The Princess in the Palace. Was she wondering when she would be a bride? Margaret's contrary remark gave a hint of her thoughts. 'You'll be next!' she was told and promptly replied: 'Mummy and Papa need me to keep them in order. What would they do without me?' As often before and after, she rejected what she could not have. Her friends say that at this stage she felt that there would not be a husband for her for quite some time which was a sound instinct. Anyway, Elizabeth's wedding was fixed for November 20th, 1947.

When Sunninghill Park, the home Elizabeth and Philip had chosen for themselves burned down – it was completely gutted – it was almost as great a blow to Margaret as to them. The young couple accepted the King's hospitality to start married life under his roof at Buckingham Palace. Farewell to Margaret's dream of being number one. If it was not a great tragedy it was still an irritant gnawing at her consciousness even while there was so much to do and to think about. While Elizabeth tried on her wedding dress, Margaret was in and out of her sister's apartment with a host of seamstresses and servants including another Margaret – the real name of Bobo MacDonald, Elizabeth's maid.

Then there was her own bridesmaid's outfit. She was in constant touch with the other bridesmaids, six of them in their early twenties and only the eleven-year-old Alexandra of Kent younger than herself. As she ranked above the others, mostly cousins, her ideas about colour and design had to be respected. There was a good deal of girlish chatter about bride and bridegroom but Margaret did not hint one word of the secret which the family was jealously guarding until it was publicly announced the day before the wedding : that the King had made Philip a Duke and a royal prince : Prince Philip, Duke of Edinburgh Earl of Merioneth and Baron Greenwich to give him full new title.

That day, the new-baked Duke, his bride, the King and the Queen, Margaret and the other bridesmaids went to the Abbey to rehearse the wedding ceremony. In the evening Buckingham Palace glittered with the most brilliant party since the outbreak of war. Elizabeth looked radiant, her bright eyes competing with the magnificent diamond necklace, South Africa's wedding present. Margaret proudly wore her new diamond bracelet. As a junior hostess, she moved smoothly among Europe's royals, the world's most eligible young princess well aware of the discreet scrutiny to which she was subjected. Was there a royal parent who would not have welcomed her as a daughter-in-law? Where Philip had conquered, could others not follow?

Among guests she exchanged pleasantries with was young Michael of Rumania with whom her name was rashly linked; he was only too patently in love with Anne of Bourbon Parma who was at his side. Margaret looked up, literally, to her great-uncle, the tall King of Norway, and had a word with the King of Denmark and his tiny wife. Among the younger foreign royals (some of them ex, like Peter and Alexandra of Yugoslavia) were Juliana of the Netherlands and her husband Bernhard, a German princeling and friend of Philip's. There were the Luxembourgs, the Swedes and Greeks galore . . .

Post-war austerity which the King had wisely taken into account when setting the tone of the occasion did not put a damper on the proceedings. No stands in the Mall – shortage of labour and materials – no extra facilities in the Abbey for more than the statutory two and a half thousand guests. Lounge suits and service uniforms were the order of the day. But in the event there were huge crowds and British flair for royal ceremonial triumphed over the restrictions. Margaret was not the only one who loved the sight of the Household Cavalry who were exempted from the austerity restrictions and resplendent in their full dress scarlet tunics and gleaming breastplates.

A little nervous and anxious to perform their duties correctly, Margaret and the other bridesmaids were at the West Door of the Abbey. The girls' chatter subsided as the clatter of horses' hooves signalled the arrival of the royal escort and the bridal coach carrying the King and Elizabeth. Looking neither left nor right, Elizabeth had her emotion well under control but Margaret could sense the tension and the excitement below the surface. She was herself taut as she followed the bride and her father into the Abbey where the rest of the royal family and the guests were already in their places. The crowded congregation, the sharp brightness of the newsreel lamps heightened the atmosphere of expectancy. So many thoughts crowded Margaret's mind that she saw the brilliant scene only hazily . . .

The previous week they had been discussing the marriage vows in the family circle and Elizabeth had said that, of course, she did not mind in the least promising to obey her husband. Apart from the ceremonial frills, hers would be like any other marriage. Margaret had raised her eyebrows and made a flippant remark but had quickly realised that it was no joke to her sister. How different they were, Margaret who took few things seriously, and Elizabeth with the built-in stabiliser in her mental make-up !

As the small procession fell into place, Margaret walked immediately behind the two little pages – William of Gloucester and Michael of Kent – who carried the bride's train. By her side was Alexandra, gawky but already quite as tall as she. Throughout the ceremony, Margaret's eyes were on Elizabeth and Philip as the Archbishop of Canterbury pronounced them man and wife and gave them his blessing. She followed the couple to the High Altar and, in rhythm with the choir, her lips formed the words of the sixty-seventh Psalm 'God be merciful and bless us...' Then the Archbishop of York gave his address.

Except for the two central figures in the Abbey few of those present could have responded to the solemn rites with greater intensity than Margaret whose strong religious involvement was an unexpected strand in the tapestry of her personality. As if communing with the Almighty she was still deeply preoccupied when joining the family in the Edward the Confessor Chapel to sign the register. Only little Michael of Kent getting his foot caught and stumbling roused her from meditation, but she was so far away that the King stepped in before she made a move to deal with the minor crisis.

It was all very dream-like. She vaguely remembered driving back to the Palace behind the newly-weds, the King and the Queen, Queen Mary and the Princess Royal ... Presently she was out on the balcony with her parents, with Elizabeth and Philip, Philip's mother, the bridesmaids and pages, infected by the high spirits of a happy wedding group and thrilled by the exuberant cheers from below. Elizabeth's eyes were shining with a hint of tears and the bridegroom was visibly moved when he heard the crowd shouting: 'Good old Philip!'

Relaxed at last, Margaret exchanged impressions with the other girls, cousins all but two – Margaret Elphinstone, Diana Bowes-Lyon, Caroline Montagu-Douglas-Scott, Mary Cambridge, Pamela Mountbatten and Elizabeth Lambart. She led the way to their table, one of fifteen for one-hundred and fifty guests in the first-floor ballroom, but only toyed with the *Filet de Sole Mountbatten*, the *Perdreau en Casserole* and the *Bombe Glacée Princesse Elizabeth*. Next came a surprise which appealed to her Scottish instincts – the King's Pipe-Major at the head of four pipers from Balmoral marching up and down the room playing 'The Green Hills of Tyrol' and other traditional airs. Standing close to the couple when they cut the four-tier cake with Philip's sword, she was one of the first to toast them in champagne after the King's brief speech.

As Elizabeth was leaving, Margaret, the King and the Queen led a cavalcade of bridesmaids and guests across the quandrangle to bombard the bride and bridegroom with rose petals before

53

they reached the open landau. Within seconds they were on their way to Waterloo Station and the royal train.

As with such occasions on a lower-level, the spin-off from the royal wedding was a burst of social activity for the bridesmaids, and for Margaret more than the others. 'A royal wedding', wrote Bagehot, 'is a representation of a great universal truth,' and if he was right the truth of the matter was probably that this wedding marked a turning point in the national condition, a backlash against restrictions and shortages and long faces. That Margaret caught the imagination of the British people – more than the heiress to the throne – was largely due to her being in the vanguard of this popular reaction. To Hell with austerity was the motto, and before long Margaret implemented it to the hilt.

It did not happen overnight because she was still officially a schoolgirl supposed to pursue her studies, but reading was already a hobby rather than organised work. Once the clock struck noon, the day's serious business was concluded and Margaret looking despondent was at a loose end hanging around with nothing to do. In Palace parlance, she did not seem to be settling down to any consistent routine, had no job, no duties, no programme. There were winks and nudges in the direction of the King and the Queen but the King did not respond and the Queen did not think there was anything wrong with her younger daughter. Grandma England was recruited for a campaign to put her to rights and exchanged views with Crawfie who described Margaret naively as 'a little girl with no one of her age to play with'.

No one to play with, indeed! Before the Queen had finished saying with motherly compassion: 'Without Elizabeth, it's lonely for her here,' the object of common concern started to remedy the situation. Via the idle teenager's umbilical cord, the telephone wire, Margaret was in touch with scores of friends and as a result invitations began to arrive by the dozen. They were avidly accepted. Come the weekend, Margaret was off to the country estates of one noble family after another vying with each other to organise house parties for the young princess's enjoyment and titillation. Mostly it was harmless fun. One way or the other, many of the hosts and quite a number of the guests were relatives, anyway. The main ingredients in these top-class, social pressure-cooker mixes were standard-size eligible young aristocrats who were difficult to tell apart – same clothes, same hats, same small-talk, same hobbies – hunting, shooting, fishing – and same thought in mind : how to bag a royal princess.

Early off the mark in this pursuit was the Duchess of Gloucester's clan, the Duke of Buccleuch's heir, the Earl of Dalkeith, a war-time naval officer like Philip, who had a good start through his sister, Lady Caroline Montagu-Douglas-Scott, one of the royal bridesmaids and a friend of Margaret's. Before their flirtation had gone beyond a little close dancing, gently risqué, post-prandial party games, a brush of hands at late-night private film shows – no tripping along deserted corridors at night – his name was, in the contemporary phrase, linked with Margaret's. A personable, handsome twenty-five-year-old with political ambitions which took him before long to the House of Commons as member for a 'hereditary' Tory constituency, he was an eminently suitable prospective royal son-in-law and would have made a good husband.

So, no doubt, would Tom Egerton although he was a commoner. The son of the King's racing manager, he was encouraged to keep an eye on Margaret and took his duties seriously and personally but did not get much further than escorting her to race meetings and amusing her with anecdotes about famous men, women and – horses. Before long there were many more recruits to her entourage, mostly ex-Guards officers in their civilian regalia of bowler hats and rolled umbrellas who were such a feature of the English scene it is surprising how soon they became extinct.

Considering Margaret was all of eighteen years, it was a considerable feat of personality for her to show the way to the good life in a country weakened by the exertion of victory in an exhausting war. Mountbatten was extricating the Crown from the Indian connection and assisting with the birth of two new Commonwealth countries. Elizabeth was giving birth to her first baby (November 14th, 1948) who was christened Charles. Something to celebrate ! Her bandwagon rolled on gathering momentum travelling along new routes to London's West End on regular nightly excursions.

Between her eighteenth and twenty-first years, Margaret's name became linked with the more exclusive night-spots where her patronage boosted business. A decade still separated London from the 'swinging sixties' but Margaret's London of the late forties and early fifties made a good stab at it. Bright lights, discreet gloom – take your pick! Outstanding in this landscape of late-night watering holes was the '400' Club in Leicester Square, the darkish, comparatively sedate haunt of prosperous young men and society girls emerging from the chrysalis stage – and international roués casting their nets to catch attractive butterflies for their private collections.

Only a respectable amount on the table or a recommendation from an obliging West End hotel concierge was acceptable as a substitute for a membership card. Drink was available on the 'bottle party' principle which by-passed the awkward licencing laws enabling customers to feed on their own liquor or champagne bottles until the early hours. At the '400' Margaret recaptured some of the prewar gaiety her elders were always talking about.

To catch the flavour of the period, one must have seen, as I have, Margaret, at the head of a party of eight, ten or twelve, sweeping regally into another of her regular amusement arcades, the Milroy Club – a contraction of the names of manager John Mills (no relation to the actor) and bandleader Harry Roy, once Margaret's favourite. If there was something outlandish about the Milroy which catered successfully for the native gentry, it was the powerfully built John Mills himself, one of the exiled-Polish ex-servicemen who graduated from waiters and head-waiters to dominate London's night-life (even the linkmen at the entrance were ex-colonels who employed sergeants to whistle for cabs). Mills now owns 'Les Ambassadeurs' which took over where the Milroy left off.

'Margaret was amazing,' my late friend Count Alex Poklewski-Koziel used to say over and over again. 'Not yet twenty but more sophisticated than girls five or six years older, and quite a handful for the chaps who qualified as escorts – she was still careful with whom she showed herself in public.' Grandson of the Czarist ambassador who sold Alaska to the United States, Alex was the model for Marina of Kent's painting, 'A Young Man', and taught the current Queen the rhumba. Like most men of his generation who came into contact with Margaret, he was a little in love with her and could never hide his surprise at finding this vivacious, temperamental, uninhibited girl struggling to free herself from the strait jacket of her royal status: 'She wanted to know everything, hear everything, see everything,' he said with a smile. Already her escorts could risk mentioning some way-out Soho place they had discreetly visited only if they were prepared to take her there as she was bound to demand – many of them kept their tongues but Margaret still visited a lot of 'boites' in which no princess had set foot before or since.

Savouring her special position, Margaret cultivated her own rules of the sex game: 'She had a way of showing her preferences,' Count Koziel explained. 'A man would know that she wanted to dance with him. Nothing too obvious – a quick, meaningful glance often out of the corner of one eye, an expression, a gesture, a move . . .' Now it would be called body language. She spoke it fluently, unobtrusively but unmistakably. 'She enjoyed herself although her poker face could fool you. If she looked bored, it did not always mean she was.' The Count knew Townsend but regarded him as one of the scores of personable men with whom Margaret flirted violently.

One of her problems was how to shake off her loyal, hard-pressed personal detectives who groaned under the burden of their 'glamorous' job. She succeeded frequently. Often one of them was left standing at the kerb when Margaret roared off in a boyfriend's car. That they almost always caught up with her testifies to their intuition, know-how and dedication. As they performed their arduous duty, the coachmen of her desire – the chaps who carried her away – were often in a worse predicament. One after another desperately wondered whether he was reading the signs correctly, whether Margaret was in a receptive mood: 'How do you respond?' was Count Koziel's rhetorical question. 'How could you be sure? How far could you go? Misjudgment could lead to a terrible mistake. It could mean ostracism, social suicide, banishment from the royal circle and all associated with it.'

That all the small talk across Margaret's table in the strident voices of Mayfair and Belgravia – in the late forties and early fifties only the lower and upper classes brayed, the middle classes whispered and mumbled – camouflaged such thoughts, mostly in anticipation of a situation which might never arise, tells more about her than the alert gossip writers at her heels ever discovered. They did not give up. Already much of the information in circulation about her came from members of her own circle. News about her doings began to take up more and more space in the newspapers which coined a name for the people around the young princess – The Margaret Set.

CHAPTER FIVE

The Margaret Set was making headlines – or rather paragraphs in the gossip columns. Too fluid to allow a proper assessment by reporters – not for want of effort – it created its own mystery and romance. Which of the men was she dancing with? Into whose eye did she gaze soulfully? Who drove her home – or elsewhere? These were some of the questions pondered by Fleet Street's 'London by Night' experts. Everything she did made copy. Margaret going back-stage at the London Palladium where Danny Kaye, blazing a trail for American stars, gave a stimulating performance; Margaret kissing him on the cheek and he greeting her with 'Honey!' when they met again; Danny being asked to lunch at the Palace ... Did she? Was it possible? Were they more than 'just good friends,' a phrase which was coming into vogue.

Margaret spent weekends in Sussex with the Hartingtons – he the heir of the Duke of Devonshire – and the Egertons, parents of Tom who was forsaking the Guards for other pastures—scientific farming. The Hartingtons, the Egertons and Margaret went to church on Sunday ... Although Tom Egerton kept his distance, reporters could hear wedding bells. They could hear them again a few weeks later at the other end of the country when Margaret went weekending with Lord Dalkeith at Drumlanrig, the Buccleuchs' Scottish Castle. And, incredibly, there was even talk of a possible marriage to the (then) young Hugh Fraser, M.P., brother of the gallant commando leader Lord Lovat and a frequent weekend guest at Balmoral. It was some time before it occurred to people that Margaret was not likely to choose a prominent Catholic as a husband.

It was just as well that girls, apart from Jennifer Bevan who shared much of Margaret's fun, also came into the picture. There were Caroline and Rachel and Laura : 'I spend far more time in their company than with anyone else,' Margaret said. Caroline was Lord Dalkeith's sister, Rachel Brand lived with her parents near Marble Arch and worked in a hospital, and the tall, handsome Laura answered to the name of Smith, of 'W. H. Smith', and was the eldest daughter of Lady Hambledon, the Queen's lady-in-waiting.

The most congenial girl-friend the pleasure-seeking Princess acquired around this time was Sharman Douglas from Arizona, the blonde, fresh-faced daughter of Lewis Douglas, the American Ambassador. Breezy and informal like most American youngsters but too impressed with the aura of royalty to become over-familiar, Sharman was so full of the joy of life that she animated every party she attended, a latter-day Annabel Lee, Anita Loos' historic (*Gentlemen Prefer Blondes*) heroine who, on taking the dance floor with the pre-war Prince of Wales, passed her hand-bag to a friend saying : 'Hold this while I step into a page of English history.' It happened to Sharman when she was invited to ride with the royal family in the open landau on Derby Day.

In the summer of 1949 – by which time Elizabeth and Philip had set up their own home at Clarence House – Sharman, anxious to extend the frontiers of Margaret's enjoyment, organised a big fancy dress party at her father's home in Princes Gate at which Margaret was to make an unusual appearance. Also attended by Elizabeth (as an Edwardian parlourmaid) and Philip (as a waiter), the party was in full swing when a special entertainment was announced with great flourish : 'Mademoiselle Fifi and her Can-Can girls!' Maurice Winnick's band struck up Offenbach's familiar tune and, to the accompaniment of half-whistles and raised eyebrows, Mademoiselle Fifi in lace panties, black stockings and wriggling her hips turned out to be – Her Royal Highness Princess Margaret.

The establishment as the people who mattered came to be called – were shocked when it became known that Margaret had exhibited her shapely legs and 'pantied posterior', and before long apologists put it about that she had worn so many petticoats her legs could hardly be seen. But the King was

FROM A STURDY LITTLE GIRL TO A FASHIONABLE WOMAN

(*Top left*) on her pony in Windsor Park, at the age of ten; (*top right*) two years later in her Girl Guide uniform; (*above left*) arriving at Westminster Abbey, Prince Philip behind her, for the rehearsal of her sister's wedding, 1947 and (*above right*) aged nineteen in an elegant hat on a tour of Lancashire, 1950.

Peter Townsend and Margaret during the Royal visit to South Africa, eight years before she announced her decision not to marry him.

(*below*) Princess Margaret and the new Queen drive behind the cortège as the body of King George VI returns to London from Sandringham, 11th February 1952.

pleased with her performance and remarked what a shame it was that his daughter's talent had to go to waste. The rumpus reflected adversely on Sharman who gradually slipped from royal favour. Ambassador Douglas returned to the States and Sharman went with him and visited Britain only spasmodically to hunt around for a job or any good reason to stay – the family was not wealthy enough to support the girl's ambitions.

Whether Sharman was responsible or whether, as was also suggested, it was Danny Kaye's influence which led to the generous display of royal charms was a moot point. Margaret had needed little encouragement. She was livelier than ever and quite fit although the press voiced a concern echoed in the Palace, about her 'delicate health'. It may be that echo was nothing but an attempt to curb her exuberance. If she was under any strain, it was due to a crowded official schedule being super-imposed on her active night-life.

In the span of a fortnight she attended a military concert followed by supper with the officers; visited the theatre and went on to dance at a club until the early hours; danced at a ball and again at a night-club the next night; went to a reception at the Danish Embassy where she was seen drinking 'hard liquor' (gin) with Prince George of Denmark who was also, quite wrongly, counted among her suitors. Night-club again, the Ballet, next to see a revue in Oxford while staying at Blenheim Palace with 'Sonny' Blandford, son of the house and heir to the Duke of Marlborough. A future Duchess of Marlborough? It became rather confusing when she took Lord Blandford to see Danny Kaye at the Palladium.

Inspired reports asserted that, however late she returned home after a night out, she was up bright and early next morning at nine a.m. It sounded reassuring but it was, of course, not true. The overall impression created by her frantic socialising and as avidly discussed by the foreign Press as by their British contemporaries called for some subtle correction. It was skilfully provided by John Pudney, the poet and writer, who produced a learned treatise (for the benefit of American readers) comparing Margaret with her great-great-grandmother and concluding that Queen Victoria was by no means as Victorian as was generally assumed and, as she herself recorded, did sometimes not leave a dance before four a.m.

Without being put out by press criticism, Margaret, trying to show herself in a new light, boarded a number 11 bus in the company of Mr Simon Ward, son of the Earl of Dudley, yet another young man supposed to enjoy her favour. One of a gaggle of Scottish lairds among Margaret's regulars, the closest really and, as it turned out, the most durable of her friends, was Colin Tennant, the enterprising heir to Lord Glenconner.

Whether Colin was in love with her only he can tell. If he was, he must have been a most selfless admirer because then, as twenty-five years later, he gallantly helped to put Margaret's parents, friends, police guards and the press off the scent of her real paramour, Group Captain Townsend. Colin Tennant earned Margaret's eternal gratitude by enabling her and Peter to meet at his London house without drawing attention to themselves. Those who attribute this role to Colin Tennant go further and say that not only he but all the young men around Margaret in these years only served to camouflage her association with the only man she cared for; that she encouraged gossip about all the others and even provided realistic evidence to lay false trails; and that, moreover, her flirtations never went as far as prurient imagination suggested.

This interpretation seems borne out by the number of Margaret's 'boy-friends' who married girls of their own choice, or second choice as was sometimes hinted. Lord Blandford (I am only mentioning first wives) married Susan Hornby in 1951; Colin Tennant married the Earl of Leicester's daughter, Anne, who became Margaret's favourite lady-in-waiting; and Lord Dalkeith took a model, Jane McNeill, a Hong Kong lawyer's daughter, as his bride.

Eventually, the ex-Guards were joined or replaced by men with weightier minds – the aspiring Reverend Simon Phipps, a sounding board for Margaret's religious ideas; Mark Bonham Carter, ex-Balliol grandson of Mr Asquith and a confirmed Liberal who responded to her erudition, the same function which also accounted for her close association with the highly intelligent Judy Montagu, granddaughter of the first Lord Swaythling and daughter of a one-time Secretary of State for India. Margaret often visited Judy who was five years older than she at her Knightsbridge flat until Judy went to live in Rome and married an American, Margaret becoming godmother to their little girl and taking an interest in her upbringing after Judy's untimely death. At the time, companions like Judy testified to Margaret's loftier interests. The irresistible bright lights blinded many to her devotion to the classics – Keats, Chaucer, Shakespeare – fostered by Crawfie (whom, incidentally, I recently saw compared to Governess Gruffenough of Thackeray's 'The Rose and the Ring').

Playwright William Douglas-Home, whose name was up in lights long before his elder brother, to his and everybody's astonishment, became Prime Minister, introduced her to the delights of Christopher Isherwood's works; she made friends with Douglas-Home in spite of the fact that he had been convicted for disobeying a military order in the war. (It was not long before the more tragic figure of another member of the Douglas-Home family attached itself to her...) With her literary inclinations went her abiding love of music; it was she who encouraged Elizabeth and Philip to go with her to Covent Garden and not the other way round.

She already had star quality, the elusive ingredient which is by no means the automatic birthright of a royal princess: Marina of Kent had it but the Princess Royal lacked it, the little Queen had it in ample measure but the Duchess of Gloucester – no. With youthful pride, Margaret basked in the glory of saturation coverage of her activities by the press and enjoyed playing hide-and-seek with some of the shrewdest reporters. Loss of privacy did not as yet outweigh the glamour of being so much in the public eye. But she did let slip a remark which blamed the papers for turning Elizabeth into 'the dull one' and making her 'the gay one' (this, of course, long before the word acquired another connotation).

New heights of Margaret mania remained to be scaled but the attractive and promising outline of a new royal playground could already be discerned through 'Long Tom' long-focus camera lenses. With the reading public's circulation-boosting preoccupation and the young princess in mind, editors, not only British, stripped for battle when it was announced that Margaret would visit Italy. They deployed their troops on the island of Capri (favourite gathering place of the world's homosexual elite) where she was scheduled to spend a few days. She would be living informally in an hotel, take walks and go swimming in the sea. That, a photographer frankly admitted, would give the press what they wanted – 'a view of the royal limbs.'

Margaret travelled in the company of the Queen's private secretary, the usually impeccable Major Thomas Harvey. Capri, when they reached it, was solidly occupied by the press. Pointing in the direction of Margaret, the ominously phallic 'Long Toms' sprouted on every cliff and even below the waterline where one photographer wearing a diver's helmet lurked to snatch pictures from 'an unusual angle'. Presently, the target of such concentrated attention was discovered sun-bathing on a private beach, her face shielded by a cartwheel straw hat. With the press in hot pursuit, she went for a walk along the rocky goat track, accompanied by Major Harvey, his shirt-tail unceremoniously flapping around his shorts ('Continental fashion', a royal spokesman muttered unconvincingly). While Margaret, stockingless, plagued by pebbles in her shoes and nettle stings on her ankles, was on her hike, a reporter slipped into her hotel suite and established that she was reading *Busman's Honeymoon*, using Tweed perfume and Peggy Sage nail varnish.

At long last it happened on the water front. The Long Toms picked out Margaret as she was getting into a boat assisted by the boatman and her Major. She was wearing a swimsuit. Or was she? 'My God, she's naked!' a London picture editor exclaimed when he examined his reporter's despatch of photographs. It certainly looked like it but it was actually the sun playing on a very light-coloured swimsuit. The *Daily Express* retouched the pictures darkening the swimsuit but, rather than reassuring readers, it made them only suspicious. The King let it be known that he considered the photographs 'very undignified'. *The Times* said sternly that it was time to stop treating the Princess as a peepshow. Margaret, full-bosomed, tiny-waisted with shapely legs, enjoyed it more than she dared to admit.

The press coverage of the visit set the pattern for hundreds of similar accounts. Reporters referred to her 'mad holiday' or 'semi-educational holiday' threatening to become a fiasco but they could not decide whether she had been wearing a 'two-piece', a 'tight-fitting' or a 'low-backed' swimsuit. They tasted the special 'Margaret' cocktail concocted by an Italian barman but reported that 'she ordered lemonade, drank it quickly, and called for a second'. *Il Messagero* enthused about her eyes –

'the most beautiful things she has brought to Naples ... as grey and tender as the air of Capri' but the *Daily Mail* knew better and said that her eyes were 'a very beautiful blue'. According to another report, the Italians, for no immediately apparent reason, called Princess Margaret 'Poor little one'. Less newsworthy was her demure appearance when, head covered with black lace, she visited the Pope in Rome but this, she confided to a friend, was a great spiritual experience.

From Italy to France: Paris with Nicholas of Yugoslavia, the Duchess of Kent's nephew, as a guide to such educational centres as 'Maxim's', the culinary cathedral where Edward VII had worshipped in his time, and the more contemporary 'Monseigneur' night-club and 'Jimmy's' in Montparnasse, all illuminated by flashbulbs. Margaret was startled but had no need to be apprehensive: 'Our visitor,' wrote *Le Figaro*, 'is all that we have dreamed in our childhood of a fairy princess. All France is now nostalgic for a princess.' *Paris Match* illustrated Margaret's range with photographs of her swiftly changing headwear – a diadem (as worn at the coronation of Juliana of Holland), a picture hat (in London), a stylised beret with pom-poms (in Paris), a naval hat (in Portsmouth), the black veil (in Rome) and a head scarf (in Capri) which became part of the royal ladies' regular gear. She had her fashion idiosyncrasies, favoured high-heeled shoes ('Uncomfortable?' she snapped at Elizabeth 'Never mind, I'm wearing them, not you!') and a black evening gown.

In London it was thought Margaret's excursions could be exploited to present a more dignified view of her. To promote it for the enlightenment of the British public, royal advisers chose the incomparable Godfrey Winn, Fleet Street's most eminent sob-brother, the writer with the golden pen and master of the smarmy phrase whose inclinations, furthermore, were not such as to tempt him to dwell unduly on the swiftly maturing young princess's more eye-catching attractions at the expense of extolling her royal virtues.

At a time when nobody could have foreseen that the heir to the throne would one day discuss his prospects of marriage with a reporter of a woman's magazine or that the royal family would allow a television camera to record their leisure hours, Godfrey Winn subjected Margaret to gentle questioning. Direct quotation was out of the question but the writer skilfully conveyed that his information came straight from Margaret's mouth. He was genuinely impressed, or rather surprised, by her personality. Embarking some years later on another royal feature for *Picture Post* (where I was working at the time), he recalled asking her about the de-personalising atmosphere of Buckingham Palace – these long echoing corridors and the sudden remote silences – and of her own quarters. How did it affect her? 'But this is my home!' she had answered fiercely.

She tried to counter criticism of her 'dull' speeches – did anyone expect her to get up and shout 'Hiya folks!'? Official functions were no joy-rides, she explained. The King's secretary prepared her speeches, she went over the scripts and adapted them to her own phraseology, rehearsed and tried them out on Jennifer or, once or twice, on the King. The journey, meeting a host of strangers, the small talk, reading the speech with a nagging worry whether she had done well, how it had gone down: 'Some people imagine', Margaret said, 'I lie on a sofa all day waiting for the evening to come and the next party to begin . . .' Was it a burden, then, to be what she was? 'I cannot imagine anything more wonderful than being who I am!' Brave words.

Margaret still loved to rummage in her childhood memories – much of the spoilt little brat had spilled over into adult life. Now that she was grown up she could not help wondering whether her father's devotion to her did not owe something to a feeling of guilt that he had expected a son. But nothing detracted from her own deep affection for him, nothing, not even that it was Elizabeth, and not the feline younger daughter purring or scratching as the mood took her, whom the King involved ever more in his work. Still, Margaret felt, as she had felt as a child: 'I want to be like Lilibet!' Since she could not be, she insisted on leading her own life, a curious blend of sophistication and naïveté, thinking high thoughts but raring to go out and about and enjoy herself. The thrill of lunching at a public restaurant (at Claridge's with Queen Ena of Spain) was as great now as her first ride on the underground more than a dozen years ago.

Contradictions. Much as she craved amusement, Margaret was eager to perform her public duties. Her work load increased, and so did the number of her official positions and titles. At this point she was Honorary Colonel-in-Chief of the Highland Light Infantry (and of the sister regiment in Canada), President of Dr Barnado's Homes, Commander-in-Chief of St John Ambulance Brigade Nursing Cadets, Patron of the Scottish Association of Girls Clubs, Patron of the English Folk Dance and Song Society, and Patron of the National Pony Society. Each demanded her presence at functions for speech-making, conferring honours, handing out certificates and other variations of a royal's routine. Since she did not compose her own orations it was a bit silly for people like the Minister of Education to shower her with phoney praise as he did after she had opened an L.C.C. Training College: 'I have recently heard many speeches at the openings of schools and colleges,' he blabbered, 'but her Royal Highness's was the best.' Take a bow, Major Harvey, or whoever wrote that speech.

Sometimes Margaret did not take herself so seriously and was not taken in by the sycophancy lavished on her. Dancing with a young man at the '400' club, she suddenly told him: 'Look closely into my eyes! Do you realise you are looking into the most beautiful eyes in the world!' She burst out laughing and explained that this is what an American magazine had written about her eyes. On another occasion, one of her escorts pointed to an over-informal American girl in their party and warned Margaret: 'Watch out, she'll be calling you "Maggie" next!' Margaret dined out on these stories. She made fun of a new crop of 'engagement' rumours – the press was predicting that she would choose Robin McEwen, and, for good measure, his brother James: 'Am I supposed to be marrying both of them?' she asked with a twinkle in her most beautiful eyes.

It was not so easy to talk away another young man who had been around so long that neither of them remembered where and when they had first met. Like a banker in a pools permutation, he was included in every list of the Princess's prospective fiancés. Tall, gangling but elegant with beautiful manners, a sense of humour slightly above the average in this circle, and a great deal of money, he was Billy Wallace, son of the late Captain Euan Wallace, one-time Tory Minister, and his wife Barbie whose second husband was Herbert Agar, prominent American publisher and historian (*A Time for Greatness*). They lived in some splendour at Beechwood (Lavington Park), originally Cardinal Manning's house, on the fringe of the Sussex Downs.

The Wallace-Agar wealth was estimated at many millions and their life-style was up to that standard, but when Margaret went to spend a weekend at Beechwood it was presented as a retreat into a simple, quiet country atmosphere. Only her visits to nearby Cowdray Park to watch her young host playing polo gave the game away. Billy's stepfather interested Margaret in topics closer to his heart than polo ponies and discovered that she was better informed on many subjects than most other weekend visitors. She enjoyed his challenge to her intellect.

Billy Wallace worshipped Margaret and she loved his company. His polo playing, dancing, beating up London town disguised a debilitating liver disease so well that he was regarded as an ideal partner for Margaret, and gawkers, society and press, were constantly on the lookout for signs of intimacy between them. Margaret did not disappoint them, treated him affectionately in full view of strangers, yet what there was between them emerged from a remark he made many years later after a weekend with Margaret and Tony Armstrong-Jones at Birr Castle, home of Tony's mother, the Countess of Rosse: 'Thank God', Billy sighed, 'Margaret and Tony have found each other ... She won't need me any more to cover up for others!'

The first time Billy got involved in a typical Margaret situation was in 1950 when her friendship with Peter Ward was thought to be blossoming into something more. Friends since they had been contemporaries at Oxford, Billy and Peter shared a flat in Chesterfield Street where servants in powdered wigs and knee breeches waited on the guests. Margaret had attended some of their parties without attracting attention until one of her visits, for reasons impossible to discover, created a tremendous stir.

Though no different from previous occasions, the party was publicly described as a 'secret dinner' to mark Margaret's engagement to Peter Ward. It was said that she had sent her car and her faithful bodyguard, Police Sergeant Ashbrook, away – though, of course, he would not have gone even when asked, simply made himself more unobtrusive. As a piquant detail it was added that Peter had driven her home in his red sports car. It raised a lot of dust but it was sheer fantasy. The party, it turned out, had been to celebrate Billy Wallace's return from a lengthy visit to the United States. There had been no – repeat : no – engagement, and, besides, it was not Peter but Billy in his own almost identical red sports model who had brought Margaret back to Buckingham Palace. Ah well, said the *cognoscenti*, then the engagement party had been for Margaret and Billy. Exasperation in the Palace was reflected in a curt statement saying that the Princess had returned home in a royal car.

Mercifully, there were no complications when Margaret went to a more conventional function, the coming out of Lady Anne Coke, daughter of the Earl and Countess of Leicester, at their Norfolk home. The King and the Queen were among the guests, and so was Margaret's friend Colin Tennant who had his eye on the attractive young debutante (and eventually married her). But there was a public row in the wake of a wedding reception Margaret attended (in her mother's company) at Glamis Castle, her birthplace. The happy couple were Anne – Lady Anson – eldest daughter of the Queen's brother, the Honourable John Bowes-Lyon, and Prince George of Denmark, the acting military attaché at the Danish Embassy.

The point which did not have the significance for Margaret it assumed a couple of years later was that the bride's first marriage to Viscount Anson had ended in divorce. The Queen and the Princess attending a divorced person's wedding – it provoked a lot of criticism. An added piquancy was the presence of Lady Anson's, or rather Prince George of Denmark's, eleven-year-old son Patrick whom we shall meet again as a grown-up, celebrated social lion, royal photographer and bosom pal of Margaret.

An element of balance could be discerned in Margaret's social and official engagements. Returning from a tour of Cornwall with the King and the Queen she went straight to a Sinatra concert; from a wedding reception in a stately home it was on to a dance at the Dorchester, and from prize-winning goats at the Royal Norfolk Show to the Village Homes of Addleston whose first patron had been her great-grandmother, Princess Mary Duchess of Teck.

Another weekend at Drumlanrig produced the predictable

comment : 'People close to Court circles are saying that Princess Margaret's engagement to the Earl of Dalkeith will be announced before the end of the year' (*The Star*, October 10th, 1950) which provoked one defender of her privacy to the titillating rejoinder : 'I should urge that what is essentially a private affair should be allowed to remain so until the right moment comes.' The right moment never came. What happened while Margaret was in Scotland was that Elizabeth gave birth to a daughter – Princess Anne – who, in the passage of time, would attract some of the public attention currently devoted to her aunt.

Margaret, as usual, taunted the inveterates who saw romance ahead for her at every step. Turning up at London Airport to fly to Malta, she wore a scarf with a big inscription on it : *'Toujours l'Amour'*.

CHAPTER SIX

Friday, August 17th, 1951 – four days before Margaret's twenty-first birthday, a turning point more significant for a royal princess than for any other girl about to get the key of the door. All morning, in jodhpurs and brown hacking jacket, a bright yellow scarf around her throat, she was out riding in the grounds of Balmoral with Group Captain Townsend. Losing themselves in the wooded country, Margaret and Peter could enjoy precious privacy without the subterfuge and deception they had to practise in London.

Once of age, she would receive an annual allowance of £6,000 – compared with Elizabeth's £40,000 and Philip's £10,000 – which would enable her to buy a car and spend a little more on clothes. Her financial affairs would be administered by Sir Arthur Penn, the Queen's Treasurer, and her official life managed by the Queen's new secretary, Captain Oliver Dawnay. She would be mistress of her own destiny – up to a point. But she would still have to get her father's consent if she wanted to marry.

Margaret's cheeks were flushed, not from the exertion of keeping control of a capricious mount, but by the emotional undercurrent in their conversation. It turned to the state of Peter's marriage which was heading for the rocks – not necessarily Margaret's fault. It was an intricate constellation. While the elder, gossip-prone courtiers frowned on their tender feelings for each other ('What did I tell you? No good could come from introducing this kind of chap into royal service!') the royal family loved and spoilt Peter who basked in the hothouse atmosphere and glitter of court life.

The crisis came to a head in Peter's own backyard when he suspected that his wife Rosemary feeling injured and neglected had sought solace and compensation in other arms. Like many a man in such an emotional tangle, Peter seized on Rosemary's infidelity to justify his own infatuation with another woman although Rosemary has always insisted that her affair with another man was over by the time Peter became aware of it. Yet he could or would not forgive – as deeply religious as Margaret at this stage, charity was not a virtue he practised – he would not even admit to himself that his own behaviour might have contributed to his wife's lapse. Rosemary's efforts to mend the marriage were in vain. A psychologist might have concluded that Peter needed his wife's 'guilt' to salvage his conscience. As he saw it, the disintegration of his marriage was Rosemary's fault and he was entitled to a divorce. It would have come sooner had the royal connection not demanded restraint. But now, Peter told Margaret, proceedings were under way. He was suing his wife. A problem? Of course! Embarrassing publicity? Unavoidable! Yet, Margaret of age and Peter free – it opened up a sensational prospect.

Years later a story circulated according to which Margaret was at this point praying for God's help which was in effect praying for forbidden fruit. She was, one of her contemporaries said, praying for a life with Peter whom she craved with the painful passion of a first love.

Royal training stood her in good stead. Except for the Queen and Elizabeth, nobody sensed Margaret's predicament. The King was still pondering the meaning of a puzzling incident when, some weeks earlier, he had run into Peter who was carrying Margaret up the stairs in his arms. 'I asked him to, Papa! I ordered him!' Margaret insisted when the King looked angry. A youthful prank? Later the King talked sharply to Peter but it did not occur to him how close his younger daughter and his equerry already were. (Luckily, he had not seen the two on another occasion driving away from the Palace in Peter's car flushed and looking like a couple of kids stealing – kisses.)

It was with a heavy heart that Margaret prepared for the birthday celebration. While Peter would have to take a discreet back seat – if not too far away – the best places would be reserved for the hardy annuals, the principal characters of the 'Maggit' Set – Billy Wallace, Johnny Dalkeith, Peter Ward, Sonny Blandford, Colin Tennant, Lords Ogilvy and Porchester, to name some of the 'Ten Little Nigger Boys' who, one by one, would presently become engaged, married, boring, over-ambitious or disrespectful and fall by the wayside until there were only nine, eight, seven – none. Altogether there would be twenty-five guests including parents, Elizabeth and Philip who was not in the best of spirits when Peter Townsend was around.

The great day started with Margaret going through her mail and stacks of congratulations and reading the newspapers with their highly imaginative stories which greatly amused her. Elizabeth and Philip came over from Birkhall to add their good wishes before Philip went off with the King for a morning's sport on the grouse moors. The King cut short the shoot when it was time for a picnic lunch at Corndavon, a beauty spot not far away. The queen and her daughters in almost identical pleated tartan skirts, headscarves and thick-soled shoes, strode out manfully to join the guns. It was a convivial gathering. The empty baskets were hardly back in the castle when the staff called the guests for afternoon tea with a huge birthday cake crowned by twenty-one pink candles. And already Ruby MacDonald (sister of Elizabeth's maid, Bobo) was laying out Margaret's fussy evening gown for the big dinner party.

The King's six pipers played some of the birthday child's favourite Scottish airs, she danced to the Queen's choice ('The Dashing White Sergeant'), sang 'The Silver Dollar's, her current favourite, accompanying herself on the piano, then went to look at the huge beacon which illuminated the grounds. After dinner a cavalcade of cars took the young guests to Birkhall for an impromptu dance, the 'regular' escorts taking their turn with Margaret – not Peter who had dutifully or tactfully stayed behind with the King.

Love became Margaret who was blossoming forth in spite of the implicit complications. She gave, in the words of Sir Louis Greig, a little glamour to a drab world, and the country responded to her personality which triumphed over a certain lack of elegance. Who was to blame for that? I remember Norman Hartnell wringing his hands in his old-maidish manner: 'I have difficulty in getting bows past Her Royal Highness,' he complained. 'More and more she demands simplicity without fuss of any kind.' So it was Hartnell, getting a few bows past her before she could assert her own taste, who was responsible for the over-decorated bustline of her birthday gown which Cecil Beaton, lapsing from his own standards, allowed her to wear in several of her official birthday photographs for which he was responsible. Not that the great British public minded. It snapped up half a dozen or more souvenir books, one selection boasting '327 lovely photographs of H.R.H. The Princess Margaret.'

In the back of the family's mind was a deep worry about the King's health – Margaret was, if anything, more concerned than the others. It cast a shadow over the gathering in Balmoral although the King himself made light of it, had made light of it ever since, two years earlier, doctors had identified his complaint as Buerger's Disease, a tightening of the arteries which also gave him leg trouble. As if nothing was amiss, he went out shooting – and returned with a big bag – but breathing was getting more difficult. The Queen, with the help of Dr Greg Anderson, the royal family's Scottish doctor, persuaded him to consult a specialist.

In the first week of September a lung specialist, accompanied by a radiologist, travelled to Balmoral and examined the King. They agreed that it was essential for him to come to London for a more thorough investigation in their consulting rooms. He went obediently, if reluctantly, submitted himself to another examination which produced a definite diagnosis – bronchial carcinoma. It required an operation with the least possible delay. For a few more days, the King went out shooting – September 14th was the last time he shot in Scotland. In the meantime arrangements went ahead for the operation to be performed at Buckingham Palace on September 23rd.

That day the King underwent a lung re-section which was successful as far as it went. Eight doctors signed the bulletin. For the period of his physical incapacity his functions were taken over by a Council of State of which Margaret, along with the Queen, Elizabeth, the Duke of Gloucester and the Princess Royal, became a member. In the circumstances, the King's recovery was remarkably swift and his doctors, while keeping their own counsel about the long-term prospects, raised no objection when it was decided that Elizabeth and Philip should leave for a tour of Canada (and a brief visit to Washington and President Truman) as planned on October 7th.

As the King's health seemed to be improving, Margaret briefly resumed her 'normal' life. She went to several parties and at one of them commandeered a young partner to dance the Polka with her although he protested that he could not do it : 'Neither could I,' she told him, 'until they forced me to learn.' So far her reputation for 'independence of spirit' or a 'rebellious streak' rested on nothing more than a few childhood escapades. Now, as if girding herself for all sorts of confrontations, she began to challenge custom, if, in the first instance, in small ways. One was to light a cigarette in public, the first royal lady ever to do so. According to old Queen Mary ('I never called her "Grandma England",' Margaret protested which was probably just a lapse of memory) smoking in public was not ladylike : 'James I described it as a filthy novelty,' she claimed but her erudite granddaughter countered that Sir Walter Raleigh had encouraged Elizabeth I to take a puff of tobacco. In the end Queen Mary suggested that the girl should at the very least use a cigarette holder. Margaret obliged and soon sported outsize holders which only succeeded in drawing more attention to her smoking habit.

She followed the Pytchley Hunt (in a car), brushed aside complaints from the anti-bloodsport lobby with a curt 'I regret ...' and went on hunting. Hissing 'To Hell with Hartnell' under her breath, she acquired a stunning Dior creation of sheer organza and magic. Triumphantly, she took possession of her new Daimler (cost £3,000) – not bought with her own money after all but a birthday present from her parents.

As a matter of fact, her £6,000 allowance was not yet settled. It appeared that she had been left out of the Civil List Act of 1937, and there was opposition to her inclusion which required parliamentary sanction. Clement Attlee, leader of the opposition, objected and Scottish Labour members staged a protest demanding the allowance of the Scottish princess be cut by half. Singing the praises of the royal family, Winston Churchill talked of their toil and duty in tones almost as ringing as his war–time speech about blood, sweat and tears. He won the day – for Margaret.

Although the family, aware of the King's condition, implored him to take things easy, he wanted to lead as normal a life as possible and attend to his work. He dissolved the Council of State – as per December 10 – and went to Sandringham where he studied official papers but also rested a good deal. He looked forward to Christmas with the family, all the family, and to his broadcast, however arduous the chore. He was quite determined to make it as he had always done. In the event it was a painful experience for the family and for the country to hear him speaking with the voice of a dying man, hoarse, uncertain, labouring, battling for breath. Vulnerable beneath her astringent manner, his younger daughter watched his tragedy developing into the greatest crisis of her young life.

More and more in these days, Margaret and the King himself leaned heavily on Peter Townsend. When out shooting – the King pursued his sport as if he were in the pink of condition – or over the after-dinner port, Philip was a more congenial companion; but when it came to pouring out his heart, when it was a matter of discussing his daughters, and Margaret in particular, it was Peter, the son he would have liked, whose understanding and advice sustained the ailing monarch. The King's tremendous regard and Margaret's love for that man combined into something precious, something almost conspiratorial father and daughter shared. The implication was so obvious, it is not surprising that Philip did not like it.

Though his lined face and furrowed brow told the sad score, the King kept up the brave pretence that all was well with him, or soon would be. There could be no question of Elizabeth and Philip cancelling their tour of the Commonwealth due to start at the end of January – for them to insist on staying would have been tantamount to telling the King that they expected him to die. Instead, Philip joined in whenever the King, a crack shot – and 'Glen', his faithful gun dog – went out to shoot pheasants or hares. Johnny Dalkeith was one of the younger men who came down for a few days' sport.

On January 31st, the King, the Queen and Margaret drove to London Airport to send Elizabeth and Philip on their way. It was bitterly cold but the King refused to wear an overcoat. He looked dreadful. Across twenty-five years, I still remember the sad photograph of him waving a melancholy farewell as he watched the *Argonaut* disappear in the distance. As all who saw the picture, I could not help feeling that his days were numbered.

Back in Norfolk, he continued to work a little and shoot a lot and nobody tried to stop him from doing what he enjoyed. Every morning, for the next few days, he went out after hares, rabbits, pigeons – unsatisfactory targets though they were, the King's power of concentration was undimmed and his marksmanship consistent to the last. On February 5, 1952, he was out with a party of twenty, got nine hares at the last stand, and three with his last three shots. Margaret saw him when he returned to the house tired but content. That night the King died.

Although he had been shy and undemonstrative and never encouraged Margaret's impulsive gestures of affection, the family was aware of the deep bond between them. His loss hit her hard and only self discipline blunted the force of the shattering blow. Peter Townsend tried to comfort her but she was inconsolable. Later she talked of her sense of loneliness after the King's death and how, more than in his lifetime, she suddenly realised how truly irreplaceable he was in her world. If she cried, her tears remained unobserved and unrecorded, unlike Elizabeth's who broke down when the sad news caught up with her at Nyeri, Kenya, after a visit to the romantic Treetop Hotel where she had spent her last night as a princess watching jungle animals converging on the famous waterhole.

The young Queen and Philip returned home by the first available flight and, on February 8th, went through the Accession formalities. The Queen spoke of the consolation she derived from the sympathy her people felt towards her, her mother and sister. Sitting in her apartment at Clarence House, she saw herself on television being proclaimed, while at Sandringham Margaret watched the screen as intently, her thoughts wandering from her father whose body was still in the bedroom where he had died to her sister who was the Queen. For her and for her mother, it needed a major psychological effort to adjust to the new situation.

Could the gulf opening between the two sisters ever be bridged? Would not the mystique of the throne come between them and separate them still further? And – a thought that could not be banished – what would have been had it been she, Margaret, instead of Elizabeth who was ascending the throne?

77

Would she have liked to become Queen? Inappropriate as the question sounded at this stage, the answer from her own lips (to which a number of friends testify) was an unequivocal 'Yes!' These same friends have made no secret of her view – a mistaken view, to my mind – that she would have made a better Queen.

With the Queen's arrival at Sandringham, reality took over from fantasy. While Margaret had been to say farewell to the King, Elizabeth, according to Stanley Clark (in *Palace Diary*), did not enter her father's room. Both watched the coffin being carried from the house to Sandringham Church. (Charles and Anne who had been staying at Sandringham while their parents were in Africa were back at Clarence House.) On Monday, February 11th, the King's body was taken to London to lie in state at Westminster Hall where the Queen, Queen Mother, Queen Mary and Princess Margaret attended a short service.

Presently court ceremonial took over. To a better understanding of Margaret it is important to visualise her controlling her sorrow, grappling with her emotional attachment to Peter Townsend, yet playing her part, serene and disciplined beyond her age, in the formalities which on such occasions ruthlessly relegate a royal person's true feelings to the background. The show had to go on. Royal visitors, heads of state, dignitaries from all over the globe were converging on London for the King's funeral, and Margaret had a part to play. It was nerve-racking, tiring, yet she thought her sister was reaching the limit of her strength after a day of relentless public duties welcoming the foreign mourners. Only Margaret accompanied the Queen and Philip to Westminster Hall that evening to see the King lying in state.

The country grieved genuinely for the good man. But the royal funeral was also a spectacle with an irresistible appeal to the morbid, the curious and the habitual royalty watchers. Yet, the pageantry and the martial splendour could not drown Margaret's pain. Pale under her veil, almost frail, she girded herself to accompany her father on his last journey – from Westminster to Paddington, to Windsor and the castle where the coffin was lowered into the royal vaults under St George's Chapel.

While deeply involved in the complicated mechanics of the

funeral, etiquette and logistics concerning eminent foreign mourners, Peter Townsend did not neglect the practical, mundane problems of the domestic arrangements for the Queen Mother and Margaret who, in their bereavement, put themselves and their affairs totally into his hands. He, the King's closest confidant, was the stable pillar in the shifting scene around them and best able to guide them through the momentous changes in store. Together, the three – Margaret, her mother and Peter – looked beyond their memories of the man who was more to them than a King.

A lover on whose shoulder Margaret could lean, a substitute father in charge of the household, Peter had his work cut out organising the move to Clarence House to dovetail with the Queen's installation in new quarters at Buckingham Palace. Fortuitously this also separated him from Philip who, as the Queen's consort, was already emerging as a new force at court. His bland, boyish features unmoved and only a wrinkled brow betraying strain, Townsend managed to cope with his complex duties, with Philip's hostility and his own domestic crisis at the same time. But his marriage had broken down long ago and what remained were only legal formalities. He was citing John de Laszlo as co-respondent, and Rosemary (through her lawyers) agreed not to contest his petition for divorce which minimised the risk of publicity. It was arranged that Peter should have custody of, and financial responsibility for, their two boys who would continue to live with their mother.

Peter found comfort discussing his problems with Margaret who, while so much younger and able to feel sheltered and secure in his presence, was basically a much stronger personality and character than the smooth courtier. The bereaved Queen Mother, competent and resolute as she was, also confessed that she could not have done without Peter. He helped to supervise arrangements to take account of the changed financial circumstances, the King's will involving tremendous amounts, the distribution of the royal family's considerable private fortune, and the official emoluments which had to be allocated and administered. The Queen was, of course, the main beneficiary but considerable assets went to the Queen Mother and to Margaret.

Peter's services were even more personal when it came to redecorating Clarence House (at a total cost of £55,000).

Margaret left him to choose the colour-scheme for her private suite – cream-coloured walls, homely black window frames and doors. Although he spent every free minute with her, the crackle in the grapevine, whispers, talk, gossip about them at Clarence House and 'Buck House' remained hidden from the outside world (until much later when foreign papers hinted at the situation) because courtiers would tittle tattle among themselves but had such a vested interest in the integrity of the monarchy that they were reluctant even to voice their disapproval.

The press was still busy marrying Margaret off to one or the other remaining 'little nigger boys' and, while divorce was severely frowned upon at court, completely failed to grasp the significance of the news that the marriage of Group Captain Townsend and his wife Rosemary had been dissolved, and that he had been granted a decree nisi. It was not long before Rosemary quietly married the co-respondent.

Although Margaret disappeared from public view after her father's death, the air was thick with inside information that she had 'changed' and that 'her smile had vanished'. It was surprising that people expected her to resume her rounds of pleasure before the end of the three months' official court mourning. Reporters waited anxiously for her reappearance and eventually spotted her with the Queen at the Badminton Trials. It looked almost as if it was back to the old routine when she turned up at the theatre to see 'Call Me Madam', and went backstage to meet Billie Worth, the star. She asked about a line the Lord Chamberlain had censored – 'Even Margaret Rose goes out with Danny Kaye' – as if it signified the end of the class system.

But the general mood was still low-key. Royal smiles were sparse and Margaret looked sombre even at Ascot where she wore the comparatively sober post-mourning outfit in which she was seen again on her next theatre outing. She resumed her dreary duties – inspecting cadets in Wiltshire, visiting youth organisations in the West Country and hospitals in the Folkestone area, the N.A.A.F.I. and the Dockland Settlement.

She had wider scope to demonstrate that her charm had not lost its appeal when she flew to Oslo to attend the wedding of Princess Ragnhild of Norway to a commoner, Erling Lorentzen. Was this not a good omen?! Wearing one of the Queen's tiaras and draped in a white mink stole, she yet produced one of her most dazzling smiles when Prince Bertil of Sweden escorted her to the church. No, Prince Bertil was not courting her. He was in love with another English woman, a Mrs Lilian Craig.

News leaked out – probably deliberately – that Margaret had attended a very high church service 'incognito'. It was seen as a growing involvement with religion and gave rise to a report which first circulated far away – in Australia – but was not so far fetched : that she was studying Roman Catholicism. Nobody as yet associated her preoccupation with the church with a practical issue vexing her – whether there was an acceptable solution for a Christian woman wanting to marry a divorced man whose first wife was still alive.

The truth was complex enough, romantic, dramatic, intriguing – in the original sense of the word. Also more complicated. Margaret's curiosity about Catholicism did not diminish her interest in the established Church. She attended a course of eleven half-hour lectures on 'The School of Religion' at St Paul's, Knightsbridge, and went to post-confirmation classes at the vicarage. Sometimes, dressed inconspicuously in black suit and beret, she turned up at the church at the crack of dawn slipping unobtrusively into her pew. In this 'religious phase', friendship with her 'private curate', the Reverend Simon Phipps, blossomed. Son of one of the late King's courtiers, he had been chaplain at Trinity College, was industrial chaplain to the Coventry Diocese, and, strangely, a member of the Amalgamated Engineering Union. He was also an uninhibited social butterfly who amused Margaret with poems like the one entitled 'Can Anyone Think of an Original Sin?' which included this verse :

> What can anyone do that is the least bit new
> And hasn't been done before?
> Wouldn't it be nice to discover vice
> That is not just a terrible bore?
> I long to break out and make a sortie
> In a world that is mildly naughty.

The lines fairly accurately expressed Margaret's sentiments but her association with Simon was by no means entirely frivolous. They talked a great deal about serious matters and Margaret poured out her heart to him – though it was not formal confession.

She was clearly in need of solace and comfort. It looked as if hopes of a happy ending for her and Peter were receding. Far from moving towards a blissful climax, powerful forces were at work to abort it. The King's death had robbed the lovers of a supporter who loved them both as much as they loved each other. When Margaret wanted to keep her spirits up she said: 'Papa would have found a way', which meant that there was a way. But it is highly unlikely that the staunch Defender of the Faith would have blessed her union with Peter if it had come to the crunch in his lifetime (any more than his successor did in the event). Yet, protesting their deep religious loyalty, both Margaret and Peter were confident that the church would support them, much as Edward VIII and Wally Simpson had expected the country to back them. Margaret was as wrong as her uncle had been. She refused to heed the warning signs even when a well known cleric plucked up the courage to tell them – Margaret and Peter – that they should not count on special treatment because of their status; the church would not condone re-marriage of a man whose first wife was still alive nor would it allow them back to communion.

It was not long before Margaret, without a compassionate father to shield her, began to feel exposed to a stiffer wind whistling around her ears. Opposition to Townsend was consolidating in very influential Palace quarters which were confident that the Queen's worldly-wise husband, even if there were no old scores to settle, would warn her of the damage it might cause if the fact of Margaret's liaison became more widely known: 'It will cause a scandal!' courtiers warned.

'He ought to go!' said the man closest to the Queen's ear. As alert eyes could see, Townsend was not only always in the picture when Margaret appeared in public, and never far away during her free weekends; reports of clandestine meetings between the two increased in numbers – one afternoon Peter took her to his sister's for tea; in the evenings they slipped away from official functions and escaped into small cinemas; Colin Tennant and other friends offered them shelter. Margaret and Peter had a great deal to talk about, were coping with tremendous pressures and desperately trying to find a way out of their predicament.

The Queen was as yet reluctant to hurt her sister unless her situation posed a real threat to the monarchy. Some influential people not too well disposed towards Peter Townsend, or Margaret for that matter, thought the Queen's hand would be forced when the public became aware of what was going on, and argued that, in this case, it might be better if the truth became public. They kept their eyes peeled for the slightest indiscretion – it was bound to come sooner or later. It came at a most inconvenient time – the hour of the Queen's apotheosis.

CHAPTER SEVEN

The 'Margaret situation' rumbled on, hot, volatile like lava under a deceptively peaceful landscape while preparations for a great national celebration went ahead. A few with their ears close enough to the ground sensed the bubbling undercurrent which was bound to erupt sooner or later. The Coronation Council chaired by Philip was putting the finishing touches on the elaborate plans for June 2nd 1953, studying precedents, consulting records, analysing constitutional implications. It was all laid down, every detail pre-ordained—except for a new element arising immediately out of the Margaret situation.

What, courtiers asked, if after the Coronation—surely Margaret was not going to diminish its impact by any sensational move beforehand—the Queen's sister should decide to marry a commoner and divorcee and be obliged to renounce her royal prerogatives (as laid down in the Regency Act of 1937)? Although Margaret, until she reached the age of twenty-five, required the Queen's permission to marry—which might or might not be given—they pressed on. What of Margaret's place on the Regency Council and her designation as Regent if tragedy befell the Queen before her children came of age? Should the position not be clarified—now?

The questions had only to be asked for a subtle anti-Margaret manoeuvre to be mounted in harness, as it were, with the perennial anti-Townsend campaign. 'Force the girl's hand!' was the slogan under which the smooth-tongued, iron-fisted enemy rallied the faithful for the battle. Margaret off the Regency Council! And – here was the crux – Philip on to the

Regency Council! The idea had no sooner taken root when it became known to the leading political reporter of the day, Derek Marks, who followed the thread of the conspiracy through the corridors of the Palace to the corridors of power but stayed his hand until it became a political issue.

Margaret was sweet-talked into accepting the changes. She did not like them but had no intention of rocking the boat, not before the Coronation, anyway; she had waited so long – it was almost ten years since she had first run into Peter – a few more months would make little difference. But it is not difficult to guess what her attitude might have been had she known that at this critical stage, the Palace – no names, no pack drill – had promoted the changes by leaking information about her infatuation to the leaders of the political parties and hinted at the complications which could arise.

Details were only revealed when government and opposition had agreed to amend the Regency Act and drop the principle of 'next in succession' (which had given Margaret her special status) in favour of new arrangements. Prince Philip – and the Queen Mother – would join the Regency Council and there was no provision in any circumstances for Margaret to become Regent. Margaret was out. It seemed a reasonable, logical arrangement but it left the Queen's sister with a vague grudge.

Philip's position was also quite properly strengthened in other respects. To begin with, he was given precedence 'next to Her Majesty', i.e. ahead of Margaret – she saw something sinister in the rise and rise of her brother-in-law, and he was no longer hiding his dislike of Townsend. Yet, far from trying to grab more of the spurious power attaching to the throne, he followed his inclinations most of the time – travelling, flying, spending convivial evenings with friends such as my late colleague, photographer royal Baron (Nahum), whose studio accommodated some fairly Bohemian parties. Coincidence fantastic – one of the young men working for Baron was Antony Armstrong-Jones who was being initiated into the arts of photography. And it so happened that around this time Margaret had her portrait painted by Simon Elwes (who thought she was an excellent sitter). The artist gave a party in his St John's Wood house to show the finished work to friends, among them interior decorator Oliver Messel who brought his nephew along – Antony

85

Armstrong-Jones. Margaret attended the party but though Dominic Elwes, one of the painter's two sons, used to boast that Margaret and Tony first met under his father's roof, it must be recorded that, while Tony – as everybody else – had his eyes on her, Margaret did notice him.

A brief shadow fell across the pre-Coronation scene when the health of the grand old lady of the British Empire deteriorated sharply. Late evening on March 24th, the flags were lowered over Marlborough House. Queen Mary was dead. The Duke of Windsor made a rare trip to London to pay his last respects to his mother, and met his royal relatives including Margaret but twenty-six years was too big a gap across which to maintain a childhood hero worship or any sort of personal empathy with her favourite uncle. Still, the encounter, even in such melancholy circumstances, brought it home to Margaret that, like Uncle David in 1936, she too might be heading for an uncertain future, renunciation of her rights, separation from her family, perhaps exile if not disgrace. Was she over-dramatising the situation? Not necessarily, in the context of the time.

Royal life went on. On the morning after Queen Mary's death, the Queen tested the specially designed Coronation chairs. She was kept busy with a thousand and one details of the forthcoming occasion, and so was Margaret. The old Queen's funeral on March 31st marked the end of an era. Remote as she had been in life, an awesome figure to her granddaughters, she had generously provided for them and, much as she had disapproved of some of Margaret's activities – the press just then was as critical as she had been of the young princess smoking in public – left her enough leeway to give her a measure of independence. Independence was what Margaret wanted – to be a person in her own right, independent even of the Queen. The sisters saw little of each other because the Queen and Prince Philip were at Windsor while Buckingham Palace was being made ready for the Coronation junket, and Margaret's relations with Philip could, in any case, best be described in the hackneyed phrase as 'strained'. That's what they have remained ever since.

The country's mood brightened in anticipation of the Coronation, and Margaret entered into the spirit. As if to taunt the 'marriage brokers' who were still foisting husbands on her, she turned up for the Red, White and Blue Ball at the Dorchester Hotel with seven possibles all at once – three Lords (Dalkeith, Hambledon, Patrick Plunkett), three commoners (Billy Wallace, Tom Egerton, David Naylor-Leyland) and one Prince (Nicholas of Yugoslavia). She opened another Ball, this time at Wimbledon : 'Must go out dancing more often', she breathed quite incongruously, then went to see Eddie Fisher at a midnight gala cabaret and asked him to join her at her table and sing, or whisper, 'Outside of Heaven' into her ear. With such social diversions, she tried to still the pangs which heralded the impending crisis.

The steady rain did not deter the thousands who came to watch the Coronation and were lining the route long before the dawn of June 2nd. That day, with precision timing worthy of the event, Edmund Hillary's British Himalayan Expedition conquered Everest, and Roger Bannister added more gloss by running the mile in under four minutes breaking through a barrier against which the world's greatest athletes had battered in vain.

With the crowd tuned in to the young Queen – impossible to take one's eyes off her when she was in view – Margaret and the Queen Mother attracted less notice when, attended by Group Captain Peter Townsend, they arrived at Westminster Abbey to take their seats in the Royal Gallery. Irrepressible as ever, Margaret was quick to point to the gaggle of cleaners with brooms and carpet sweepers who performed a private little ballet – or so it looked – as they brushed the golden carpet around the throne. A glance in the direction of Peter, and, presently, she was involved with fellow royals who filled the Gallery, among them old friends like Bertil of Sweden and Bernhard of the Netherlands.

For a seasoned practitioner of royal ceremonies like Margaret, no less than for humbler spectators, it was nerve-tingling to watch the arrival of the Queen – a picture book Queen, transfixed by her vocation – and hear the Archbishop introducing her : 'Sirs, I here present unto you Queen Elizabeth, your undoubted Queen . . . !'

Fascinated and absorbed by the elaborate service, Margaret followed the proceedings intently although, having attended the rehearsals, she knew every step ahead – the Queen kneeling before the Archbishop, the Dean of Westminster helping to clothe her in the ceremonial vestments, the Lord Chamberlain presenting her with the Golden Spurs ... The Sword of State, the Golden Bracelets, the Stole and the Robe Royal ... The Queen seated in St Edward's Chair ... The Orb, the Ring, the Sceptre and the Rod ... For an instant, Elizabeth's eyes darted in the direction of the Royal Gallery and towards her mother and sister as if to remind them that the climax of the rich symbolism was at hand, and the diamond-studded, jewel-encrusted St Edward's Crown about to be placed upon her head.

Margaret's expression reflected the deeply moving, engrossing experience of seeing her sister, slender, girlish, yet with solemn dignity holding her head high as if to demonstrate that she was well capable of carrying the weighty Crown and the weighty responsibility that went with it. Still in the grip of emotion, one emotion releasing others and relaxing her composure, Margaret found herself with Peter Townsend in the annexe of the Abbey when it was all over, reliving, recounting every phase of the ceremony. Bubbling over with excitement, gesticulating and without halting the flow of words she flicked a miniscule speck of dust from the lapel of Peter's uniform, one of those instinctive, intimate gestures which reveal a great deal. Had she been asked what she had done, she could not have answered; intensely personal as it was in this context, it was automatic and natural – like a wife sprucing up her husband. She could not have guessed that the fleeting incident had been observed by an alert reporter.

Donald Edgar who described the Coronation so graphically that he made his name with his report from the Abbey told me of his stunned surprise when he saw Margaret and Peter looking into each other's eyes: 'At first I thought this slight man in R.A.F. uniform was a member of the royal family,' he recalled. He saw the officer holding out his hands, Margaret almost falling into his arms, a half-embrace ... Overwhelmed with the impact of the ceremony they had just witnessed, other people missed the couple's first public show of intimacy but when an account of it was published, it burst open the floodgates of speculation. More than speculation. Suddenly it was common knowledge that Margaret was in love. Suddenly it was obvious that she had been in love with one and the same man all the time.

Palace reaction was predictable. That was it! This was what

old hands had long predicted – a public scandal. For the old guard it was action stations. Whatever the final outcome, the situation had to be dealt with right away. The Queen could surely no longer put her erring sister above the prestige of the monarchy. That sort of thing could not be allowed to go on under the roof of the Palace – or Clarence House or anywhere! First – shades of Townsend separating Elizabeth and Philip six years earlier – Margaret would have to take a little trip (Philip's suggestion); next, Townsend would have to be removed from royal service. With Philip supporting the anti-Townsend brigade, the handsome courtier's days were numbered.

As with heads of government or cabinet ministers who always have a sheaf of invitations or a special occasion – an inauguration, an anniversary, a national holiday – to choose from when opportune, so with the royals. The Rhodes Centenary Exhibition at Bulawayo, Southern Rhodesia, which warranted a royal presence, was conveniently remembered. That was ideal for Margaret – with the Queen Mother going along for comfort and as a chaperon. They would be going before the end of the month. As to Townsend, another job would have to be found for him without delay. Winston Churchill, alerted by the Queen's Secretary Alan Lascelles, agreed and was said to have told the Queen bluntly: 'Get rid of him!' There was a vacancy for an Air Attaché in Brussels? That was very suitable, very suitable indeed.

In the meantime, something would have to be done to stem the avalanche of rumours at home and abroad and fortunately the Palace could count on friends in Fleet Street to lend a hand. First off the mark with a storming rebuttal was *The People* (June 14th, 1953) 'Stop These Scandalous Rumours!' the loyal headline screamed. 'The story (of Margaret's infatuation with Peter) is, of course, utterly untrue!' the popular Sunday pronounced. Of course! It called on the authorities to issue an official denial. When less compliant and credulous contemporaries continued to publish the scandalous rumours, the Church of England newspaper chipped in with a stern rebuke accusing them of violating the canons of good manners. The *Catholic Herald*, on the other hand, seemed to accept the speculation at face value and demanded – unkindly, considering the lady's Catholic sympathies – that the Princess should be made to surrender rank and status if she married divorced Captain Townsend. The 1936 precedent – Edward VIII preferring life with the twice-divorced woman he loved to the throne – came naturally to mind. But the London *Times* grumbled that 'based on the flimsiest structure of supposition' the Margaret-Townsend story 'had been given unforgivably the shape of scandal'.

Tribune, the left-wing journal, told its readers that the Queen had sought the advice of the Cabinet whether Margaret should marry the airman and the Cabinet had answered 'No!' This was the cue for Parliament to get into the act. 'Can we have an assurance that the British Cabinet has not interfered with Princess Margaret's private life?' asked Labour M.P., Marcus Lipton ('Amazing how Labourites spring to the defence of any royal who kicks over the traces', was one comment I heard at the time) and Chancellor of the Exchequer R. A. B. Butler replied: 'Such matters have never been brought before Her Majesty's advisers.' When Peter Townsend's appointment as an 'Extra Equerry to the Queen (signifying his retirement from active royal service) and appointment to Brussels was duly announced, another Labour M.P., Emrys Hughes, wanted to know why it was proposed to send an air attaché to Brussels. Because there had always been one and there happened to be a vacancy now, was the government's bland reply.

Although the Queen was distressed and anxious about the effect of the affair on the monarchy, she did not have it in her heart to reproach her young sister. If she was in love ...! Try ing to be helpful, the Archbishop of York only succeeded in confusing the situation when he demanded greater charity on the part of the Church of England in its attitude to divorce and said that adultery should not be regarded as the one unforgivable sin : 'Many who have gone through the divorce courts have a right to our sympathy and not our blame,' he said making no apparent distinction between guilty and innocent parties. The lone voice of support was cold comfort for Margaret who was deeply shaken by the church's implacable opposition – opposition to her happiness, as she saw it. Disappointed, disillusioned, she felt the church was asking too much of her. Her religious fervour was dampened and did not flower again until happier times came within reach once more, though by this time the church's attitude towards marriage and divorce had changed. By this time, friends sensed Margaret's strong feeling that, since the church no longer appeared to believe in its own strict rules, her sacrifice had been in vain.

To some extent, perhaps, the intensity of public interest in this upstairs-downstairs romance in the Palace was due to the slack period in world affairs. The full implications of Stalin's death some months earlier had not yet been grasped; Europe was fumbling with a futile Defence Community; the Korean War was approaching its end – an armistice was signed in July within a week of the *Daily Mirror*, the world's largest circulation newspaper, coming out with an eight-inch tall, single-word headline – YES. It was the readers' answer to the question : 'Should Princess Margaret be allowed to wed Peter Townsend?' 70,142 voted, and their verdict was – Yes : 67,907; No : 2,235 (or 96.81 as against 3.19 per cent). "Yellow journalism,' retorted the rival *Daily Sketch*, green with envy over the *Mirror*'s circulation-boosting impertinence. Once more, as at the time of her Capri holiday, Margaret was becoming a royal peepshow.

The Queen, while recalling her own resentment at being despatched to Africa at the height of her involvement with Philip, had little difficulty in persuading Margaret to remove herself from the centre of the storm – the accepted way of dealing with a royal romance. Whatever Philip or anybody else thought or said, the Queen was known at this stage to be reluctant to slam the door in Margaret's face. And Margaret alternating between despondency and optimism finally convinced herself that, in spite of inevitable tribulations and delays, there would be a happy ending for her. Peter, now that their cover was blown, would have to go, alas, but she looked upon the impending separation in the spirit of absence making the heart grow fonder . . .

When, in the middle of the crisis, the Queen, Philip and Margaret went together to the opera, there were stiff upper lips all round. Like civilised people, they did not exhibit family problems in public and, besides, royal fraternisation meant as little in 1953 as at the time when the Kaiser kissed Queen Victoria's hand. Nothing disturbed the Queen's triumphant Coronation tour of Scotland which coincided with a rumour reaching Margaret that her sister intended to give up Balmoral – too little privacy, too old-fashioned. The boot was on the other foot and the rumour was traced to the Queen Mother's search for a Scottish home of her own, to be shared with Margaret, which resulted in her buying the Castle of Mey, a bit further to the north. More significant were the whispers which spread when the Queen Mother went to inspect Marlborough House. Was she going to move into Queen Mary's old home making way at Clarence House for Margaret – and her husband?

Group Captain Townsend's last official duty before leaving for his new assignment was to accompany the Queen on a visit to Northern Ireland. It was an opportunity to talk to him and she was said to have spoken in specially friendly terms which reflected her memory of her father's affection for his courtier rather than her sister's infatuation with him. On their return to London, the Group Captain took his leave from the sovereign at the airport. In full view of the usual gathering around her, the Queen shook Peter's hand warmly, demonstratively and with a smile which looked like a token of encouragement. The farewells between Margaret and Peter, on the other hand, were discreet and, one gathered, not altogether sad. Both felt a sense of relief that the thing was out in the open and told each other that the stuffed shirts in the Palace would be obliged to surrender before long. But Peter kept out of the way when the Queen and Philip went to London Airport on June 30th to see the Queen Mother and Margaret on their way to Africa. The aircraft took off at two-fifteen p.m. precisely. That, less than three-quarters of an hour later, Philip was at Wimbledon watching the tennis, shows that he did not linger one minute to discuss his sister-in-law's departure with the Queen. It was an embarrassing subject.

With the Townsend affair the world's most popular topic, Margaret's every gesture and expression was being scrutinised as she went about Southern Rhodesia. Did she look gloomy, dejected, depressed? The day she and the Queen Mother visited Bulawayo, the contrast between the elder lady's unflagging charm and Margaret's sullen apathy struck some people who, unaware of the Princess's swiftly changing moods, searched for hidden reasons. The truth was that she looked miserable not because she was pining for Peter but because she was freezing in the intense cold of the Rhodesian winter. Dancing Scottish reels to the accompaniment of an African band a couple of days later she was in high spirits, laughing readily and chatting amiably with all and sundry.

Friends said she was in constant touch with Peter Townsend telephoning him twice a day but, though it was quite likely, there was no authentic confirmation of this particular piece of intelligence. But she did expect to see him on her return and have a few days with him before the enforced separation. The powers at the Palace were not having it. They pressed, cajoled and finally got Lord de Lisle, the Air Minister, and the Foreign Office (in view of his new diplomatic status) to issue orders for his departure – not later than July 15th. It happened to be the day before Margaret's return. He, too, had been anxious to stay and see her once more but he had no choice and reluctantly obeyed orders.

Much of Margaret's bitterness could be traced to a disappointment at not finding him there when she came back. She was angry about 'the dirty trick' that had been played on her. Yet she was soon back in the old groove. Her diary listed a great many public engagements largely because the Queen was on a tour of the Commonwealth and every available royal had to take a share of her official duties. Still Margaret spent much time with a remarkable trio of lady friends, all of them wives of gentlemen who, at one time or another, had been expected to marry her – the gentle Marchioness of Blandford, the Countess of Westmorland (famous for her 'magnolia skin') and the Countess of Dalkeith whose sweet face matched her nature. From such decorous get-togethers, Margaret went on to see a harmless American comedy, 'The Moon is Blue', which had acquired a reputation because Cardinal Spellman had condemned the film version and some moronic American naval officer had described it as 'unfit for sailors to watch because it was immoral'. It all revolved around the word 'virgin' which had not previously been uttered from the stage. Margaret had seen stronger stuff in her time.

She went out with Robin McEwen – his being a Catholic brought out a new crop of religious gossip. They had dinner at a restaurant in Charlotte Street, Bloomsbury, duly chaperoned by two members of the royal household, Miss Iris Peake, daughter of the Minister of Pensions and granddaughter of the Earl of Essex, and Captain Oliver Dawnay, the Queen Mother's

Private Secretary. There was no question of Margaret falling for Robin, no hint of romance that evening unless one could have seen ahead to 1963 when Oliver Dawnay and Iris Peake were married. Margaret's private file of outrageous press reports soon sported two contradictory entries – one, that she would shortly announce her engagement to Robin McEwen, and another, that the Queen was about to confer a dukedom on Peter Townsend.

When we tested public opinion in these days (at the request of foreign editors) we encountered the most endearing British phenomenon – support for the underdog. The heavy hand of the church, the Palace campaign, state interference and the prissy establishment trying to crush the love of the glamorous Princess and her humble hero provoked a backlash in the lovers' favour. 'Never was Margaret more popular', wrote Hans Tasiemka, the perceptive London correspondent of a German newspaper. It was felt that Townsend had had a raw deal and that, anyway, Margaret was closer to the spirit of the times than her adversaries and seemed to be purposefully striding towards what came to be called the permissive society. Not that she accepted this reading.

The pattern of her private life was disrupted without Peter. She missed the one person to whom she could talk freely and who appreciated her biting accounts of her tedious official duties – silly local councillors tying themselves in knots trying to make conversation, county women falling over each other to be 'recognised', children being pushed forward to be noticed. Without Peter's willing ear at the end, she performed listlessly, the fixed obligatory smile on her sensuous lips even less credible than before. Yet, life without Peter was less taut, no more fear of discovery, no more guilt feelings, no temptation to steal apples because there was no (forbidden) fruit on the tree. With her natural hedonism she turned to old pursuits and adapted the showbiz slogan of the royal scene – 'The show must go on!'

Talking about showbiz, just then her wise friend Judy Montagu came up with a suggestion that she should take an active part in a theatrical venture in aid of charity. The plan was to stage a play with a large cast to be filled by as many society types as could be mustered. Their appearance on stage would attract not only their families and friends but a host of prosperous, forelock-touching royal fans who would not mind spending five guineas a head to watch the hoi polloi disporting themselves on either side of the lights. In view of the commotion caused by her appearance as Mademoiselle Fifi, the idea of Margaret's taking one of the parts was quickly dropped. Instead she could help to produce and direct. Who had seen more plays than she had? Her experience would be invaluable.

After much heart-searching, the play selected for this dilettante excursion into the performing arts was Edgar Wallace's thriller 'The Frog', which had an outsize cast and a totally confusing plot. Margaret and Judy spent hours compiling lists of suitable performers and came up with virtually every member of their circle, all titled, naturally, with the exception of Billy Wallace. A professional director, Alan Jefferson, was persuaded to lend his services, and Margaret was officially appointed 'Assistant Director' until Alan insisted that it was 'infra-dig for a princess to be an assistant' and up-graded her to 'Associate Director'.

One of the leading parts went to 'dear Porchy', as they called Lord Porchester, others to Lord Norwich, Mrs Gerald Legge (the future Lady Lewisham, Dartmouth and Spencer) and the rest of the 'Maggit Set'. Maggit herself dutifully attended rehearsals, enjoyed gossipy 'Take Fives' with democratic sandwiches and sausage rolls, gave her view on where performers should stand on stage and how they should or should not say their lines. The rest of her days was taken up with telephoning all round, visiting, consultations and arguments.

Top people were clamouring for tickets, among them such contemporary scene stealers as Noel Coward and Lady Docker, who, with her gold-plated Daimler and diamond-studded husband, was at the height of her headline-grabbing career as a 'personality'; Sarah Churchill, Sharman Douglas (on a brief visit) and the glamorous Aly Khan competed for the gawkers' attention. Missing from cast or audience was the hapless Nicholas of Yugoslavia who was still being talked about as a gigolo unworthy of Margaret's friendship when news arrived that he had lost his life in a motoring accident.

As the first of the scheduled three performances went across the stage at the Scala, an American impresario offered to put up £7,000 to take the show to the U.S.A.: 'I'll double it if the Princess comes along,' he said. The offer was declined. The exclusive audience studied the elaborate programme with one of Osbert Lancaster's inimitable drawings – the creator of 'Lady Littlehampton' did not have to abandon caricature when portraying the leading members of the cast, Lords and Ladies Littlehampton one and all.

What the audience saw was a production which would have graced a village hall but, in the heart of London's theatreland, was highly embarrassing stuff. Having watched the show from the director's box, Margaret went on stage to make a curtain speech telling the spectators what fun it had all been. Like a real trouper, she decided to wait up for the first editions of the national newspapers with their reviews and went to the '400' Club. She did not know what to expect – how remote the royal clique was from the world outside. The critics' verdict was devastating and might have been worse had some of them not tried to spare Margaret utter humiliation. 'Oh, how silly it all was!' was one typical comment. 'It would have been a relief . . . to find that the saga of the Princess and the Frog was just a fairy story. Unhappily, the whole bad dream is sadly, ridiculously true.' Margaret's foible cost £3,500 to produce but raised a respectable £10,000 for charity.

She also, incidentally, helped to raise funds for a worthy cause when, a few weeks later, she attended the performance of a masque – 'Porci Ante Margaritam' – at St Hilda's College, Oxford, where she was presented with a copy of Apollo's address to her :

> Fairest of pearls, the world Thine Oyster,
> We from our academic cloister
> Have come to serve Thee, take us not to task
> For the sad quality of this our masque . . .'

Her presence helped St Hilda's considerably. The humility of the academic performers, however, made her wonder about the view she and the aristocratic cast of 'The Frog' had taken of their own effort.

Reverting to higher forms of stage craft, Margaret hugely enjoyed Marlene Dietrich's performance at the Café de Paris, the pre-war society haunt which had been hit in the blitz by a Nazi bomb when scores of fine young officers and their girlfriends were killed. Recapturing its old glory, the Café de Paris lured such stars as Margaret's admirer, Noel Coward, who would entertain her and her friends for the pure joy of it. Watching him and Marlene made Margaret itch to go out there and perform – she might have done better than the un-talented 'Froggies' – but she reserved her repertoire of ballads and American hit songs for private occasions.

For a vivacious young woman with her active mind and in-telligence, the mixture of official duties and private pleasures was not satisfying and often left her frustrated and bored. She spent many lonely hours doing crossword puzzles as came to light when she entered one, from *Country Life* magazine, in a competition. Sigmund Freud might have interpreted it as a cry for sympathy ... She promptly won a prize. An even more wel-come escape from the treadmill was an invitation to visit the 3rd King's Own Hussars at Bad Eilsen in Germany – it was one of the half-dozen regiments of which she was Colonel-in-Chief (apart from holding office in twenty-three civil bodies).

The Germans had always taken an almost proprietorial interest in 'Margaret Rose, die schöne Prinzessin', and not even the prospect of lunch with such ageing Teutons as Chancellor Konrad Adenauer and President Theodor Heuss spoiled her cheerful anticipation. The visit ran true to form. Accompanied by Iris Peake, Margaret was whisked from function to function including an inspection of the Royal Navy's 'Rhine Squadron'. It ended with a regimental ball with her hosts, the Hussars, complaining that R.A.F. types were monopolising her – it was not fanciful to suggest that she saw Peter Townsend in every Royal Air Force officer she danced with. She was in a happy frame of mind. As always when she was in a good mood she created much goodwill among her British hosts and the Germans.

For the British people, Townsend was already old hat. Out of sight ... This was the explanation for a new rash of marriage rumours around her traditional summer trip to Balmoral where – also something of a tradition by now – Colin Tennant was one of the house guests. 'Imminent announcements' were bandied about by the press but Margaret emerged from the celebration of her twenty-fourth birthday unengaged, and Colin returned to the arms of the girl he was to marry soon.

A week later, Margaret went to Edinburgh to look in on the

Old Vic's Festival production of 'A Midsummer Night's Dream', blissfully unaware of an anonymous telephone call, possibly from a Scottish Nationalist extremist, threatening that 'something would happen' if she went to the theatre. Fred Crocker, her detective, organised security – and nothing happened. One of the more pleasurable events of her royal business took her to the stateliest of stately homes, Blenheim Palace, where the Duchess of Marlborough played hostess to Christian Dior and his attractive models. Two thousand people paying the obligatory five guineas each (in aid of the Red Cross Society) saw a hundred Diors, among them a wedding gown which Margaret inspected with interest – much tittering in the crowd.

By way of contrast and with the English upper class woman's inalienable talent for defeminising herself, she turned up in a hideous pixie hood and assorted shapeless winter garments once the first frost touched the air around Drumkildo House, Meigle, Perthshire, the estate of her cousins, the Elphinstones. One of these we shall encounter before long as plain Mrs Jean Wills, wife of Major John Wills, playing hostess to Margaret at the climax of her deepest personal crisis.

How handsome Margaret looked when she peeled off the protective garb to exhibit a new hairstyle, her girlish curls gone. Straight hair, sophisticated, very attractive. Alas, the frosty winter look was more symbolic of the year ahead of her than Dior's wedding dress.

CHAPTER EIGHT

Margaret's future was much in Churchill's mind. A passionate royalist, he was emotionally involved, if not as deeply as in the 1936 abdication crisis, and anxious to save the monarchy embarrassment. Although his public pronouncements had been ambiguous, he had never, in his heart, approved of Edward VIII's plan to marry Wallis Simpson. But he had been of the opinion that, given sufficient time, the King would have changed his mind and that therefore abdication would not have become necessary. That events had proved him wrong, that the king had been determined to marry the twice-divorced American lady whatever the consequences did not affect his view of the Margaret–Townsend crisis. This, surely, would be solved in time without the need for any drastic step on Margaret's part.

And time was what he worked for. He persuaded the Queen to play it cool and not to exacerbate matters at this stage by putting pressure on Margaret. Philip was in favour of a more radical solution and against what he called pussy-footing. He, too, was aware of 1936 and the traumatic effect the abdication had had on the monarchy. Margaret demanding to marry Townsend – not to speak of her actually marrying him – could only involve the Crown in new controversy and open up old wounds. The best way to deal with the situation was to separate the couple, put distance between them – not a love test such as he and Elizabeth had had to pass but a permanent separation which would soon bring the lovers to their senses, would cool Margaret's and Peter's ardour and the end of the affair would be nigh. Why not give Margaret some interesting new assignment, tempt her with an irresistible proposition – send her on her first solo royal tour. What a good idea! The Queen took it up and asked to see the royal travel programme, plans in the making, invitations in hand. She came up with an imaginative suggestion, a tour of the Caribbean – Trinidad, Jamaica, Barbados, Tobago . . . Even hedged in with protocol and with every move pre-arranged, it promised colourful people, new impressions, the sea and the sun, adventure, magic. Margaret who had never been to the Calypso Islands jumped at the opportunity.

Prompted by the Prime Minister, the Cabinet quickly approved the trip. The Colonial Office was instructed to work out the itinerary in consultation with local governors and mayors who were asked to put forward suggestions for detailed programmes and provide information about places she ought to visit and about the 'paunch-and-curtsey' brigade she would be expected to meet. Margaret kept in close touch with the preparations. The start of the journey was fixed for January 30th, first stage – London to Port of Spain, Trinidad – by air. In the Caribbean, the royal yacht *Britannia* to serve as her base and take her from island to island.

Never before had the assembly of Margaret's wardrobe been so complicated. Victor Stiebel and Norman Hartnell shared responsibility for outfits in Caribbean gold and, less appropriately, Bermuda blue, five a day for each group of islands over a period of four weeks. With less funds at their disposal, similar problems confronted the ladies of her entourage – Iris Peake and twenty-eight-year-old Elizabeth Cavendish, do-gooding sister of the Duke of Devonshire – and the men as well: Brigadier Sir Norman Gwatkin, a mature but lively member of the Lord Chamberlain's office, and Oliver Dawnay, the Queen Mother's trusted watchdog in her daughter's camp. Crocker – Detective Inspector Fred Crocker of the Yard – would be going along and so would 'Ruby', Margaret's maid. Minor characters brought up the party to twelve.

As with most things throughout their geographical separation, Margaret kept Peter Townsend informed about the involved planning for her first solo overseas tour. A wistful note crept into their telephone conversations when, according to her friends, Margaret sighed that, much as she looked forward to the trip, what would have made it perfect would have been for Peter to accompany her and share the experience (as they had shared the joys of the African tour of 1947). A forlorn hope. While she would not have passed up the tour for anything, she was at the same time apprehensive because it marked a watershed in her life. She would have to make up her mind, make a decision as soon as it was over. The prospect concentrated her mind, the issue became more clearly defined than it had been. Yes, she did want to marry Peter Townsend. No, she did not want to give up her status and her privileges. Neither would she accept that her two aims were irreconcilable although she thought she could notice a change in her sister's attitude. Only a few months separated Margaret from her twenty-fifth birthday when she would no longer need the Queen's permission to marry but even so . . .

However tight security, however discreet the royal family, important topics under discussion at the Palace, as Margaret knew only too well, had a way of filtering through the safety curtain and becoming public property, distorted sometimes, mistaken in detail but only too often surprisingly accurate. The effect was to add a new dimension to Margaret's quandary. History, tradition, family, politics, palace feuds, public opinion built up into a formidable drama threatening to relegate the principal character to a minor role or – to change the metaphor – reduce the Queen's sister to a pawn on a many-sided chessboard. Margaret, though she tried not to show it, felt hemmed in to the point of claustrophobia – every Tom, Dick and Harry was grappling with her intensely private problem. She resented it and was doubly anxious to get away. The Caribbean was a good place to be while her future was in the melting pot.

So clear were the sub-sonic signals from the Palace indicating that something sensational was afoot that even the serious newspapers wanted to cash in on whatever might come to pass. In this spirit, even the ponderous old *Observer* (so much livelier in years to come) published a profile of Margaret, unsurpassed in pomposity and humbug, presenting this intelligent, hard-pressed girl who had been kicking cheerfully over the narrow royal traces most of her life, as a paragon of virtue. Castigating more informative newspapers by invoking the spirit of Wilkes as a vile distorting mirror of royalty, the anonymous sycophant praised Margaret's 'fastidiousness in the choice of her friends'. Sounder commentators described the dreary fellows she had been associating with as 'witless wonders'; indeed, in the passage of time, fastidiousness was the last word one would have applied to Margaret's choice of friends.

All this was behind her as the Caribbean trip, while not releasing her from the grip of a tight royal schedule, transported her into a new and captivatingly attractive setting. The tour got off to a splendid start when she was greeted on arrival at Port of Spain, Trinidad, with a chorus of strong voices and the twang of a steel band rendering a surprisingly perceptive calypso.

> Lovin' sister of Queen Lilibet
> Is Princess Margaret.
> She ent married, she ent tall,
> Like to dance, like to sing,
> Like to try out anything.
> If she been boy, she been king.

Although there were grumbles on her behalf that the crowded programme did not leave her much time to do her own thing between receptions, official luncheons and dinners, Margaret thoroughly enjoyed herself. She entered into the spirit of the Caribbean and, being stimulated, in turn revitalised the traditional atmosphere and gave people something to cheer and sing about.

Self-conscious about some prominent, if rather attractive, features of her figure, she was most careful to choose a secluded, well-guarded beach from which to go for a swim in Tobago (while Mesdemoiselles Peake and Cavendish and Monsieurs Gwatkin and Dawnay splashed about in less remote parts of the coral seas). Photographers were sternly warned off – if they dared to trap the swim-suited princess in their lenses, their cameras would be confiscated and their accreditation to the royal party withdrawn.

At Grenada Government House, Margaret showed that she had her wits about her even during the dullest formalities. When Governor Sir Edward Beetham introduced a lady to her adding (mistakenly) that the husband was regrettably indisposed, and the husband turned up for presentation a minute later, Margaret greeted him: 'I congratulate you on your quick recovery.' In Jamaica she floated down the Rio Grande on a bamboo raft and whiled away the night at stimulating beachside picnics, the beginnings of one of her most enjoyable pastimes.

She sounded genuinely happy – 'sounded' is the operative word – as her host, Jamaica's Governor Sir Hugh (now Lord) Foot discovered. When, one morning, he called out to his servant: 'Turn that radio off!' it so happened that what he heard was not the radio but Margaret singing in her bath. 'She does burst out singing suddenly,' the Governor remarked. Her party was infected with her high spirits. The immaculate Brigadier Gwatkin was observed in a calypso shirt performing an African dance . . . Among distinguished people contributing to Margaret's amusement were Adlai Stevenson and the ubiquitous Noel Coward, the tax-exile who waxed nostalgically about his native country. At Antigua, steel bands, 'Brute Force' and 'Hell's Gate', made sounds which did justice to their names.

At St Vincent, against the background of 'La Sulphiere', the sulphorous volcano, Margaret swam in the sea, bathed in the sun, presided over sumptuous barbecues, listened to songs. She was enchanted. At night, the drums in the bush and the roar of the waves, matched the grandest orchestra: 'That's where I should like to live . . .' she sighed. The spark struck at this moment burst into a flame years later when she bought her island home on Mustique, near St Vincent, and became involved with another man arguably even less suitable as a consort than Peter Townsend.

She returned home to a friendly reception, protected from the English weather by a mink coat and sporting a deep tan that did not suit her. Her Rolls Royce, the first she owned, with a P.M. (for 'Princess Margaret') on her personalised number plate, took her to Clarence House and hours of pleasurable recall for her mother's benefit of the hectic month in the Caribbean. Though Philip and Elizabeth, who had now come round to her husband's view, hoped that the excursion had pushed her preoccupation with Peter Townsend into the background, the Queen Mother was still turning a blind eye.

What was new at home? Well, it looked as if the family's fatherly friend Winston Churchill was about to step down and hand over the reins, how sad. His successor – obviously Anthony Eden. The name instantly conjured up his marital position. Had he not divorced his first wife in 1950 and married Winston's niece Clarissa Churchill two years later? So the country would have a Prime Minister who had gone through the divorce courts! If the occasion arose, it would seem but a brief step to a princess marrying a man who was an innocent party in the break-up of a marriage.

Anticipation of significant developments in Margaret's affairs was bound to express itself. *Time* magazine had started the ball rolling a month earlier while she was still abroad but the story had been eliminated from the English edition. Now the British and the continental press gave themselves up to an orgy of speculation, views from all angles and comment, not all uninformed. What had been a discreet Palace ploy – to send Margaret to the Caribbean to help her resolve her personal problem – was now out in the open. The Queen could no longer hold back. She had to tell Margaret that this world-wide gossip about her undermined the dignity of the throne. She is said to have talked gently but it was impossible to miss the firm resolve behind her gentle voice.

The Queen quoted chapter and verse of the Royal Marriage Act of 1772 which stipulated that members of the royal family required the sovereign's permission to marry before the age of twenty-five; and that after that he, or she, had to give the Privy Council a year's notice of intention to marry when it was up to both houses of parliament to sanction the marriage or block it. The consequences of defiance would be very dire.

It struck Margaret as not very tactful of her sister to remind her of the old Act which, as she knew full well, had been introduced by George III (as binding on all descendents of George II) because his own brother, the Duke of Cumberland, had married a disreputable woman, a certain Mrs Horton, and another brother had been secretly married for years. But Margaret also knew that the Act had been bitterly attacked by Walpole, among others ... Anyway, what relevance did it have in modern times? Margaret would not accept that she could not marry Townsend and retain her status once she was twenty-five and parliament approved. She still thought she could have her cake and eat it.

A few days later, clutching at straws, she raised the subject of Eden's divorce. That was a different kettle of fish. Confirming Eden as Prime Minister was a political act, a far cry from the Queen acquiescing in her sister contracting a marriage of which her Church disapproved. But was the issue all that clear-cut? The Archbishop of Canterbury was blowing hot and cold. Some months earlier he had written: 'I do not find myself able to forbid good people who come to me for advice to embark on a second marriage. I tell them that it is their duty as conscientiously as they can to decide before God what they should do.' But he had also said more recently that if the Church were to marry divorced persons it could not bear effective witness before the world to the standard of Christ. What Margaret knew full well was that the Archbishop had been active behind the scenes and discussed her position with the Queen and the politicians.

That Eden, too, representing the view of the Cabinet was against the marriage, that the Commonwealth leaders thought it inadvisable to tamper with the line of succession which had already been broken by Edward's abdication were factors which did not register as strongly with Margaret as the Queen's opposition. Because she had, in spite of all the warning signals, counted on her sister's support, her disillusionment was all the deeper. Elizabeth had let her down. The Queen was making common cause with her enemies. The Archbishop, the courtiers, even Winston Churchill! And the one who was the chief culprit, the architect of her predicament – it was Philip. Philip was the bogeyman! She would never forgive him. One of her intimates put a different construction on her 'pathological hatred' of Philip – she would not admit it but she was already, so his theory went, halfway towards giving Peter up because the alternative was too unpalatable; and she needed a scapegoat to banish her feelings of guilt about her change of mind and heart with which she could not come to terms. It could have dawned on her that she did not after all love Peter enough to change her life, enter into a hole-in-the-corner marriage outside the established Church, banished from court or, worse, like Uncle David an exile in a foreign land and a pathetic stranger to the British people. She had said it before and she felt it as strongly as ever – it was wonderful to be a royal princess and she did not want to be anything else.

No one believed more firmly than she in the mystique of the monarchy, and her recent trip had strengthened her conviction. Ovations such as she had enjoyed, veneration, cheers, curtseys, the entourage of ladies and gents waiting on her, the flunkeys at her beck and call, what they symbolised above all, the royal princess bit – could she give it all up and live happily ever after? Her emotions, even those she later tried to articulate, are difficult to describe in precise language because, even if her love for Peter was waning, the mounting obstruction made her rebellious and belligerent.

Peter Townsend did not weather the crisis well. At first he kept out of harm's way and avoided the press, then switched tactics and seemed anxious to unburden himself: 'I'm fed up hiding in my apartment like a thief,' he growled within the hearing of the horde of reporters who were congregating in Brussels. The result was a spate of interviews, an avalanche of fumbling, inconclusive or contradictory statements some of which he retracted claiming to have been misrepresented. They left the overall impression that he expected Margaret to give up everything for him. Indeed, when a reporter told him in March 1954 that the whole of the British people would understand if Margaret gave up her position for the sake of love, he replied: 'That's good to hear.' They were no longer on the same wavelength. Pressed further he let slip an indiscreet and over-optimistic excuse for his reticence: 'The word must come from elsewhere,' he said.

The immense goodwill Margaret enjoyed was expressed by the large crowd which acclaimed her when she went to a 'Welcome Home' luncheon at the Mansion House. She showed herself on the balcony and the crowd roared: 'Good luck, Margaret!' At the lunch she found herself sitting next to Dr Fisher, the Archbishop of Canterbury, who talked to her deedily throughout the meal but it was fanciful to assume that they discussed her private affairs on this public occasion. There was little doubt, however, that they were very much to the fore when the Archbishop went to Buckingham Palace a few days later for a private lunch with the Queen and Philip, and stayed for two hours. 'There is nothing unusual about the visit,' he said. His evasive answer produced further speculation in the press which threatened to get out of hand. *Punch* published a cartoon which reflected the Queen's reaction. It depicted the throne and the steps leading to it littered with sensational front pages. 'The Dignity and Honour of the Throne', was the caption.

By this time, Peter Townsend, no longer as iron-willed as in his heyday as an R.A.F. hero, was getting rattled. When friends told him that Margaret was beginning to crumble under the war of nerves – if she had not already succumbed – he refused to accept that her love might not have stood the test. He telephoned her to say that he was taking a fortnight off and coming to London. 'Under no circumstances!' she snapped back. His presence could only complicate matters. While he, understandably, took this to mean that she was afraid his return might harden opposition to their plans, the truth was that she did not want him around while she was wrestling with a desperately difficult situation. Perhaps she did not want him to try and reverse the painful decision she had already made. Asked about his holiday, Townsend said that he was about to take it but was not sure whether he would visit Britain.

While he was still in Brussels and moaning that he was under an awful strain, Margaret bore up well but her patience was sorely tested when the Chaplain to the Queen, the Reverend P. Gillingham, included an ominous passage in his sermon (a parallel to the Bishop of Bradford's initiative in 1936): 'Christian duty', he pronounced as Margaret listened with a stern expression, 'is not always – in fact is seldom ever – pleasant or easy or what one wanted from life. The road is hard, straight, and must be taken!' His meaning was clear, his philosophy open to question. Before long, Bishop Blunt, a veteran of the battle over Edward VIII's marriage, raised his crook once more with menace and said: 'I do not see how the Queen could consent to such a union.' It looked as if ecclesiastical tanks were moving up with the Palace artillery in a concerted assault.

Margaret was livid because they would not even allow her the privilege of making her own decision. While pressure was mounting, public and press were still completely in the dark. 'Townsend to be promoted Marshal of the Royal Air Force', one prophet predicted, and the *New York Post* carried a banner headline: 'PALACE CIRCLES SAY MEG, FLIER WILL WED.' When nothing happened, when Margaret did not announce the hotly expected 'decision', public and press, as if exhausted by their sustained concentration on the subject, turned wearily in other directions.

Margaret gave the impression that she was trying to get away from her own shadow and plunged into traditional entertainment. She went to the theatre with Billy Wallace to see 'Kismet' – saw it four more times for some unfathomable reason – and, a few days later, spent a very enjoyable evening with the English Folk and Dance Society in Camden Town. She was on the dance floor for three full hours changing partners frequently. Her next outing was to attend the premiere of 'The Dambusters', a thrilling film of one of the war's most spectacular R.A.F. raids on Germany. As always, the audience watched her as intently as the screen. The most notable change they discovered was another new hairstyle – with a kiss curl.

Not much was read into it when she then disappeared briefly from public view. Perhaps nobody cared. Had Margaret watchers not relaxed their vigilance and hot pursuit, they would have discovered their quarry at the country house of a friend not far from an R.A.F. airfield where a little later a small, slender man with a familiar face stepped from an aircraft to be driven to a secret rendezvous with Margaret. It was Peter Townsend on a clandestine visit – for once the secret was not betrayed nor is much known about what passed during their brief meeting but it seems certain that Margaret was anxious to explain to Peter as graphically as possible what the outlook was.

The legal position, the risk of another year's delay even if she gave notice of her intention to parliament (and the possibility that the Commons and/or the Lords might raise objections even then), what the future held in these circumstances, were all points which must have conveyed to Peter that love was not the all-conquering consideration. If no more, their talk brought him from a dream world down to earth. Margaret seemed visibly relieved when she showed herself again at the Windsor Horse Trials playing 'Aunty' to Charles and Anne.

The state of play could be judged by all who paid attention

to some reliable indicators. One was Godfrey Winn's taking up where he had left off four years earlier and preparing a piece on Margaret for (Sir) Edward Hulton's *Picture Post*. He had seen the Princess, he told me, and his article would make her position perfectly clear – one marvels at the skill with which the royal *enfant terrible* already manipulated the press via her favourite reporters, Winn in 1955, Nigel Dempster twenty years later. What appeared under Godfrey Winn's name a week or so later culminated in this prediction: 'Do not imagine', he wrote, 'that this fairy-story princess in real life would exchange the destiny that is hers by birth and upbringing for any other kind of future in the whole wide world.' It could be interpreted in two ways – that she would wed and retain her royal status or that there would be no marriage.

Insiders reading Godfrey Winn's words nodded in agreement. Was there, then, no hope of a compromise? Could the Royal Marriage Act of 1772 not be changed? And would parliament wish to veto a royal marriage in this day and age? Similar thoughts occupied Margaret's mind as her twenty-fifth birthday (Sunday, August 21st, 1955) dawned to mark yet another turning point in the tortuous search for a solution. Everybody thought it was at hand when Anthony Eden went to visit the Queen at Balmoral where Margaret was also staying, but Eden arrived and went and once again nothing happened. The next significant visitor to come into view was Lord Mountbatten, everybody's favourite uncle but the royal family's most trusted friend did not influence events either. Townsend muddied the waters by saying that he would be in England in the middle of October therefore suggesting that there would be no birthday engagement. Undeterred, three hundred reporters bivouacked around the Queen's Scottish residence and the nerves of some Fleet Street editors were stretched to breaking point.

The one who gave way was the Editor of the *Daily Mirror*, Hugh Cudlipp, most brilliant of the great popularisers, who penned the banner-headline which echoed the sentiments of his four-million-odd readers: COME ON MARGARET – Please Make Up Your Mind!' he exhorted the Princess. (More than twenty years later, Lord Cudlipp confessed that he was not proud of his headline and rude intrusion into Margaret's private affairs but, though inveterate loyalists castigated the *Mirror*, I happen to know that Margaret herself, typically, bore no grudge and was all sweetness and light whenever she met Cudlipp.) The day his blunt exhortation was published, Margaret presided over a stall at a charity auction at Castle Abergeldie.

Sunday. Margaret's birthday. Anticlimax. The handsome airman did not descend from the sky to claim his Scottish princess and there was no man by her side in the traditional birthday photographs.

These photographs, approved by Margaret before their release, showed her as she saw herself : ethereal and a little aloof toying with leafy branches; or demure, domestic, with dog; or, again, sophisticated with six rows of pearls and an evening gown revealing her well-shaped shoulders. The birthday celebrations were a muted affair, the family preoccupied and at odds with each other and Margaret, obstinate, exasperating, unpredictable Margaret, the nigger in the woodpile.

Apart from the principal members of the family, the young Duke of Kent and his brother Michael were in the party, and so was Philip's sister, Princess Georg of Hanover. Of Margaret's personal friends only Dominic Elliot was among the guests. When the press lifted their siege Margaret and the Queen went riding, looking fine, giving nothing away. Neither did Peter Townsend who was traced to Ostend where he was on holiday with his two sons and also riding – in a Gentlemen's Race. A few weeks later he was, along with Prince Aly Khan, one of the competitors in the Grand Prix for Gentlemen at Deauville but either his horsemanship or his horse failed him and, in racing parlance, he came nowhere.

August ended, September passed, October was here. At last something stirred. It was now or never. Townsend was coming to England 'on a month's holiday', he said. Margaret had told him, without going into details, that the climax was at hand and that they would have to talk and Peter, according to friends, spent a few agonising days exuberantly hopeful one moment and dejectedly pessimistic the next.

On Wednesday, October 1st, Margaret caught the night train from Scotland to London which was due to arrive at Euston at seven-thirty a.m. the following morning. At that time Peter Townsend was on his way to Le Touquet in his green Renault, with a raincoat, a saddle and two pigskin suitcases. He – and the car – took the regular ferry plane to Lydd which also carried four reporters. Back on English soil, he continued the journey in his car – his destination: London and Lord Abergavenny's house in Lowndes Square, Knightsbridge where a big crowd and a small army of reporters gathered as soon as news of his arrival got around. A similar gathering of press and public collected outside Clarence House.

It was after six p.m. when Peter emerged from the house, took his car and drove to Clarence House. He made for one of the Household doors, could not get in and went to another which opened to admit him. Blinded by a hundred flashlights, he stumbled inside and was taken to the second-floor drawing-room. Margaret was in several minds; there is some evidence that it was her fighting spirit rather than her love which determined her strategy. The fronts were drawn: supporting her were the British people, opposing her was Philip backed by the Queen, the Archbishop, even Eden (although there were members of parliament of all political persuasions prepared to champion her cause). Popular and political support might yet sway the Queen! Peter and Margaret were together for one hour and fifty-one minutes.

It was eight-twenty p.m. when Townsend left Clarence House to shouts of 'Good luck, Sir!' and drove back to his host's house. The dramatic reunion released a huge national sigh – 'Together at Last!' it echoed from rooftops and front pages. It was noted that the Queen was due back the following Tuesday, and parliament scheduled to reassemble a week later, obvious stages, it was assumed, on Margaret's progress towards a happy marriage.

Having mapped out a busy social programme for the coming days and, maybe, weeks, Margaret – with Peter going under his own steam – made her way to Berkshire the following day (Friday, October 14th) where they met up for a weekend together as the guests of Major John Wills and his wife (née Elphinstone), Margaret's cousin, at their country estate, Allanbay Park, Binfield. They talked all afternoon, then had dinner with their hosts. What snippets of information escaped from the privacy of Allanbay Park indicated that John and Jean Wills took a much gloomier view of prospects than Peter and Margaret.

Peter was up and about at seven-thirty a.m. next morning, drove to Miss Wilmot's stables some two miles away, saddled a three-year-old which answered to the name of Juliet Jones and went for a short sharp gallop. Margaret was out in the grounds when he returned. 'They seemed happy,' was the concensus of those who saw them but who could really tell? For the rest of the day they stayed indoors.

On Sunday morning, seven-year-old Marilyn Wills, Margaret's godchild, acted as spokesman and told reporters that Margaret was still in bed. Not for long, though. She and her cousin drove to Windsor and went to the Royal Chapel which was empty except for a few royal servants. The Queen Mother came over from the Royal Lodge to meet Margaret as she left the church. They embraced and went for a walk while Jean Wills waited in the car. Later Margaret said that in these days her mother was the only member of the family who understood her. They talked for forty minutes, then Margaret joined Jean and they drove back to Allanbay Park where Peter Townsend was waiting for them at the entrance. That afternoon, there were guests for tea – Margaret was gathering the faithful around her to relieve the growing tension of her *tête à têtes* with Peter. It did not look good but what was there to say?

The awkward weekend proceedings were concluded on Monday morning. Margaret was the first to take off. Buried in the back of the Rolls and looking straight ahead, she had no smile for the photographers and reporters who thought she was looking sad. They were still prepared to put their shirts on an early engagement when a different message reached them from Denmark where King Frederick after waving goodbye to Prince Philip who had been staying with him, made a Delphic pronouncement with the authority of an insider : 'I know how the affair will end,' he told some people, 'It will not end as you think.' What did Townsend think? He was back in his Lowndes Square pad at two-fifteen p.m. and four hours later was collected by Mark Bonham Carter, the only member of the old Margaret Set to become involved, who drove him to his own house in Victoria Street, Kensington. Mark was no stranger to the problem of divorce and re-marriage because his wife of a few months, Leslie, daughter of the Condé Nast *Vogue* dynasty had obtained a divorce from Lord St Just a few months earlier. They were waiting for Margaret whose car flew out of the Clarence House gates at an unusually high speed. She was wearing a mink jacket over an evening dress and evening sandals as if for a formal occasion. In Victoria Street, Inspector Crocker knocked at the door of the Bonham Carter house which was opened to admit the elevated guest. It was dinner for four; they stayed together till well after midnight.

Things were obviously not running smoothly. No news was bad news. But there were studied leaks from the Palace – addressed to Margaret as much as to foreign newsmen – which poured cold water on overheated imaginations. The American press promptly gave voice to informed whispers: 'Meg, Peter, Dine as Dark Clouds Gather,' was the *New York Daily News* headline; 'Family Tells Meg to Think it Over,' the burden of another fairly accurate situation report. That morning, the Queen returned from Balmoral with Charles and Anne. In the evening Margaret went to Claridge's for an R.A.F. function but those who had hoped she would be accompanied by Group Captain Townsend were disappointed – he was visiting the Motor Show. Did they not want to be seen together in public? Instead, Peter went to Clarence House where he arrived just as the Queen Mother was leaving. They only exchanged a few words. Much as she liked Peter, the situation brought back too many memories of David (Edward VIII) and Wallis and, come to think of it, neither as Queen nor as Queen Mother had she received the twice-divorced Duchess of Windsor.

Although showing signs of weariness, mental rather than physical, Margaret continued to fulfil her official engagements but leaned heavily on old friends. Among those who sustained her were John and Jennifer Lowther (Jennifer Bevan, her erstwhile lady-in-waiting) and Michael Brand and his wife, sister of Lord (W. H. Smith) Hambledon. They helped to clarify her mind, reminding her – it was easier to take from friends than from biased relatives – that whichever way she turned she could not escape her royal obligations or her birth as a princess of Britain. They were unanimous that she should not cut herself off from her heritage.

Pressure also came from the Marquess of Salisbury whose voice carried much weight. The situation was getting intolerable.

Townsend could not stand much more of it. Here he was, a royal servant by inclination, training and habit, upsetting the royal applecart, flying in the face of everything he had stood for in the last twelve years. He lacked the strength of Margaret who, in the meantime, got on with her job. On Wednesday (October 19th) she presented colours to the First Battalion, Highland Light Infantry, at Bulford, Wiltshire, and was back in time to join the family for a royal occasion – painful and embarrassing under the circumstances – a service of rededication of the war-damaged chapel at Lambeth Palace, followed by dinner with the Archbishop. The Queen, Philip and the Queen Mother were there. The Archbishop was to have steered tactfully clear of the explosive issue but there is no way of knowing what he said to individual members of the royal family.

On Thursday, the opening of a new hospital department in the Home Counties demanded Margaret's presence, Friday belonged to Peter Townsend and her friends, and Saturday to another opening ceremony, the new Church Community Centre of St Nicholas and All Hallowes at the East India Dock. Long before dockland became the backcloth for a happier and more relaxed phase in Margaret's life, she could count on a friendly welcome in the East End – Cockney women gathered, cheered and shouted: 'Good luck, Maggie! You marry him!' Margaret engaged a gaggle of curates in spirited conversation about sin and charity, then drove to Windsor Castle for a weekend with the Queen and the Queen Mother who came over from Royal Lodge.

A confrontation took place between the Queen and her sister in which the Queen was as vigorous in defence of her offices and dignities as was Margaret in the assertion of her personal rights. It was said, that to avoid a total break with the Queen, Margaret shifted the weight of her attack towards Philip and blurted out some tittle-tattle about him, and a car accident in which he was supposed to have been involved with an unnamed lady, which had no substance in fact. She repeated some silly rumours about Philip's lively friend Baron, the photographer, their get-togethers at Baron's Brick Street (Park Lane) studios, and about the 'Thursday Club' of which he and Baron were members, meeting at Wheeler's Oyster Bar in Soho every Thursday for a private lunch and some harmless frolics.

To repeat to the Queen's face this kind of malicious gossip could only widen the breach. The resulting coolness between the sisters lasted for over a year (until the Queen publicly restored Margaret to favour) but some courtiers doubted whether the previous relationship would ever be restored. With Philip, not surprisingly, it left a deep resentment against his tempestuous sister-in-law.

Though nothing was finally resolved, a solution could not be delayed much longer. The new week resounded to a crossfire of telephone conversations between Clarence House and Buckingham Palace (and/or Windsor), between Buckingham Palace and Lambeth Palace, between Lambeth Palace and the Palace of Westminster to which members were returning for the beginning of a new session of parliament. At Tory watering holes, in Fleet Street offices and pubs, in the country, the Commonwealth and Europe Margaret was a favourite topic of interest. Press and people were clamouring for authentic news – there was no shortage of views.

What was going on? Was Margaret's arm being twisted, and by whom? Was she being bullied – by the Queen, Philip, the Church, the Establishment? Or was she still stubbornly insisting on marrying 'him' (to use the appellation favoured in certain circles) and offending against the rules? When no answers were forthcoming, curiosity turned into irritation. The Palace was at the receiving end of some harsh criticism. The *Daily Mirror* castigated the royal advisers, the *Sydney Morning Herald* denounced the 'disastrous silence of the Palace'. More public heat was being generated than at the time of the abdication.

On Tuesday, October 25th, President Lopez of Portugal arrived for a state visit, and Margaret dutifully lined up with the rest of the royal family at Westminster Pier to greet the head of the country which is Britain's oldest ally. The good President could have been excused for being a bit confused at finding himself caught up in a family quarrel, constitutional crisis, political problem – whatever it was. The Queen, handsome and majestic, moved as if surrounded by icebergs and anxious to avoid a collision. There was a nip in the air which was not strictly seasonal. From the sidelines, people kept their eyes, not on the President of Portugal, poor chap, but on the royal party, and compared notes on who was talking or not talking to whom.

If President Lopez expected *The Times* to mark his arrival with a leading article, he was sorely disappointed. That morning the voice of the establishment addressed itself to Princess Margaret. With scant regard for the views of ordinary people who either wished her and Townsend 'the best of British luck' or could not care less whom she married, *The Times* (October 6th) pontificated: 'If the marriage which is now being discussed comes to pass, it is inevitable that the reflection (of the Queen's family life) becomes distorted. The Princess will be entering into a union which vast numbers of her sister's people, all sincerely anxious for her lifelong happiness, cannot in conscience regard as a marriage.' The people of the Commonwealth would see her step down from her high place with deepest regret, the sermon went on. That she would have to step down was regarded as a foregone conclusion.

Margaret was by no means friendless in Fleet Street. The *Manchester Guardian*, as it was then called, rebuked its august contemporary: 'If we have a Prime Minister, cabinet ministers, and judges who are innocent parties, we can, without feeling unduly disturbed in our moral fibre, give the same latitude to the Queen's sister,' the liberal paper said. And the *Daily Mirror's* irrepressible Hugh Cudlipp asked whether *The Times* would prefer 'this vivacious young woman to marry one of the witless wonders with whom she has been hob-nobbing these past few years?' The question might have raised another one – in what way was Peter Townsend so different from Margaret's other friends?

Pros and cons were so fiercely argued that Margaret's romance was like a millstone around her neck. People's moods are variable and many began to blame her because the Church vacillated, the Palace dithered and the politicians were at odds about what should be done or said. Whatever the British monarchy was – symbol of ancient legitimacy, emblem of Commonwealth unity, personification of glory – it was first and foremost a family affair. Every spinster was its maiden aunt, every shopgirl its kid sister, every vicar its parish priest. But the family was getting tired of the Margaret affair and beginning to wish that the nasty taste it created would go away. Even the jokes were getting derogatory, like the one about the little boy choosing his career: 'Soldier, sailor, group captain...' and a comic on the B.B.C. read a spoof news item: 'They had tea together again ...!' Margaret was in danger of becoming a bore and even the Queen Mother was being criticised for letting her younger daughter slither into this situation.

Margaret was at the end of her tether. The table in her sitting-room was covered with newspapers when Peter Townsend called on her. It was there and then that she admitted defeat. Neither she nor Peter have ever revealed in what terms she told him but the burden of her message was that 'they' would not let her marry in honour, that she could not let the royal side down or endanger the Commonwealth which hung together only by a hair-thin thread. Neither could she bear to take Uncle David's way out. She consoled herself, I am told, as royals do, with the thought that her sacrifice served a higher purpose but it is possible – and some of her friends thought so – that the sacrifice was not as great as it would seem. She and Peter had survived two years apart during which bonds had loosened even while superficial attraction remained. They would survive the years ahead. Princesses, grown-up princesses, don't cry. Although he had felt the drift and the end did not come as a total surprise to him, Townsend, one gathers, did wipe a little tear from his misty eyes.

The following morning, Margaret called Lambeth Palace and said she was coming to see the Archbishop. Assuming that she intended to consult him about her marriage plans, the Archbishop had all books of reference spread around him, annotated with cross references to historical precedents, canonical law and learned commentaries. Margaret strode into his study, saw the volumes scattered over the tables and addressed him with a magnificent phrase (which may have been invented by Randolph Churchill to whom I owe this version): 'Archbishop, you can put your books away. I have made up my mind already.'

Randolph publicised this sequence of events to defend the Archbishop against accusations that he had robbed Margaret of happiness. Suspicions about the high cleric's role lingered, however, until only recently (early in 1976) when his Chaplain, Eric G. Jay, confirmed that the Princess had only gone to

Lambeth Palace to tell the Archbishop what she had already decided. Margaret drove to Buckingham Palace and, in a curt sullen exchange told the Queen that she was not going ahead with her plan to marry Peter. She said she would be issuing a public statement which would make it quite clear that she still loved him . . .

A mood of despondency seemed to envelop the royal family when it assembled once more to give their guest from Lisbon a final treat. Margaret looked sombre, the Queen sad, Philip defiant as they, with the Archbishop and Anthony and Clarissa Eden – and President Lopez – took their seats in the royal box at Covent Garden for a gala performance of Smetana's 'The Bartered Bride'. The bartered bride! Margaret seemed isolated, and the foreign guests noticed that none of the family talked to her or vice versa. She and Philip sitting side by side did not exchange a single word throughout the performance or in the interval. Margaret did not bat an eyelid when she heard the soprano evocatively singing to a forbidden lover: 'Nothing in the world will ever part us!' There were other suggestive passages – 'We have been talking of your future', 'I have not changed my mind!' – but they were out of date.

Away from the make-believe of Covent Garden, Margaret, with her sense of the dramatic, opted for a spectacular finale: a last, if not lost, weekend with Peter. On Friday, October 28th, she and Peter entrusted themselves once more to the tender care of John and Jean Wills, this time at their town house in Knightsbridge. The evening turned into a wake. A fair amount of liquor was consumed, so much in fact that the hosts had to send their son Andrew to the 'Nag's Head' around the corner for a bottle of whisky. The landlord could not oblige: 'We haven't even enough for our own guests,' he said. Young Andrew Wills could not very well tell him that it was for Princess Margaret . . .

On Saturday, the scene shifted once more to the country, this time to Sussex and Uckfield House, home of Lord Rupert Nevill (Abergavenny's brother) and his wife Anne Camilla, daughter of the ninth Earl of Portsmouth. The sands were running out for the lovers. They spent most of the morning con-cocting the statement Margaret had in mind. The first draft was an emotional document which mirrored their long association – twelve years of crush, infatuation, passion, joy, hope, fear, doubts, defiance and sacrifice – and the tragic decision at the end of it. It underwent many changes until it was whittled down to something less personal but only just.

It was time for the cruel mechanics of parting, and the attractive setting and the civilised manner did not help to dull the pain. It left wounds which would not heal easily, scars which, like those of old soldiers, would flare up time and again for ever after. Some people would rather walk away abruptly in opposite directions without looking back, hide themselves and take refuge in the future. Others savour the agony tearing themselves apart slowly, dramatically. Walking hand in hand in the grounds of the estate, Margaret and Peter acted out their destiny in full view of the press cameras.

No sooner had they returned to the house when Captain Oliver Dawnay arrived to collect the draft statement. The Queen Mother's secretary studied it and without revealing his instructions to try and persuade Margaret not to make any public announcement at all proceeded to edit it and cut it down until they reached the point when he ventured to suggest that she might withhold it altogether. The Princess refused and Captain Dawnay took the draft to London where it was studied by constitutional experts and the Queen's personal advisers. As amended by the Captain, they found it acceptable except for one or two expressions which, they thought, had better be toned down – the word 'devotion' figured prominently and was said to have been the main stumbling block. Margaret was in no mood to compromise and when Captain Dawnay went to see her again on Sunday morning, he could not change her mind.

Monday (October 31st) saw the final act. Peter dropped in at Clarence House where Margaret was still agonising over the statement which marked the end of the affair. No eye remained dry when the non-marriage announcement was finally published. It pointed, ingeniously, unmistakably, the finger at the defenders of an outmoded concept of marriage and a crumbling empire who had exacted the sacrifice from her :

'I have decided,' it said, 'not to marry Group Captain Peter Townsend. Mindful of the Church's teaching that Christian marriage is indissoluble, and conscious of the Commonwealth, I have resolved to put these considerations before any other.

'I have reached this decision entirely alone, and in doing so I have been strengthened by the unfailing support and devotion of Group Captain Townsend. I am deeply grateful for the concern of all those who have constantly prayed for my happiness.'

The tear-stained view of a broken romance dims powers of analysis. If Margaret had been so mindful of the Church's teaching, someone asked rudely, what had she been doing playing around with a married man all these years? Was it only now that she had become conscious of the Commonwealth? Her renunciation under enormous pressure, one cynic remarked, was made to look like a hardened sinner's death-bed repentance.

Peter Townsend had tea with Margaret formally and decorously at Clarence House later that week before departing for Brussels.

CHAPTER NINE

Margaret did not pine. Parting from Peter proved less painful than the fear of parting had been; it also relieved the pressure. A war lost, but at least an end to the fighting – apart from a few scores to settle. Not now, though. Now she wanted above all to get away, away from the family, the root of her trouble. The Queen was burdened with a great deal of work and ceremonial duties and did not in any case show much inclination to have Margaret around. The Queen Mother posed a different problem. While the Townsend crisis did not seem to have greatly affected her relations with Margaret, the interlude left an element of embarrassment behind – silent memories, eloquent silences. Besides, at twenty-six, a girl went through a phase of not enjoying living under her mother's eyes.

How long could two entirely different life-styles continue in the narrow confines of Clarence House, two sets of friends who had little in common, two routines which were bound to clash? The one dining-room which the Queen Mother and Margaret had to share could be as irritating as it could be for two women sharing a kitchen in a humbler home. While it had worked reasonably well so far, Margaret was so irritable and uncompromising in the wake of the Townsend troubles that minor disagreements added up to a lot of bad blood. Yet, for an unmarried royal princess to set up an establishment of her own was as yet unthinkable.

In one respect, Margaret almost envied Peter who went on a world tour in his faithful old Peugeot. When he reached the Caribbean, he was thought to be following in Margaret's footsteps as if hoping to catch up with her somehow, some place, some time. But reunion could not have been further from Margaret's mind as she resumed her own travels on the familiar round-about. From lunch with Simon Phipps in his rooms at Trinity College, Cambridge, and some spiritual refuelling, she turned to spirituals of a different order at the jazz temples of London and, better still, at the B.B.C.'s Lime Grove studios which she visited while a big variety show was being recorded, a potted, packaged version of all that was best in the genre.

Unaware that the likes of Danny Kaye, Eddie Fisher and Noel Coward kept her supplied with the latest records, her B.B.C. hosts were surprised to hear her joining in the Lizzi Borden chorus from the revue: 'New Faces': 'You can't chop your Momma up in Massachusetts!' Margaret thought a day at the studios was better than a week watching T.V. at home. Not much later she was entertained by Louis Armstrong ('Your Princess is one hip chick') and Lena Horne. She went to see Count Basie's first and second performance at the Festival Hall in one day.

She seemed to be doing things to draw attention to herself but when she went to a newsreel cinema in the Charing Cross Road and remained unrecognised as she walked down Oxford Street with Billy Wallace and Judy Montagu she was thrilled by a feeling of privacy in public. Similarly, she welcomed the sight of Alexandra of Kent growing up into a very handsome young woman and going out with her own circle of friends, soon to be hailed as 'Alexandra's Band' although they did not, as the press hoped, become a substitute for the much-missed 'Margaret Set' – not enough personality to match Margaret's.

Still, the press would not let go of her. Deprived of Townsend and other retainers, most of them solidly married by now, the gossips 'linked' Margaret with a thirty-five-year-old German princeling, Christian of Hanover, brother of the Duke of Brunswick and Queen Frederika of Greece, and a relative of Philip. The rumours came on so strong that the Palace, still smarting under the attacks for its fumbling silence about Townsend, over-eagerly issued an official denial. There was more such silly nonsense when Margaret joined the Queen and Philip in Sweden where the local newspapers ('Dare we hope ...?') revived the hoary old tale about her and Prince Bertil.

Not surprising really since the public was still being fed on the awful pap prepared by professional royalty watchers, in this instance the inveterate Charlotte and Denis Plimmer, who saddled Margaret with their vision of her future: 'Royalty must always be prepared to marry for dynastic reasons,' they proclaimed. 'It is obvious that she will marry in the royal sense "suitably".' Will she, now? Before long, from the opposite end of the gallery, Margaret-expert Audrey Whiting, who still gets angry when others take an interest in royal lives, came out with a prediction, supposed to be based on authoritative information available to her exclusively, that Margaret and Townsend had taken their parting so hard that they had vowed never to marry.

The melancholy expression in the photographs Margaret selected for publication on her twenty-sixth birthday reflected the atmosphere of vacuity around her which inspired public demands that she be given a rôle to play or a job to do such as Governor of the Caribbean or a similar office – shades of the Duke of Windsor's war-time governorship of the Bahamas. The clamour overlapped intensive preparations for her next big tour which were already well advanced. It would take her to East Africa – Kenya, Tanganyika, Zanzibar, Mauritius. *Plus ça change* ...! The *Britannia* was again mobilised to ferry her around and she was flown to Mombasa, starting point of an excursion into the world of rapturous Africans and Asians (most of the latter belonging to the old Aga Khan's Muslim Ismaili sect): dusky sultans with colourful robes and bejewelled swords, their sultanas and white-suited colonial officials. Open Land Rovers transported her from tribal meetings to 'purdah' (read: hen) parties. Escorted by governors, a species on the verge of extinction, she saw the local sights, swam in the sea and even enjoyed the blazing tropical sun of Mauritius. Her easy-going attitude failed to bring down traditional barriers and she was meticulously protected against untoward sights such as the famous Wakamba women dancing, as was their custom, with their ample brown bosoms uncovered. The ladies were obliged to perform for her with their outstanding charms modestly obscured. Local leaders showered gifts on Margaret who accepted them with unflagging enthusiasm. She made one African chief very happy by acknowledging his present of a fly whisk – the third fly whisk she had received within minutes – with a genuine sounding 'Terrific!'

A past-mistress of the royal art, she was all eager eyes and ready smiles and lent a gracious ear to official mentors as she proceeded according to plan until there was (in the official idiom) 'a flap on' when the name of the British District Commissioner of Arusha, Tanganyika, turned up among the worthies to be introduced to her. It was Francis Townsend, Peter's thirty-five-year-old brother. Should he be presented? Did she want to meet him? Yes, she did. Bronzed, taller and more robust than Peter, Francis came at the head of a group of Masai tribesmen, his protégés. His introduction was formal and brief. Margaret could not very well ask him what was behind the current reports of Peter being involved in a new romance with a Countess van Limburg-Stirus.

Throughout the tour, Margaret delighted and bewildered people of all stations with her own brand of earthy royalty. She got on well with Governor Sir Evelyn Baring who was taking his leave of her rather formally on one occasion when she dismissed him with a jaunty: 'See you later, alligator!' The puzzled Governor asked his aide-de-camp what it meant and after some hurried consultations was advised that, should Her Royal Highness say it again, the correct reply was: 'In a while, crocodile!'

Had she, instead of trudging all over East Africa, been at home, she would have heard that Philip, in loyal memory to his recently departed photographer friend Baron, had introduced the latter's erstwhile assistant, Antony Armstrong-Jones, to the Queen who had looked over the young man's portfolio of photographs, mostly theatrical and fashion, and agreed that he could take pictures of Charles and Anne. If they were satisfactory, they could be released on Charles's eighth birthday in mid-November. (They came out very well indeed, particularly the one in black and white cut-out style showing the children's handsome profiles.) Actually, the aspiring young photographer's first royal client was the Duke of Kent who had met him through Jane (Sheffield), the wife of Jocelyn Stevens who knew Tony from university.

Again, had Margaret been at Clarence House where the newspapers were brought to her in bed together with her morn-

With Billy Wallace at Royal Ascot, weeks before her 21st birthday, and (*below*) with Lord Ogilvy (brother of Angus) and Lord Dalkeith at the Perth Races in 1950.

Dining with Colin Tennant, the future 'founder' of Mustique, at the Dorchester in 1954 and (*below*) at a sale of work near Balmoral: helping her on the stall is Dominic Elliot.

ing tea, she could hardly have missed an announcement in the *Daily Express* – keeping their ears close to the Palace grounds, editors were quick to cash in on royal trends – of the impending debut in its columns of 'a cameraman with the magic touch, London's most talked-about photographer, twenty-five-year-old Tony Armstrong-Jones'. (He first came to our attention', said former *Express* picture editor Frank Spooner, 'through our theatre critic. He was very talented.' 'When Armstrong-Jones brought his first picture late one night,' explained Roy Wright, now Editor of the *Daily Express*, 'Frank Spooner said he was not interested in a fee but desperately wanted to have the photograph credited to him – I agreed.')

Suddenly all London seemed to know what a rare find Tony was : sensitive, gentle, diffident, quite different from the run-of-the-mill Fleet Street cameramen in these days; and, what's more, Eton and Cambridge and a rowing Blue. He was so slight and small, he could only have been a cox and had, in fact, coxed Cambridge to victory over Oxford in the 1950 Boat Race. Being in vogue, half his personal life was opened up for general inspection, the other half being much discussed in Fleet Street and Shaftesbury Avenue long before it became familiar to Margaret. Unorthodox girl-friends, male companions, the studio, a converted ironmongery in Pimlico (Aubusson carpets, paper chains, parachute silk, that sort of thing) where he lived under the shop, a hole in the floor leading down to his private den, stuffed with Regency grotesques, lapis lazuli, a rifle and cartridges. His *pièce de résistance* was a looking-glass – with sharp diamond at hand – in which everybody who was anybody in Mayfair and Belgravia (including two friends we had in common, the late Dominic Elwes and the very much alive Jocelyn Stevens) had etched his signature. After her return from East Africa, Margaret learned something of his arty and aristocratic background, and his upbringing. His father was a lawyer, Ronald Armstrong-Jones (hyphen of recent origin); his mother and her second husband, the wealthy Earl of Rosse, lived in the splendour of Birr Castle in Ireland's County Offali, sister Susan married to John Vestey, Viscount de Vesci, an Irish peer, half-brothers Lord Oxmanton and Martin Parsons, and, most important, uncle Oliver Messel, the noted theatrical designer and interior decorator.

With time on her hands, Margaret agreed to have her portrait painted by Annigoni who said he had wanted her to sit for him since he first saw her in Italy in 1947. He thought she was a difficult subject, there was so much change in her face. 'A girl as beautiful as the princess, difficult?!' the sycophants cried out. She sat for him fifteen times over a period of six months, first at Clarence House then, when Annigoni grumbled about the light, in his studio. When the work was completed in the spring of 1957, Margaret's only criticisms were of a little bow on her dress and one strand of hair that was out of place. 'I made the changes,' the artist recalls. Within a year she sat for the aged sculptor Jacob Epstein who did a bust of her.

In the meantime her thoughts were on photography. One of the most sensitive 'talent' scouts of her time, Margaret registered the waves emanating from Tony Armstrong-Jones whose name was on every lip. Elizabeth Cavendish knew him from her recent association with John Cranko's revue 'Cranks' at the St Martin's Theatre into which she had put some money while Tony worked as 'house photographer'. Elizabeth, to satisfy the Princess's curiosity, gave a small dinner party to bring her and Tony together innocuously. Tony, but not Margaret, recalled that they had come face to face earlier in the year when he had 'snatched' a picture of her at the reception after the wedding of Colin Tennant and Lady Anne Coke at Holkham Hall.

Though not as brazenly as in later years, Margaret concentrated on the man who interested her to the exclusion of almost all others. It is a technique which flatters – and flattens – most men. But when she attacked Tony with a fusillade of questions, he stood up well to the interrogation, parrying difficult thrusts, dealing discreetly with explosive subjects and emphasising what they obviously had in common – a strong interest in the theatre and many friends. He was at ease, amusing and not at all over-awed, an attractive, stimulating companion. She asked him to dinner which led to other meetings on new territory where none of their respective friends discovered them.

With her acquisition of Tony as a new friend, more than just a friend, Margaret entered upon a two-tier existence, part overt, part covert. Because her association with Tony before long absorbed most of her interest and much of her energy, she gave less thought and less time to her royal programme. It was soon noticed. Her official appointments were counted – on the fingers of one hand. There were cries of anguish when the public was deprived of its daily dose of Margaret and people wondered why it was so quiet around her; whenever it got quiet around her noisy questions were asked. When no answers were forthcoming the conclusion was that she must be pining – presumably for Townsend.

She was in fact happier and more relaxed than she had been for years. It showed in small things – the way she kicked off her shoes at Epsom while watching the Queen's horse Doutelle struggling but failing to make an impact in the Derby. (Kicking off her shoes became quite a habit: she did it again while dancing in the aisles at a musical.) The Queen looked glum by contrast.

Royals are better able to protect their personal secrets from outsiders than is generally realised but they can rarely keep secrets from each other. There are detectives, servants, retainers whose lips are not sealed. Cliquish and loyal to their own master or mistress, they are yet all courtiers with the courtiers' *esprit de corps;* they meet, mingle, gossip, compare notes and pass on most of the distilled news to their principals. Margaret kept their tongues wagging more than most largely because she so often did things worth chatting, smiling or tut-tutting about. The gist of the new stories circulating around royal residences was that Margaret was involved in a new intimate adventure. The Queen and her husband had a shrewd idea of what was going on but it caused disquiet only in case it involved more unwelcome publicity – the cause of the Queen's apprehension.

If it was a matter of her public persona, there was little to worry about. She was 'called to the Bar' and dined with the benchers (she still does and at least one barrister was lyrical about her personality and her intellect); keeping up her patronage of Rock-'n-Roll, she saw 'The Girl Can't Help It' in a party which included among old faithfuls Lord Lovat's brother Hugh Fraser and his bride of a few months, Antonia Pakenham (who parted from him twenty years and six children later).

With such outings, Margaret did no more than fill in time. How she felt in these early days of her new love was no secret among her friends who often commented on the intensity of her emotions. As one with some personal experience of the situation explained: 'When she's in love, she is terribly demanding – demanding of time, effort, attention. Because she does no regular work, not in the ordinary sense of the word, and few of her associates are bound by routine, she has little understanding of other people's timetables. If she is fond of a person, she wants him around all the time. She monopolises, occupies, drains a fellow. Not every man can take it. Some who have adored her for years were emotionally crushed before they could get anywhere near; others have dreaded her favour as much as her rejection. Yet, when in love, she sparkles. To her it is like L.S.D. – her perception is clearer, her wit sharper. She is dazzling as well as devouring.'

Tony would never dream of discussing his association with Margaret – not with his family, not with his friends – but those who know and respect him have said that, while he was much in love with her, he was not the kind of man to surrender himself totally to a woman. Even in their heyday, they say, there was an element of skirmish, a ding-dong strength-testing and battling for supremacy about their togetherness. It added spice, if often too much of it. Neither of them was ideal marriage material. Their attraction was instant, and once they met something was bound to happen. But it could not last.

Somewhat less than monogamous at the time of their meeting, Tony's approach to sex was uninhibited if not all round liberated. But he had his favourites and the one who was closest to him until she was displaced by Margaret was a delightful, diminutive, eighteen–nineteen-year-old girl who looked like her name – Jacqui Chan – but came from Trinidad and was several generations removed from her Chinese origin. An actress with reasonable prospects whose filigrane figure and mobile features were most appealing, she also worked as a model. She hung around Tony's studio, he peddled her photographs in Fleet Street. They were very attached but made no claim on each other, an arrangement that suited them both but faded out – if not their friendship – when Margaret appeared on the scene.

Margaret loved nothing better than to be asked for advice on matters of taste and Tony would not have been worthy of his reputation as a charmer had he not given her an opportunity to have her say about an exhibition of his photographs he was about to mount. Few theatrical figures of note were missing from his collection – his diffidence was supposed to have aroused Marlene Dietrich's compassion although her preference has always been for men in the Remarque or Hemingway mould. Robert Morley, Spike Milligan, Ralph Richardson, John Gielgud were some of the actors, Ionesco, Maugham and Vaughan Williams some of the creative artists he had photographed.

The exhibition was opened by Leslie Caron but Margaret could neither attend the opening nor visit it during its two months' run without giving their secret away or, at the very least, putting the press hounds on the scent. Instead – in the version which was constructed with blithe disregard for times and places – their friendship became more serious when the exhibits were returned to Tony's studio and she went to see them there. Accompanied by Elizabeth Cavendish, the indefatigable matchmaker, she drove to Pimlico and eventually descended the famous spiral staircase to Tony's private quarters where he brewed tea for the ladies.

No romance is complete without that early separation which heightens desire until the lovers come together again, never to part. In the summer of 1957, Margaret was bound for Scotland and Tony had several foreign dates on his schedule. He was due to fly to Geneva to take photographs of the wedding of Prince Sadruddin, uncle of the newly elevated young Aga Khan (and half-brother of Aly Khan) and the exotic Nina Dyer, Ceylon-born daughter of an English planter and owner of a Caribbean island, a present from her previous husband, Swiss-German multi-millionaire Heinrich Thyssen. (Tony captured the wedding mood admirably.) He was expected to go to Valletta, Malta, to discuss illustrations for a Sitwell book, and visit uncle Oliver Messel in Venice. He was enchanted with Venice and is said to have written to a friend – though I find the reverse comparison hard to credit – that Venice reminded him of Rotherhithe.

Puzzling as this tribute to one of the seamier parts of London's dockland sounds, Margaret already knew of Tony's Rotherhithe connection. He had told her that, when looking for an away-from-it-all pad to give him the kind of privacy the Pimlico basement no longer afforded, what he had in mind was some place by the river far removed from a fashionable photographer's usual haunts, preferably in Rotherhithe, London, S.E.16. A year or so earlier, enlisting the help of an old Rotherhithe resident, journalist William Glenton, he had searched among the warehouses, council flats and old sea captains' homes for his ideal hideout. From Glenton's house by the river, not far from where Charles II was believed to have come ashore on his way to Nell Gwynn, they toured the old Limehouse pubs, button-holed knowledgeable locals – and came up with a blank. But Tony had an idea. He implored Glenton to let him have the apparently empty downstairs room in his house, a kind of ground-floor attic with contents to match and a view on to the River Thames : 'You would hardly know I was there; I'm as quiet as a mouse,' Tony pleaded. Since he also offered to make considerable improvements to the room, a deal was quickly struck. Glenton was sworn to secrecy at the time but later wrote a book, *Tony's Room*, which told the whole story.

A skilled, do-it-yourself fanatic, Tony went to work on his room, chucked out the rubbish and, with the help of a couple of local boys, stripped and painted the walls. Sometimes he relaxed over a sandwich and a bottle of wine or in the local, sometimes he went out to photograph roaming youngsters and grizzled dockers. He scoured antique shops for furniture, choosing pieces for character rather than value, bought special matting to cover the floor and brought in some outsize bric-a-brac until the room reflected his idiosyncratic taste. Jacqui Chan – they were like a double act on stage – was around a good deal to share the domestic chores. By the time Margaret was invited down to Rotherhithe, everything was ship-shape in Tony's room – and Jacqui safely out of sight. Landlord Glenton who had left his lodger tactfully to himself most of the time could still not help noticing some of his preparations (more expensive paper in the first-floor landing lavatory which they shared, for instance) for the visit of what, in his judgement, could only be a lady of considerable importance.

Margaret was thrilled with Tony's refuge which was like nothing she had seen before. Primitive, perhaps, no servants, Tony making the arrangements for tea or dinner, serving, opening bottles, clearing the table, washing up – before long Margaret also had her hands in the sink. Although Tony usually took her to Rotherhithe in his inconspicuous little Morris 1000, her detective easily caught up with them. Margaret brought Elizabeth Cavendish along once or twice, told the Queen Mother a little about her excursions to the river before asking her to come and see for herself. By this time the Queen was completely in the picture. Margaret was obviously in it again up to her eyes, a new worry. It was not a matter of the man's merits – neither the Queen nor Philip ever heard anything worse about Tony than that he led a rather unorthodox life (by their standards) – it was the risk that another Margaret romance with some alarmingly novel features would create another scandal. Whether the Queen actually used the word or not, raising the subject with Margaret along these lines was enough to spark off an argument, supposedly more heated than any previous controversy between the sisters.

In strange contrast to her highly animated private life – the romance with Tony, the quarrel with the Queen – Margaret's public picture faded until she virtually disappeared from the front pages. But published early in the year in a humorous German magazine was a cartoon commenting on the embarrassing and abortive Suez intervention by Eden and the violent attacks on Britain it provoked in the foreign press. It showed Margaret in the bath and the Queen sitting with her: 'Say, Margaret,' the Queen was quoted as asking her, 'could you not do something to distract the horrid world press from our Suez débâcle?'

By the end of 1957, while Margaret was very close to doing just that, royal togetherness of that sort was unlikely. Margaret smarted under the new royal 'interference' in her private life, and it would have been unlike Margaret had she not found a way to demonstrate her reaction for all the world to see. The occasion she chose to achieve her objective with a bang was the Queen's tenth wedding anniversary on November 20th. As with the dog that did not bark in the night, it was a case of the Princess who was not there on the night. It would have been astounding enough for Margaret to just absent herself from the joyous anniversary dinner at Buckingham Palace where the Queen and Philip celebrated with the Queen Mother and the Mountbattens – Mountbatten père, daughters, son-in-law. But not content with a negative gesture, she went out of her way to show that she was not celebrating with her sister.

Wearing her headline-grabbing Williamson brooch, dahlia-shaped with a cluster of two-hundred and fifty diamonds, a present from South African diamond mine operator Dr John Williamson, Margaret was on public view sitting in the stalls at the Coliseum watching 'Bells are Ringing' in a party of eight which included Iris Peake and the Michael Brands. Was she going on to Buckingham Palace after the show? She was not. Her friends took her to the Savoy where they were kept waiting in the Grill Room foyer while the table was prepared for them. They wined and dined in ostentatious high spirits until Margaret rose around midnight and, deciding to observe the minimum proprieties, drove to the Palace but stayed less than an hour. Perhaps her attitude to the occasion would have been less glaringly obvious had she stayed away altogether. Although the terms in which she expressed her sentiments were quoted to me in several versions, their gist, as addressed to the Queen, was; 'It's all right for you to celebrate ten years of marriage – thanks to you I am still unmarried.'

The Queen was understandably shocked, the rift ceased to be the private concern of two sisters and raised some awkward questions. Suddenly it occurred to a lot of people what was already the talk of the court, that this was by no means the first royal party Margaret had recently snubbed. She had kept away from the Royal Variety Performance, had given the Royal Film Show – 'Les Girls' – a miss although she had been expected to be there with the Queen, and, what's worse, gone to see the film privately with friends a week or so later. Still the press was totally off beam. With all the authority at their command, professional soothsayers revealed the existence of a new problem due, they said, to Margaret having renewed her request to be allowed to marry Townsend and having been again turned down by the Queen. According to them she was still in close touch with her ex-boyfriend wherever he was – Rio today, B.A. tomorrow – and she was hell-bent on resuming where they had left off two years ago. Nothing was further from her mind but the press continued in that vein following the old precept which had guided their Margaret coverage : 'Cherchez l'homme !' They were right, of course, except that they picked the wrong man.

Far from helping them to find the right one, Margaret was soon involved in a complex plot to keep them looking in the wrong direction and settle a few scores in the process. What follows are the bare bones of her scheme which she put into operation in March 1958 when the Queen and Philip were on a state visit to Holland's Juliana and Bernhard. At that very moment, Peter Townsend, a group captain in name only since his resignation from the R.A.F. in 1956, was arriving in London at the end of his five-hundred-and-twenty-one-day tour which had taken him sixty thousand miles across Europe, India, Malaya, Australia, Japan, U.S.A. and South America. He had been in touch with Margaret and had sent her the occasional souvenir.

It was this coincidence of the Queen's absence and Peter's return that spawned the plan of a spectacular cover-up and manoeuvre comparable to the British war-time ruses to confuse the Nazi enemy. To begin with it ought to be said that Margaret's romance with Tony was going strong – the Queen's misgivings were the only jarring note in this first chapter of her new love story. Margaret was smarting under her sister's warnings which she regarded as another interference in her private life: 'My sister does not want me to see Tony – or any other interesting man!' Margaret, giving vent to her bitterness, was reported to have said. She was convinced that, had she been attracted to any of Philip's clan – some German prince or duke – all would have been well . . .

The devil in Margaret inspired a double ploy. Press reports were still harping on her changed life, 'Part-time Princess', was one of the sobriquets applied to her; 'Margaret giving up social life', ran a headline of a story bemoaning her absence from the limelight. Would it not be fun to give people something to talk about, particularly if it kept them away from her secret love, and to taunt her sister a little into the bargain?

Her first move was to let Peter Townsend know that he would be welcome for tea at Clarence House if he cared to be there on Wednesday, March 26th, at four p.m. Having arrived that morning and settled in at Whitehall Court, a block of short-term rented service flats, Townsend, looking bronzed, fit and cheerful, was at Clarence House at three fifty-six p.m., had tea with Margaret and the Queen Mother, told them about his world tour and departed three hours later. No matter what was said by way of official explanation – 'No significance', 'Nothing has changed since the Princess's statement two years ago' – the incident galvanised the wire services and reports of the sensational reunion circled the world much faster than the man in the centre. Once more it was – 'Together Again!'

Reaction in the Queen's camp in Holland was stunned surprise and impotent anger: 'It's just a case of perversity on the part of both of them!' said a court official in the Queen's entourage. 'Foolish!' 'Unwise!' were some of the other strangulated cries from Amsterdam. Perversity? Never before had a royal princess been criticised in such violent terms by her sister's officials. 'The Queen Irked', said one of the sedater reports.

Whether the Queen really believed that there was any romantic significance in Margaret's invitation to Townsend (which is doubtful since she was aware of Tony) and whether that worried her are questions that were avidly asked. But what really mattered, what did infuriate her and her officials was that Margaret – deliberately, no doubt – had stolen the headlines from her while she was on a goodwill visit to a friendly neighbour. Who would want to read about the dreary encounters of two goody-goody royal couples when there was all this exciting news about naughty Margaret on every page? Since state visits are public relations exercises, Margaret's success in displacing reports of the Queen's activities in Holland had made this one, costly, time-consuming, tiring as it was, a totally futile enterprise.

Not content with the block-buster reaction to her tea for Townsend, Margaret proceeded to rub it in. She changed into a glittering gown and, no sooner had Townsend taken his leave, was ready to give the world more of her to see and talk about. That evening she drove to the West End for the first night of a new David O. Selznick spectacular, the film of Ernest Hemingway's *A Farewell to Arms*. The function was not much different from scores of others she had attended and might not have attracted so much attention had it not followed immediately on the afternoon which was already agitating people's minds; and had she not skilfully and cunningly arranged for virtually all the principal characters in the Townsend drama of 1955 to be present and jog memories.

John and Jean Wills (of Allanbay Park) greeted her on arrival at the cinema, Lord and Lady Rupert Nevill (of Uckfield

House) were in her party, and so were the Brands, all of whom had given her and Peter comfort in the critical weeks of November 1956. For the benefit of reporters and photographers, Margaret wore her most radiant smile, and they dutifully recorded that 'she looked happier than she had looked in years' or, more precisely, since she and Peter had parted. 'Will he join her ...?' was the question on all lips. Everybody was on the lookout.

Although her putative leading man did not appear (but told reporters that there would be no further meetings) Margaret's production of the whole occasion was wicked but brilliant. And successful. No wonder she looked so dazzling. She had upstaged the Queen, bamboozled the press, confused the gossips and kept Tony safely under wraps.

CHAPTER TEN

In public Tony Armstrong-Jones was discussing the kind of photographs he would like of his own children (if he had any); his conversations with Margaret already turned on the question of who might become the mother of his children, and between them they were moving towards agreement on this point. Margaret so recently denied happiness – it did not matter in this context whether by the Queen, Philip, the Archbishop or herself – was determined not to let it slip for a second time. If there were dynastic or other obstacles, they worried Tony more than they worried her. He was having other problems. His landlord noticed that he was getting very secretive about his visitors – Tony was clearly upset when Glenton recognised the shadowy figure of a woman slipping into his room as Princess Margaret.

Tony was already being included occasionally and unobtrusively among the guests at Margaret's dinner parties and visits to the theatre. Billy Wallace entertained them at his home offering himself as a target for all rumours about Margaret's romantic inclinations. She spent some weekends with the Nevills at Uckfield – shades of Townsend – while Tony was with his grandmother all of twelve miles away; he drove to Uckfield without attracting attention. They were deedily discussing family problems like the break-up of his father's marriage – Carol Armstrong-Jones parted from her husband after twenty-three years (and soon married a Spaniard). Margaret commiserated with Tony who fretted about artistic setbacks such as the crushing reviews of Cranko's 'Keep Your Hair On' for which his stage designs had come in for some harsh criticism.

The show was a flop. More confidently, they discussed his new project, a volume of photographs entitled 'London' – he was assisted by the talented Mark Boxer (who was later instrumental in getting him his job with the *Sunday Times*). Once when *Vogue* published a set of Tony's photographs under a pseudonym he explained to her that editors sometimes tired of using his name to which she promptly replied; 'I wish they'd tire of using mine!' Just as well editors did not know about the intimate occasions when Margaret snuggled up to Tony in the cinema at Clarence House.

In the euphoria of this phase, Margaret's chief concern about publicity was that it should not disturb her idyll. What did it matter if a French magazine produced a girl in a mini-bikini whose only claim to fame was that her measurements were supposed to be exactly Margaret's? Or that the Scots were again going on about her ascending the throne of the Stuarts, an early move towards Scottish independence? She bid farewell to her faithful G.A. (Gentleman Attendant), Brigadier Gwatkin, who said 'I never quite knew myself what a G.A.'s duties were'; at the age of fifty-eight, he had decided to marry a nurse twenty-three years younger than he. His successor as Margaret's G.A., thirty-nine-year-old Major Francis Legh, had an impeccable royal service pedigree. She was in need of congenial companions – Billy Wallace was in hospital.

For one weekend in the wake of the unpleasantness over the Townsend visit, Margaret joined the Queen Mother at Royal Lodge, Windsor. The Queen was at Windsor Castle – it was clearly time for a talk – and drove the two miles along the 'Long Walk' to join her family. She and Margaret were closeted together for nearly an hour. That evening the Queen and Philip dined alone at the Castle while the Queen Mother and Margaret remained at Royal Lodge.

The time for Margaret's next tour to the Caribbean was approaching. Although it was difficult to think of her as other than frivolous, it involved her in a great deal of earnest preparations to which she applied herself conscientiously. The Cabinet had agreed that she should read the Queen's Speech at the opening of the Parliament of the new Federation of the West Indies, an uneasy superstructure to cover divers social conditions and political aspirations. She read papers prepared by the

Foreign Office acquainting herself with the complexities, and studied pen-portraits of leading Caribbean personalities including such committed anti-imperialists as the Jagans (Dr Cheddi Jagan, Chief Minister of British Guiana, and his wife Janet who held several portfolios in his administration.) There was a problem about colour because the royals were suspected of operating a subtle colour bar, a difficult situation in British Honduras which was under 'threat' from Guatemala (pressing territorial claims). There was the usual string of official functions, state banquets, dinners, dances as well as visits to schools, hospitals . . .

Apart from the political homework, her wardrobe required thought and time. The outstanding item was a satin gown, embroidered with gold thread and studded with rubies and sapphires to wear at the opening of the parliament – it made her look like the Queen's double. She could count on top colonial administrators to guide her through the maze of protocol and procedure – Governor-General Lord Hailes and, in the first instance, Sir Richard Beetham in Trinidad. For political advice there was available no less an expert than the Under-Secretary of State for the Colonies, John Profumo, who was going with her.

There is an inevitability about royal functions which tends to reduce them to tired routines. Margaret was energetic, enthusiastic and assertive enough to infuse some life and glamour into the job. Arriving at Port of Spain, Trinidad, on April 20th, a day before the Queen's birthday, she was easy on the eye – they cheered her to the blue skies. She looked truly regal when, in her queenly gown and glittering tiara, she spoke from the throne on the dais of the Legislative Chamber. With no hint of the shyness that took her sister many years to overcome, she was almost exuberant. Her trip reached a peak of excitement when she arrived at Belize, Honduras, where local demonstrators and Guatemalan interference might have spoilt the occasion. The British government, slightly over-dramatising the situation, sent an R.A.F. squadron to roar over the city – just in case. In British Guiana, on the eve of her return home, Margaret dealt in her own characteristic way with the colour problem, dancing with one and all of the coloured officers of a volunteer regiment till two a.m. in the morning.

She was hardly home when the boring Townsend saga claimed new attention. The gallant airman went to visit Margaret just when the Queen was entertaining another foreign president, Gronchi of Italy, but Margaret was present and correct with the other members of the royal family at the splendid reception at Lancaster House. She still kept the Townsend record turning for all it was worth, and had him for dinner a few days later, the Queen Mother playing gooseberry. He stayed for six hours. What did they do all this time? They did not spend it as some people with overheated imaginations visualised.

Most of their time was taken up with the study of the draft of a manuscript entitled 'The Story of Peter Townsend' by Norman Barrymaine, one of Peter's Fleet Street friends, who had spent much time with him in the crisis weeks of 1955. Since Peter was the chief source of information, the book was at once authoritative and discreet and large sums were offered for publication rights in volume and serialisation. The German editor whose magazine eventually published large extracts gave much prominence to the material – he was convinced that Townsend was getting a cut of the proceeds. While freely commenting on the contents and amending several passages, Margaret did not object to the publication, even encouraged it. When Townsend's good taste in associating himself with such a story was questioned, he produced as good an excuse as any – his ex-wife, Rosemary de Laszlo was reported to have been offered half a million dollars to tell her side of the story. But for her part, even if such an offer was on the table, she had no intention of accepting it.

The Queen drove to Clarence House the following morning and stayed for three-quarters of an hour, fitting the pattern of Margaret's stepping out of line and the Queen's trying to get her on course again. It was also enough to shorten the odds on a new Townsend crisis developing. Taking a more relaxed line this time, courtiers suggested that the royal ladies had probably discussed Margaret's request to let Johnny and Pipkin, her Sealyhams, exercise in the garden of Buck House with the Queen's Corgis (Sugar and Susan) and the Queen Mother's Dachshund Rikki, and Roly, the King Charles Spaniel, a perfect picture of royal harmony.

Tony was in the game, too, and strengthened Margaret's hand like a sound bridge partner playing a trump card of his own. He drove to London Airport and, as conspicuously as he could make it, embraced Jacqui Chan who flew in to appear as a leading dancer – a new venture – in the cast of 'Simply Heavenly'. She was visibly surprised by his fiery welcome which, it was said, raised quite a few eyebrows, the purpose of the exercise. Margaret did not have to wait long to see proof that they were achieving their object of keeping the wolves from Tony's door. The indefatigable Audrey Whiting was prompt to announce, via the *Sunday Pictorial*, that 'Margaret is at this moment deeply in love with Townsend. She would like to marry him – or nobody!' Only the Swiss daily, *Tribune de Genève*, which came out with another 'Marriage imminent' report was regarded as important enough to warrant an official denial.

Let us, at this point, make a mental leap across the next short five months – to October – and look at another interesting foreign press item, a lavishly illustrated report in *Paris Match* which suggested either that Peter Townsend was a philanderer who had accomplished a remarkably rapid emotional shift of scene or that – as we already know – there was no substance in what the papers said about his and Margaret's feelings for each other. For here, spread over six pages, were photographs of Peter Townsend at Knocke-le-Zoute in unmistakable *tête-à-tête* with the handsome, nineteen-year-old heiress of a considerable Belgian fortune, Marie-Luce ('Ma-Luce' as he called her) Jamagne. There were variations on the theme of a love-in and happiness – Peter lying in the shade of a tree with his head in Ma-Luce's lap, bathing, boating, riding together or drinking at the bar. The magazine's headline announced what the photographs made obvious : *'Peter Townsend a oublié Margaret.'*

For Margaret, in the meantime, it was back to official assignments – and preparations for another foreign tour, this time to Canada for British Columbia's centenary celebrations. Hartnell and Stiebel were joined by Rayne and Mirman to create a suitable wardrobe for her. She tried to be fashionable but it was her misfortune that high fashion just then was that most unbecoming of ladies' garments, the Sack or Balloon look, best forgotten. It so happened that Tony who was always looking for new ways to express himself had recently taken to fashion designing and produced some imaginative winter sports clothes which struck Margaret as stylish and original but which did not catch on.

Ten thousand British Columbians had grown beards to re-capture the world of their ancestors and gave Margaret a rapturous welcome. She criss-crossed the country from Vancouver to Montreal going competently through the routine imposed on visiting royalty. The smile never faded, the temper never flared, yet whether in Saskatchewan or Ottawa, her hosts felt that her heart was elsewhere (or that, perhaps, she bore a grudge because Canada had strongly objected to her marrying Peter). She seemed in a great hurry to get back home. The tour would not have run true to form had it not thrown up at least one young man, a lawyer by the name of John Turner, son of the Lieutenant-Governor of British Columbia, who seemed to stimulate her more than others. They were observed together, photographed together, the usual thing. After gracefully accepting the gift of an island, Portland, which was renamed Princess Margaret Island, she departed. She never saw the island again but John Turner did eventually turn up in England.

As abroad, so at home. Impossible to chronicle Margaret's life without referring to some of the old skeletons which rattled fearfully but disintegrated on closer inspection. If, as the clever-clever acid tongues suggested in noisy whispers, she had had a special relationship with every man with whom she was seen rubbing shoulders or even cheeks, she would have been a phenomenon – or, put more bluntly, a nymphomaniac – and not a lively twenty-nine-year-old unmarried woman with normal instincts and inclinations. But one who ought to be recalled was Robin Douglas-Home whose uncle later became Prime Minister. Notwithstanding his noble background, Robin was a dilettante labouring in several vineyards – Mayfair, Fleet Street – for a time he had earned his living as a piano player. He had caused a stir when he visited Sweden and courted King Gustaf's grand-daughter, Princess Margaretha, and there was talk of marriage. But the Swedish royal family had scotched that and had, more or less tactfully, sent him packing. Robin graduated to a place among Margaret's *amours de coeur* ('Her most handsome escort since Townsend . . .') when he accompanied her to Covent Garden and was seen dancing with her at the Travellers Club and the Casanova where his former employer, bandleader Tony

Kinsman, played up to him and his high-born partner. Margaret would be meeting this melancholy, lachrymose character again before his tragic, almost pre-ordained end.

Relations between the royal sisters were bound to mellow with time. In and out of the public eye, they were once more at ease in each other's company and, before long, Margaret could report to Tony that she and the Queen had been taking a leaf out of his book when they had spent a day at Badminton and photographed everything in sight, the Queen shooting away with as much fervour as Margaret with her 'special interest' in photography. Tony met the Queen again when he was asked to tea at the Royal Lodge. He was made to feel very much at home. There was a strong architectural resemblance between the Lodge's Gothic drawing room and his mother's salon at Birr Castle where he had spent most of his youth. The Queen thought that Margaret was deeply serious about Tony and approved. Tony was different, he was discreet, seemed, above all, the kind of man to keep Margaret on the straight and narrow. She decided to consult the Prime Minister (Harold Macmillan) and to let one or two Commonwealth leaders know that there was a possibility . . .

One reason why Margaret looked forward to her next excursion – a visit to Rome – was the prospect of a reunion with Judy Montagu who had been closer to her than most other girl friends over the last few years and was one of the few people with whom she could discuss Tony. Judy was spending much time in Rome and planning to settle there for good. The tour turned out to be stimulating in other respects as well. Inevitably dubbed 'Margaret's Roman Holiday' – after the popular film with Audrey Hepburn – it projected Margaret into a riot of principes, principessas, cardinals – and the Pope – with the Queen Mother going along to confer dignity on the trip. Judy's artist and literary friends promised Margaret a glimpse of the less conventional side of Roman life – if not quite *la dolce vita*.

She met them at a very 'hip' party Judy gave for her on an island in the River Tiber, and mingled with more conventional society when Sir Marcus Cheke, the British ambassador, entertained her with a splendid supporting cast of cardinals and aristocrats. She was intrigued by the Italian princes who were ten a penny, some wearing their title like a precious jewel, others using it to cloak their penury. The prince who emerged as the 'escort of the week' (walks in Roman gardens, *paparazzi* snatching intimate photographs suggesting this or the other) was Henry of Hesse, whose father was a relative of Philip and whose mother was the brave anti-Nazi, Italian Princess Mafalda. With such a background, it would have been surprising if he had not been singled out as yet another 'prospective husband'. Margaret had an audience with Pope John XXIII who was in rollicking form – they hit it off splendidly. The press tried to make something of Margaret's visit to Ostia Antica, the old port of Rome (some two miles inland) on the tenuous ground that she passed the spot where Wilma Montesi, a girl of the society-and-drug-*dolce-vita* set had been found murdered years earlier but the shock waves of the Montesi scandal had long since subsided.

Visits to the catacombs and seven churches revived the chatter about Margaret's 'religious mania' which spawned some curious flowers of the imagination about her fondness for dressing up in a nun's habit and – to complete the absurd tale into which it developed when she was seen pillion-riding in the English countryside – racing on a motorbike in this highly unsuitable, flamboyant attire. Where will it all end, as Margaret's favourite gossip writer asks about his own most outrageous stories.

Margaret loved every minute of her stay in Rome and Romans reciprocated her affection – except for the Italian couturier Giulio Schubert who dismissed her clothes as 'out of date' with other unflattering epithets. (It was a recurring theme among the more avant-garde clothiers; when some English gallants came to her defence she did not help them with her appearance at Ascot where, in the popular phrase, she 'looked a right mess'.) Margaret was not bothered – by temperament she adjusted better to the Italian scene than to most others except the Caribbean.

Next on her schedule was a trip to Portugal which went off as free from irritations as her Roman holiday. The Portuguese police under-estimated the popular appeal of a British royal princess, and no sooner had she set foot on terra firma when she was engulfed by a wildly enthusiastic crowd. As she was driven to the famous Cato di Roca, the most westerly point in

Europe, clusters of Portuguese in their Sunday best waving union jacks and led by local padres who had promised them a view of the British Queen's sister were stationed along the route.

Margaret lolled in the pool of her host, Viscount Antonio Asseca, while police ordered every window over a wide area around to be shuttered. Her meeting with Don Juan, the Spanish Pretender, in Estoril (he never made it to the throne having to give way to his son) was amiable enough. Count Nova-Goa offered her the hospitality of the stables on his estate and she rode off contentedly into the country. The visit reached its happiest moments at the fishing village of Nazare where students, in the spirit of Sir Walter Raleigh, made a carpet of honour with their coats for her to walk on.

Back home again, Tony was allowed to surface briefly and take her official birthday photographs. One of them, very artistic with starkly contrasting light and shade was published by the *Daily Mirror* with this comment: 'We print it because the princess is a lovely girl, because it marks her birthday and because it's the latest picture available. We wish there was another to give you a better idea of what she is like.' Perhaps Tony saw her differently from the picture editor; perhaps the *Daily Mirror* was not too friendly inclined towards a photographer prominently associated with a rival newspaper. Still, nobody spotted the link between the two disparate lovers and, for them, it was just as well that John Turner arrived from his native Canada and was received at Clarence House which gave everybody something to talk about.

Tony confused the issue further by publishing a selection of photographs of Chinese beauties including Jacqui Chan. Ah ha! But just then (October 1959) press and people were obliged to bid farewell to their 'favourite' among Margaret's partners – Peter Townsend announced his engagement to Marie-Luce Jamagne. From here on, I shall let him go his own way confident that, whether or not he and Margaret meet again from time to time, his forthcoming memoirs will put the most innocuous construction on romance with his sovereign's daughter.

That Margaret would before long provide some fascinating new talking points seemed a foregone conclusion when Major John Griffin was appointed to the staff at Clarence House as a press secretary to the Queen Mother to deal with 'matters relating to Princess Margaret'. Even so some close friends did not guess what was behind it. Neither did they recognise the Borgward parked so frequently at the back entrance of Clarence House as belonging to 'someone special', and when Tony Armstrong-Jones occasionally joined a royal party it looked as if he was simply enjoying the privileges of a court photographer. Nobody was aware that he spent a couple of days as the Queen Mother's guest at the Castle of Mey – and went on to Balmoral carrying with him an engagement ring made to his own design. Had Tony's tiny presence been noticed at all, it might at this moment not have aroused much interest anyway because the Queen revealed a secret of her own which more than satisfied the voracious popular appetite for romantic royal news – on her return from Canada it was announced that, nine years after the birth of Princess Anne, Her Majesty was expecting another baby.

Royalty like to take their most joyful steps slowly, deliberately, one by one and keep the lid on as long as possible – until every angle has been examined, every risk assessed, every obstacle studied. Margaret and Tony agreed that the engagement they celebrated in the royal family circle at Balmoral – Margaret was said to have been uncharacteristically emotional – should not be made public until the complicated preliminaries to a royal marriage had been completed and some important decisions had been taken. The marriage of a royal princess to a commoner raised matters of status which had to be resolved. Being third in line of succession, Margaret's marriage plans had to be discussed with the Commonwealth, and the position of her children, if any, to be determined. Tony did not want a title, not yet, but the real problem was that the Queen suggested an earldom while Margaret wanted him to have dukedom (like Philip's). The Queen would not budge.

Tony's future – he could not very well carry on as a commercial photographer but he was reluctant to become a royal puppet with courtiers pulling the strings and sending him off to public functions on his own or by the side of his gracious princess. He and Margaret never thought this problem through and it ticked away under their marital bed like a time bomb. There was the question of a suitable residence for them. Marlborough House was too big and pretentious for Tony. Kensington Palace was a much better idea although the only available accommodation in the big complex of grace and favour homes was bound to prove inadequate. They decided to take it until something better could be provided and the Ministry of Works undertook to make adaptations costing around seven thousand pounds. They would not come out of Margaret's pocket; on the other hand, her allowance on marriage would be increased to fifteen thousand pounds.

Margaret was delving more deeply into Tony's background (while the Special Branch looked discreetly into every aspect of his personal history) – it was fun finding out new details. Casual and informal as he was in many ways, he was as family conscious as any aristocratic or royal person, full of stories about his maternal grandfather Linley Sambourne who drew cartoons for *Punch* and relied for verisimilitude on a collection of some twelve thousand photographs which may well have inspired Tony's choice of a career. For Margaret's benefit, he enumerated his seven godparents to whom he owed his near-royal string of Christian names – Antony Charles Robert Owen Lloyd – and one of whom was the Countess of Seafield, Britain's richest woman. Grandfather Armstrong-Jones had been a distinguished medical man specialising in mental diseases, and Papa Ronald Armstrong-Jones, Q.C. was a colourful character. His marriage to Tony's mother in 1935 had not lasted long but he seemed to have been happy for most of the twenty-three years he had been with his second wife, former Australian actress Carol Coombe. But she had recently left him and he was already heading for his third marriage – to Jenifer Unite, a B.O.A.C. air hostess, at thirty-two the same age as his daughter Susan. Ronald Armstrong-Jones still maintained the family residence in Caernarvonshire, a county with which Tony would forge another association before long.

Tony's mother and her second husband Michael – the Earl of Rosse – were no strangers to Margaret. The Countess had cut a fine figure at the coronation in a spectacular robe dating back to the coronation of William IV, and her emeralds, the most fabulous in Britain. Margaret knew that Tony's mother had been regarded as the most beautiful woman in Mayfair, and that his stepfather was still known as the 'Adonis of the

146

peerage'. Michael Rosse's money came from the family's coal-mines in Yorkshire where he maintained an estate (Womenly Park, near Leeds) besides his town house in Knightsbridge and Birr Castle.

In the passage of time Margaret established a good rapport with Tony's half-brothers, twenty-three years old Lord Oxmanton and the boisterous Martin Parsons whose coming-of-age party towards the end of 1959 was a big event in Birr. Withal, they were an attractive family to marry into even for a royal princess.

Tony's record at Eton provided some amusement. It was ideally summed up by one of his masters who noted : 'Maybe he's interested in some subject but it's not a subject we teach here.' Contemporaries also recalled that Tony showed early entrepreneurial instincts at school making crystal wireless sets in matchboxes and selling them at five shillings each. In the holidays he had made pocket money working as a waiter in Brighton or for a housing agency in London. He made light of the attack of polio at sixteen which had left him with a slight limp and occasional twinges in the leg; it did not slow him down and he continued to hustle and bustle in a most un-royal manner. The thought and work he devoted to handicapped people belied the impression that he was a cold fish. Margaret was fascinated when he talked about people they both knew because he invariably knew them better than she did. With none of her biting wit, he told some amusing tales about some of his sitters such as the beautiful French Vicomtesse de Ribes, a friend of Onassis', or Madame Suzy Volterra, the famous racing lady.

Discreetly – for the time being – Margaret was introduced to Tony's intimate friends, Jeremy and Camilla Fry, with whom they spent some spirited weekends at their house, Widcombe Manor, near Bath. Tony chose Jeremy as his best man and Margaret readily agreed. The circumstances under which Jeremy had to withdraw – an old story dredged up from the gutter – belong to the chapter of 'social accidents' to which Margaret was prone. The official explanation was an attack of jaundice. Tony replaced him with Dr Roger Gilliatt whose wife, the former Penelope Connor, was a *Vogue* editor with whom Tony had been working for some time. Dr Gilliatt, inevitably dubbed 'the second best man', happened to be a neurologist who could, if the need arose, help Tony to cope with the acute nervous strain from which he suffered in this period. It did not stop him – Tony – putting up more smoke screens to disguise the sensational wedding plans. He started to drop hints that he was tired of photography and considering selling his business. He said he might go to live in the United States for a few years. The truth was that he loved his work and was in several minds about the future but while pretending for the sake of harmony that he might really give it up, he already had some idea of how he might continue his photography in one form or another and become a 'working' member of the royal family.

CHAPTER ELEVEN

Although the royal family treated Margaret and Tony as an engaged couple, the engagement (pending a public announcement) was strictly unofficial and the build-up to the great event was conducted under a cloak of secrecy. Whenever they ventured out together, Margaret hid her familiar face behind outsize dark glasses and a rather voluminous head-scarf (which was not so much a disguise, more a piece of standard royal attire). Her Rolls cruised for a quarter of an hour through Pimlico before she could slip unobserved into Tony's studio. Yet some obvious clues to the real state of their affair were overlooked. There was the occasion in a restaurant in Maidenhead when Tony called Margaret 'Ducky' – those who heard it literally did not trust their ears. There was also, according to Helen Cathcart, an angry exchange between Tony and Kingsley Amis who criticised Margaret within Tony's hearing whereupon he sprung to 'her defence so vigorously that he almost gave the game away.

Lest their irrepressible intimacy cause public embarrassment it was decided that they should spend the next three months apart, a conventional royal love test to which Tony submitted reluctantly. Alert observers later interpreted a series of small ads in *The Times* as an exchange of confidences and endearments between Margaret and Tony. They were reunited at Sandringham on the first day of the New Year. Again, they behaved like a couple of love birds but by this time the royal family was only concerned with the technicalities of their engagement and wedding. It was agreed that the engagement should be announced towards the end of February after the birth of the Queen's baby. Tony was getting on well with his future royal relatives. The Queen Mother's protective instincts were aroused by his waif-like manner which had a curious effect on elderly ladies.

Though he was not Philip's kind of man – too artistic and namby-pamby – the Duke gave him some useful hints on how to treat the common herd, how to march purposefully into a crowded room straight to the person of his choice before anybody else had a chance of butting in and forcing his or her company on him. Tony never really mastered the art which Margaret practised to such perfection but he learnt from Philip what to do with his hands, and, as a result, almost comically aped his brother-in-law's characteristic hands-behind-the-back but never matched Philip for the quick, if schoolboyish repartee. The Queen was demonstratively sweet to Tony and remained so throughout the turbulent marriage, blaming Margaret rather than him for the difficulties that arose.

The Queen's baby was born on February 19th and Margaret slipped from third to fourth place in the line of succession. It was decided that her engagement should be announced on February 26th and there were rumours that she was pregnant – quickly disproved when the wedding date was fixed for two months later – or that she was in a hurry to make it 'official' before the Queen could change her mind. The older generation of royal associates threatened to upset the time-table laboriously evolved by court officials. Countess Mountbatten died suddenly while touring North Borneo; two days later the Marquess of Carisbrook, Queen Victoria's last surviving grandson passed away at the Kensington Palace grace and favour residence into which Margaret and Tony would be moving before long. The Queen decided that arrangements should go ahead as planned, including the wedding of Diana Bowes-Lyon to Mr Peter Sommervel at the Henry VII Chapel in Westminster Abbey which Margaret and Tony attended separately exchanging neither wink nor word.

In a less formal wedding ceremony at a registry office, Mr Armstrong-Jones senior made Jenifer Unite his third wife. Two days later, Tony and Margaret celebrated their official engagement at Royal Lodge, Windsor. The court circular, dated February 26th, 1960 read:

'Clarence House
(WHITEHALL 3141)

It is with the greatest pleasure that Queen Elizabeth, The Queen Mother announces the betrothal of her beloved daughter, The Princess Margaret to Mr Antony Charles Robert Armstrong-Jones, son of Mr R. O. C. Armstrong-Jones, Q.C., and the Countess of Rosse to which union The Queen has gladly given her consent.'

The announcement caused genuine but by no means unpleasant surprise.

The pubs of Pimlico acclaimed Tony like a folk hero – 'Everybody's talking about the Jones boy.' Billy Wallace wished the couple well. Ma-Luce Jamagne-Townsend said she had known about this for a long time. Sharman Douglas cried with joy and the Archbishop of Canterbury was 'very pleased'. Tony's father sent a telegram from the Bahamas where he was on honeymoon, stepmother Carole Coombe, now Mrs Giuseppe Lopez, drank a toast to Tony in the kitchen of her Chelsea house. Jacqui Chan, appearing in 'The World of Suzie Wong' breathed: 'I'm so happy for him,' and burst into tears indicating that she was less happy for herself. From Buckingham Palace where the Queen was nursing her baby, it was announced that Her Majesty and Prince Philip were delighted with this obviously happy match, and Philip telephoned Margaret from Windsor Castle where he was spending the weekend with little Charles.

The British press went mad about Tony, and foreign newspapers and magazines were even less restrained. Overnight the royal bridegroom became a blue-eyed boy (his eyes really were blue), a genius with a camera, a paragon of virtue, brilliant, versatile, a modern Michelangelo, a youthful Cartier-Bresson and Walter Gropius rolled into one. The *Daily Mirror* described him prematurely as 'a former photographer' but there was enough bite left in Fleet Street for some writers to point out that Tony was making a small fortune out of his engagement –

not only were his old photographs reproduced (to show what a genius he was) but most of the royal pictures the newspapers printed on this occasion were his, too. The fees he collected were conservatively estimated at one thousand pounds.

The number of his close friends who rushed into print with personal tributes and memories was legion – fellow photographers, journalists, show-biz people. 'I am the only Fleet Street, journalist who isn't a personal friend of Antony Armstrong-Jones...' was the distinction claimed by Sheila Logue in *Punch*. The most sensible comment came from Professor A. J. P. Taylor who said that his hardened heart had softened at the news but who warned : 'Let Mr Armstrong-Jones remain what he is, a commoner who need fear no rival. Let him continue to practise the profession at which he is so accomplished!' 'Why not Mrs Jones?' asked the *Daily Mirror*.

It was not unadulterated joy. Foreign papers, with the sensationalist *France-Dimanche* in the vanguard, came up with some rather unpleasant stories. Tony, they suggested, had to get rid of some of his less salubrious friends, among them a Hindu guitarist, a publican, a social climber who had been involved in a Riviera jewel robbery and a bunch of models and cover girls. His step-aunt was unhappily caught up in a motoring accident and charged with drunken driving. Jacqui Chan soon released a record ('But No One Knows') because 'it seemed a good time'. Gossips traded accounts of 'pyjama' and 'nightie' parties Tony was supposed to have attended at the homes of neighbours. On the credit side – if that's the right expression – inveterate forelock touchers like Mr Montague-Smith completed a marital chart, a double-barrelled family tree which purported to show that somewhere down the distant line (taking the Queen Mother's family along the route) Tony and Margaret had an ancestor in common, a certain Ievan of Bron y Foel who lived in the Tudor period, and that they were twelfth cousins twice removed.

Tony contacted as many of his personal friends as he could reach and assured them that nothing would change. Some received notes written by hand saying : 'I'll be seeing you in a couple of months when all this fuss is over,' signed 'T.A.J.' – I remember one of them, Dominic Elwes, saying that he did not doubt Tony's good intentions but that, being unversed in the ways of royalty, he obviously underestimated the Palace steamroller which would soon flatten the uninhibited bohemian into the acceptable pattern. Dominic's worst fears seemed justified when Tony was given an office in Buckingham Palace to work under the eyes of the courtiers on the preparations for his wedding – and his life with Margaret thereafter.

On the last day of February he made his 'royal debut' as a guest of honour at Covent Garden which he had last visited as a photographer to portray some of the performers. This time, in hastily tailored tails, he walked, hands clasped Philip-like behind his back, with the Queen Mother and Margaret into the royal box while the audience cheered him and his intended to the roof. A battery of cameras was turned on the cameraman. Photographers of a dozen countries took engagement pictures so tritely conventional, Tony would never have released them from his own studio – he and Margaret gazing into each other's eyes, walking hand in hand into the distance, reading messages together, Margaret tickling the keys of the piano or the dog . . . Tony's thirtieth birthday not much later provoked a similar outburst of pictorial sentimentality.

One of his first jobs at Buckingham Palace was to deal with the official invitations to the wedding. Standard-size royal cards carried the standard text: 'The Lord Chamberlain to Queen Elizabeth, The Queen Mother is commanded by Her Majesty to invite . . .' and so forth. They soon became coveted documents. Leading actors who had posed before Tony's camera, among them Sir Laurence Olivier, Sir Alec and Lady Guinness, Sir Michael and Lady Redgrave, Leslie Caron and Peter Hall, received their tickets for the Abbey, and Tony's lowlier friends and associates from Pimlico and Rotherhithe, Shaftesbury Avenue and Fleet Street who did not expect it were delighted to be remembered. One remarkable feature of the guest list for the wedding of a princess who barely five years earlier, conscious that marriage was indissoluble in the eyes of the church, had renounced her divorced groom was the marital status of some of the principal characters. It suggested several interpretations – that moral standards had disastrously deteriorated since the Townsend affair, that the permissive age was engulfing the royal family or that the fuss over Townsend had been one gigantic piece of hypocrisy.

Among the guests, of course, was Tony's father, twice divorced, three times married; Tony's mother, divorced and married for the second time, Tony's step-mother number one, divorced and re-married. They would be joining the Queen's party, Tony's father and mother, separated for the occasion from their current spouses, walking side by side behind the Queen. This time, the marriage and divorce jumble evoked not a whisper of dissent from either Buckingham or Lambeth Palace.

Another batch of invitations caused embarrassment of a different order. For reasons not immediately apparent, the royal families of Holland, Belgium, Sweden, Norway, Greece – but not Denmark – indicated that they would regretfully be unable to attend the wedding. Why ever not? It was not the case, as was foolishly suggested, that the continental monarchs disapproved of a princess of the world's premier royal house marrying a commoner. The real reason for the snubs to Margaret – 'previous engagements', none of them very pressing, was the crude excuse in almost every case – was a simple tit-for-tat. The continental royals were angry because their British cousins with the exception of the Duchess of Kent had not attended any of their major social events since the war, not even the funeral of King Haakon of Norway. The Norwegians were also peeved because young Princess Alexandra had turned down a suggestion that she should marry their Crown Prince Harald – like Margaret, 'Alex' was said to be in love with a commoner. Margaret was girding herself for a royal wedding without foreign royals although, in the event, a second eleven of assorted Yugoslav and German princes turned up.

One essential chore facing Tony and Margaret was a visit to Westminster Abbey to discuss details of the wedding ceremony with the Dean, Dr Eric Abbott. Over the years, accounts of this discussion have percolated through the filter of secrecy, pin-pointing it as the first major pre-marriage conflict between the engaged couple. Recalling it, their friends invariably stress how much in love Margaret and Tony were at the time, how happy in their sexual harmony and their common interests – the theatre, the arts, and people (though rarely the same kind of people). So many exciting, amusing, stimulating things were happening to them that there was no shortage of topics to discuss, and, if both seemed determined to stick to their points of view, disagreement was as amicable as agreement except that Tony's deceptively meek, silent surrenders could be as aggravating as his forceful opposition in some cases. Margaret was greatly amused by his foibles like the birdcage he was currently working on, (the beginning of a preoccupation with cages, which culminated in his spectacular Aviary in Regent's Park, and soon gave psycho-analysts much food for thought).

Entering Westminster Abbey, Tony was halfway inside the gilded cage of his royal future but reluctant to accept captivity without a struggle. The subject of the couple's talk with the Dean revealed some fundamental differences in outlook between Tony and Margaret; the wedding service, the hymns, the technical details were of profound meaning to someone as steeped in religion and ceremonial as Margaret but irrelevant, even irritating for a non-believing, informal character like Tony. Put bluntly, he could not have cared less whether the service, as Margaret wanted, was based on the Prayer Book of 1662 (with which he was barely familiar) rather than on the 1928 version; whether she should promise to obey him or not, or whether there was to be a special blessing for the wedding ring (which the Queen had made from the Welsh gold left over from her own ring). His approach to royal ceremonial was that of a normal, intelligent adult; pleasant to watch but taking part – ugh!

He did understand, could not have overlooked, the significance of Margaret's insistence on a part of the Sermon of the Mount replacing the customary Address. 'She felt that the passage from the Scriptures in Christ's own words would be most suitable,' the Dean said. Her motive became obvious when, with so many nasty insinuations making the rounds, she chose the Ninth Beatitude which went like this: 'Blessed are ye, when men shall revile you, and persecute you, and shall say all manner of evil against you falsely, for my sake!' Tony was said to have tried hard to appear interested but only became so when Margaret suggested installing television monitors so that people in all parts of the Abbey could see the High Altar. Some friends have given graphic demonstrations of his facial expressions, a combination of pain and stifled yawns, which reappeared whenever Margaret referred to the subject in later years. The difference in outlook brought out by the talk in the Abbey troubled them at many stages of their married life.

Tony did not mind, though Margaret was angry, when in the event the old Palace guard who could no more reconcile themselves to him than to Townsend as a member of the royal family, seemed to be subtly downgrading the wedding and countering criticism with hints that they were only carrying out the Queen's wishes. Guests were permitted to wear lounge suits ('Tony's friends can't be expected to own morning dress...' was one snide comment) and the route of the procession was cut down severely – to a walking distance of seven minutes. To head off protests against such low-key arrangements, a massive flower decoration scheme was ordered in the nick of time. With an air of resignation, Tony accepted the prospect of riding with Margaret in the royal Glass Coach, and agreed to the recruitment of eight little bridesmaids including six-year-old Catherine Vesey, his sister's daughter.

The intricate process of welding the lives of the princess and her commoner together received a temporary set-back when Tony had to cry off from a party at which the two sets of relatives were supposed to get to know each other better – it had not been easy in the first place to work out the permutations for the Queen to meet Margaret's new in-laws with their respective partners. Alas, Grandma Maud Messel was sinking fast and the Countess of Rosse, Tony and his sister, Viscountess de Vesci, rushed to Holmstead Manor where the old lady, a noted Edwardian beauty, died peacefully.

Living in a half-way house between his busy professional past and his uncertain royal future, Tony was forced to make decisions without being master of his own destiny. At every step he encountered precedents; the Palace always knew best. In everything, Margaret's position had to override all other considerations. Counter-arguments were imperiously brushed aside, and it did not seem the time or the place to argue. So he said 'Yes' – how could he decline? – to the dolls'-house-size grace and favour residence at Kensington Palace, which the Queen offered Margaret and him as a home, and, without giving much thought to the cost (some five thousand pounds), approved the Ministry of Works's plans for alterations and adaptations. He produced his own design for a Do-It-Yourself work-shop and told officials that he would make his own furniture for it – 'I am a carpenter', he said rather proudly.

Margaret's 29th birthday photograph taken by husband-to-be Antony Armstrong-Jones; (*above right*) dancing with Tony at the Empire Ballroom and (*below*) photographed by Norman Parkinson with her children, Sarah and David in 1967.

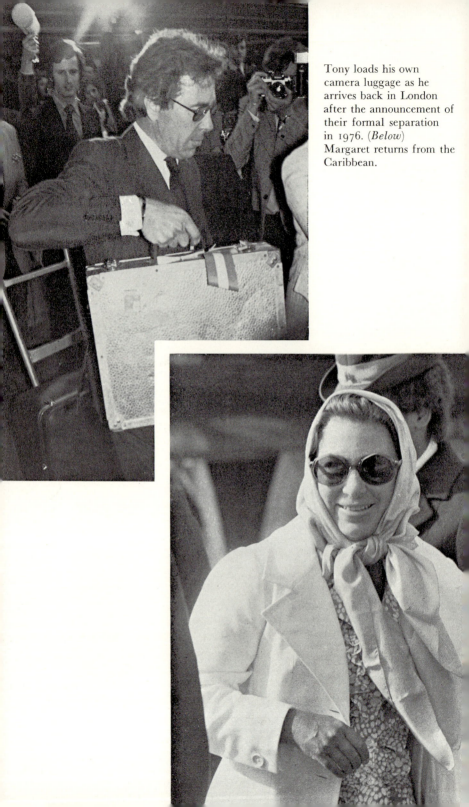

Tony loads his own camera luggage as he arrives back in London after the announcement of their formal separation in 1976. (*Below*) Margaret returns from the Caribbean.

As to staff, there would, whether he liked it or not, be a butler – the choice fell on one Thomas Cronin who had worked for the American ambassador, John Hay Whitney; a house-keeper, Miss Nora Foley, who was in her fifties; Margaret's own maid, Ruby Gordon, sister of the Queen's loyal 'Bobo'; and a married couple to serve as cook and footman. A chauffeur and 'Crocker of the Yard' would complete the domestic side but for special occasions, Margaret explained, they could count on her sister to lend them the odd servant from Buckingham Palace. Room would have to be found for Margaret's entourage, Iris Peake, principal lady-in-waiting, and Francis Legh. Tony would be keeping his faithful secretary, Dorothy Everard, to look after his affairs.

Though the groom would have liked nothing better than to do the job himself, Cecil Beaton was the obvious person to take the wedding pictures. Tony resurrected his beloved camera to act as family photographer at the christening of Prince Andrew, the Queen's new baby. As if to recapture his youth, he took Margaret to watch the Boat Race from the Cambridge launch – Oxford won. (A little later he took Margaret to Eton, another pilgrimage into his past.) They were discussing the honeymoon – it had to be the Caribbean – and, to ensure total privacy, the Queen offered them the royal yacht *Britannia* to take them to the islands. None of these seemingly simple matters was lightly decided. Subconsciously, the couple were engaged in a tug-of-war, Margaret pulling in the direction of extravagance as against Tony's modesty, the grandseigneural versus the ordinary, the royal versus the bourgeois. Margaret won on all counts.

The prospect of an increase in her Civil List allowance from six-thousand to fifteen-thousand pounds a year tempted at least one wiseacre to mention the family motto of the Armstrong-Joneses – 'To support God is to be supported' – with obvious allusions to Tony's future. How little they – or Margaret for that matter – knew him! He tended to agree with Emrys Hughes and Marcus Lipton who complained in the House of Commons about the 'wasteful expenditure' on the wedding (some twenty-six thousand pounds), a curtain raiser for the criticism that would pursue them for years.

Emrys Hughes asked questions about the royal yacht and the

cost of the honeymoon, and was told that there were twenty officers and three hundred and thirty-seven ratings aboard *Britannia* who between them were paid some four thousand pounds a week whether they sailed or not, so there would be no extra outlay for the honeymoon cruise. Hughes still insisted that this – the crew's pay presumably – was too large a sum to be spent on one couple at a time when the country was being urged to practise restraint to avoid inflation. But the Civil Lord of the Admiralty countered brusquely that the House wanted the Princess who had undertaken such manifold duties to enjoy a very happy voyage.

President de Gaulle's state visit briefly distracted attention from Tony and Margaret who did not mind taking a back seat for a day or two. Margaret attended her last public function before the wedding (opening a new department at the North Middlesex Hospital) on April 26th, the day the official wedding programme was issued. It did not bring any surprises except that H.R.H. the Bride would be given away by H.R.H. the Duke (of Edinburgh) whose German relatives were the only foreign near-royals, apart from the Queen of Denmark and Tomislav of Yugoslavia (Tony's pal, not Margaret's), making for London and the wedding.

Tony was not feeling very well, never did when under strain, and was unlikely to improve before it was all over. One of his friends thought that it was only now fully dawning on him what he was letting himself in for : not only marrying the girl he loved but getting hitched to an institution. One remark he made at the time suggested that he intended to keep his independence and carry Margaret with him into his own life, 'liberate her', as he put it, from the horsey, doggy world of the royal family.

Margaret sailed through the preliminaries with her usual panache. There was a glow about her that had been missing for years. She was trying on tiaras – in the event she chose one (the Poltimore Tiara) which was bought for her at Sotheby's for five thousand five hundred pounds. Tony was in a state. As the wedding day drew near his leg played up as it always did when he was agitated, and he visited his orthopaedic surgeon in Harley Street. Wedding presents from well-wishers were arriving by the sackful as he went out looking for a present for Margaret, preferably something in silver. By this time, that able writing duo, Robert Glenton (brother of William) and Stella King, was ready with the biography of the new royal recruit (*Once Upon A Time*) and other authors were beavering away at the same subject.

At a reception the Queen gave for the couple at Buckingham Palace two days before the wedding, Tony's personal friends, consumed by curiosity, mingled freely with the royal establishment whose members were similarly intrigued by them although the difference in background and attitude of the two sides was vastly exaggerated. In spite of his resolution to remain himself, Tony opted for 'dignity' and 'solemnity', and perhaps a little overwrought by his new status, did not easily find the right tone when responding to his old chums' lighthearted, gently irreverent manner. Bandleader Joe Loss was in tune with the mood when he treated the royal party to a jolly rendering of 'Fings Ain't Wot They Used T'Be'.

Although an early rush for costly vantage seats on the stands slackened off, the wedding had all the makings of a full-blooded royal occasion. Large crowds collected for a free glimpse of bride and groom on the eve of the ceremony when they drove to Westminster Abbey for a dress-rehearsal, and quite a few of them remained to watch the real thing. Thousands camped out along the route, traffic was heavy and the more affluent of the Queen's loyal subjects foregathered in their Mayfair haunts for a night of parties. Accompanied by his best man, Tony visited his bride but was not allowed to see her wedding gown.

By early morning crowds numbering, according to varying estimates, between one hundred thousand and half a million, craned their necks and gaped at the archways and floral themes – crowns flanked by M and A (for Margaret and Antony). Clusters of people intoned a merry 'For he's a jolly good fellow!' The general atmosphere was so buoyant as to confound the down-graders. Tony's fixed smile as he rode to the Abbey was a brave response to unaccustomed cheers. Dr Gilliatt was literally the best man to help Tony through his ordeal. Margaret was escorted by Philip who, as always when he was not at ease, camouflaged his embarrassment with a cascade of jokes and chuckled about them all the way to the Abbey.

Like all royal occasions, the ceremony went like clockwork.

Only those looking for flaws noticed that Tony was a little fidgety and nervous while waiting for the bride but responded to Dr Gilliatt's comforting words. The fanfare of trumpets signalling Margaret's arrival broke the tension but Margaret herself looked emotional for an instant as she joined the groom to kneel before the Archbishop. The Queen looked splendid but remote, the Countess of Rosse seemed the most attractive woman in the Abbey, and the Countess of Harewood wore a striking outfit – like Tony she was a commoner who had been accepted into the royal family but there was as yet no hint that her marriage to the Queen's cousin would fail to last the distance in the same way as Tony's was destined to fail.

In her obligatory Hartnell wedding dress with tiny waist and bulging skirt, Margaret more than ever resembled a dainty porcelain figurine. Eyes modestly downcast, she seemed absorbed by the gentle tune of her favourite hymn, 'The Lord Is My Shepherd'. Tony's voice was almost inaudible as he repeated the marriage vows; Margaret – 'Margaret Rose' the Archbishop called her – was guilty of a rare slip of the tongue but her promise came across clear and unequivocal. The couple moved to High Altar for the second part of the service with the Dean intoning the Beatitudes, then Tony clasped his wife's hand tenderly as they walked away. As they passed the Queen, Margaret curtseyed deeply and Tony bowed his head a little stiffly before trooping off down the aisle followed by the bridesmaids.

Two thousand wedding guests rose, among them the venerable Sir Winston Churchill leaning heavily on his stick. Tony later said he had been sustained during these strange rites by the presence of so many old friends, professional associates with a sprinkling of 'deserving cases' to prove that he was still the same good old Tony – Jocelyn Stevens, owner-editor of *Queen* magazine and personal confidant rubbed shoulders with Frank Spooner (of the *Daily Express*); Bill Glenton, his Rotherhithe landlord, was alongside Dominic Elwes and the Sainsburys, and the lower orders were represented by Betty Peabody, the loyal Pimlico char, and the postman from his father's Welsh village. The press was there in strength, some photographers concentrating on Tony's 'three mothers' for whose pictures some Fleet Street editors were clamouring but between them writers and cameramen produced a dignified record of the picturesque scene.

From beginning to end, Margaret performed like a leading lady in her own production, charming and sure-footed. Once he had pulled himself together, Tony betrayed his feelings only by the flicker of his eyes and an occasional twitch of the mouth. As he later admitted, he was intensely conscious of the overpowering atmosphere in the Abbey and the fairy-tale drive in the Glass Coach with the Captain's Escort of the Household Cavalry, the clatter of their horses' hooves ringing in his ears. To appear with Margaret and his royal relatives on the Palace balcony, to look down on the sea of faces and hear the cheers rising from below was pure magic. Margaret's expression was revealing. One who was very close thought that her radiant smile was tinged with a hint of triumph – the triumph of a princess who had carried off the man of her choice.

The wedding breakfast, though there were one hundred and twenty guests in the white and gold ball supper room at the Palace, was a relaxed affair. The Grenadier Guards and a platoon of pipers provided background music. The proceedings dissolved in the customary hilarity when the royals and lesser fry scampered after the departing newly-weds out into the Palace forecourt and showered them with confetti. In contrast to the ceremonial of the morning, only a single police car followed Mr and Mrs Antony Armstrong-Jones as they drove towards Tower Pier to board the royal yacht. Warming to the handsome couple, the crowds surged forward and pressed against their Rolls with hardly a policeman to keep the well-wishers at bay. Hooting car horns, chiming church bells, shrieking ships' sirens mingled with noisy, good-humoured cheers.

The disorganised, spontaneous ovation appealed to Tony, and his bride smiled indulgently through their chaotic progress. At last they went aboard *Britannia* – after their brief flirtation with the people, the Joneses were off on a six-weeks honeymoon in truly royal style. A last wave in the direction of their Rotherhithe love nest and the yacht made for the choppy Channel. Margaret, in scarlet sweater and skirt, and Tony, more demurely, in a blue blazer and white slacks, lounged on deck. From the top of the main mast fluttered the Princess's personal standard. Through a naval transmitter came the traditional question:

'Whither bound?' The answer – 'Destination unknown . . . !' – a symbolic forecast for the unusual marriage.

Much was made of the suggestion that Margaret marrying a commoner was bringing the royal family closer to the people, and the word 'democratic', as applied to the wedding of the year, was cruelly overworked. As with most comments at the time which hindsight has exposed as nonsense, this emphasis on Tony's 'ordinary' background missed a few points. In front of me as I write are a number of photographs of Tony – as a baby swathed in lace in the arms of his mother; as a little boy with his nanny ('Like the Princess, Tony had a nanny!' it was stressed in a different context); with half-brother Lord Oxmanton, aged five or six, in jodhpurs and hacking jacket; and dressed in the upper-class boys' regulation overcoat and cap walking with the Countess of Rosse and sister Susie, the future viscountess. From boyhood, most of it spent at Birr Castle, Tony was familiar with the sort of architectural splendour that he encountered at Windsor and other royal residences. Though without a title, he had been brought up as to the manner born; and the near-hippie habits he affected were never very pronounced and, anyway, quite in fashion among young aristocrats.

The Caribbean honeymoon came close to giving Margaret what she always wanted – the best of all worlds. She found privacy on some enchanting beaches in places like Tobago, Robinson Crusoe's island, with the famous Golden Grove Lagoon where a cabin was put at their disposal. The British press tried to be discreet but Italian, French, American cameramen were relentless in their pursuit of – *plus ça change* – Margaret in a swimsuit. One of the local photographers covering her visit was Isaac Chan, Jacqui's father who confessed that he had already thought of himself as Tony's future father-in-law.

Occasionally, as in St John's, Antigua, the honeymooners were acclaimed by cheering crowds with Tony practising the royal wave of the hand with as much grace as he could muster. Local governors and administrators reduced official hospitality to a minimum enabling the couple to go their own way, laze in the sun, sip cool drinks, walk arm-in-arm on lonely beaches and dive together into the sea. At night it was back to the *Britannia* to watch the moon from deck-chairs and listen to records, mostly Frank Sinatra and Nat 'King' Cole, or to retire to their state room with one of the books Billy Wallace had sent aboard as a goingaway gift: Joy Adamson's *Born Free*, C. P. Snow's *The Affair*, Cornelius Ryan's *The Longest Day*... Mornings they were not in a hurry to rise. Sylvia Davies, a junior from Réné's hairdressing salon, kept Margaret's hair in order – her new short-curly look, while not the most becoming for her face, was at least practical for a seaside honeymoon.

Impossible for Margaret to protect her honeymoon secrets. There was always somebody who broke the rules and intimate details were soon hawked around the globe. This is how American reporters found out that her underwear was made of hand-woven *crêpe de Chine*; that Tony called her 'Pet' or 'Sweet' or 'My love' – until he finally settled on 'Ducky' – and she addressed him as 'Darling'. On many a day, the royal yacht, leaving the curious behind, sailed towards remote and lonely spots on lesser known islands like Huevos and Mustique which, as in any gripping drama, provided the backdrop to the beginning and the end of this marriage.

Mustique, as everybody seems to know, was bought (reputedly for forty-five thousand pounds) by Margaret's old friend Colin Tennant who invested a great deal of money in the attractive island, and sold parcels of land (at around fifteen-thousand pounds each) to wealthy customers in search of romantic holiday homes. He turned a derelict cotton mill into a first class pull-up for tourists, helped regulars to build their own villas, and created an exclusive colony in an extremely pleasant atmosphere with the kind of 'primitive luxury' rich lotus eaters crave. Tennant gave Margaret a plot in Gelliceaux Bay as a wedding present, and arranged for her villa to be built.

Though Tony loved Mustique the moment he stepped ashore with Margaret, he was not happy about his wife's association with the Tennant outfit. There were several personal reasons – the one his friends put forward was that he thought the Princess was being exploited for commercial and publicity purposes but this applies to most things royals do, and, for that matter, to Tony himself when, a year or so later he went to work for the Thomson Organisation. Colin Tennant being as reticent about Margaret's Mustique adventures as Tony's employers about his work for them, I cannot see much wrong in either of these transactions.

For the time being, of course, Mustique was just another island in which Margaret and Tony enjoyed an untroubled honeymoon with nothing to indicate how such a harmless excursion could carry within it the seed of so much unhappiness.

CHAPTER TWELVE

Tony had hoped for a quiet, low-key homecoming but there was a formal reception when *Britannia* deposited him and his wife at Portsmouth on June 18th. They were cheered when they drove to the station but were hardly noticed on arrival at Waterloo. They made for Clarence House where they occupied Margaret's suite of rooms until Number Ten Kensington Palace was ready. Tony lost no time checking on progress at his future abode. Workmen were still all over the little house when he went there with the furniture van which brought some of his belongings and, typically, lent a hand unloading a few pieces. He discussed every aspect of the decorations, mostly in white, but soon concentrated on what would become a dark-room and a workshop, an indication that he did not intend to remain idle for long.

There was no question of Margaret, as rumour had it, planning to retire from public life and, as if to prove it, she flew north for a royal assignment within a week. Tony made his first appearance in his new role as a royal escort by accompanying Margaret to the Royal Tournament at Earl's Court – not much progress here with his plan to wean Margaret from horses – on the contrary, he became a regular at the horsey occasions the royal family invariably attends. Not much luck with the dogs either. Though Margaret's Sealyhams disappeared temporarily, it did not turn out to be exile but a dogs' holiday in Windsor, and Tony soon acquired a gun dog of his own. Another rumour – that Margaret was pregnant – was premature by at least six months. A week or so later, she had Tony in tow at the next garden party at Buckingham Palace to bid farewell to a battalion of the Grenadier Guards which was being disbanded. In the second week of July, The Princess Margaret, Mrs Armstrong-Jones (her official title) and Mr A. Armstrong-Jones moved into their new house, and *The Times* published the first Court Circular issued from Number Ten Kensington Palace.

Only in the flush of young married life could Margaret have overlooked the drawbacks of the new home, the lack of space, the noisy visitors to the State Apartments at the London Museum next door which penetrated the thin walls. Staff problems did not make for a quiet life either. After years in the care of a comfortable char, Tony could or would not adjust to the pompous manner of Thomas Cronin, an old-fashioned type of butler. Tony had the temerity to check Cronin's accounts and to refuse his demand for a hundred-pound float. He even – sacrilege! – presumed to tell the butler what to do and what not to do. Cronin was 'shocked' to see the master taking his lunch in shirt sleeves, and got on his high horse when Tony made whistling noises or snapped his fingers to attract the servants' attention. Tony's habits and the standards of a top-drawer butler were clearly incompatible. There were angry exchanges.

Whether Cronin was sacked ('Mr Cronin has been dismissed', a royal spokesman said) or walked out in disgust (as he later claimed) is a moot point. Though Margaret was embarrassed by the row, Tony was relieved to see the last of the man. Alas, unlike other royal employees, Cronin had not been asked to give an undertaking not to reveal domestic secrets, and promptly sold a garrulous account of his weeks with Margaret's husband which was published in a dozen countries. There was more staff trouble before long when Ruby Gordon who had been Margaret's maid for as long as she could remember, left in a huff. This time, Tony recruited a replacement from his own past, Mrs Parker, who had been Grandma Messel's maid, and who stayed on when a younger girl, Isobel Mathieson, was engaged.

For her thirtieth birthday celebration, Margaret had Tony tagging along to Balmoral where, a year earlier, their understanding had been sealed. Tony was less than happy about weeks and months of idleness and futility looming ahead, and did not make a secret of it either. A cartoon in a German magazine showing him yawning his head off, and a Soviet attack describing him as 'an unemployed at court', though they incensed Margaret, reflected his own feelings. He was anxious to work and there was no shortage of suggestions and invitations. He discussed them with Margaret who turned her nose up at most of them. For his part, he would not go with her to the state opening of parliament by the Queen, so neither of them went. But he joined the royal party for the Cenotaph ceremony, and agreed to go to Brussels with Margaret for the wedding of King Baudouin of the Belgians and Donna Fabiola of Spain.

By the strange standards of such royal occasions, neither Margaret nor Tony was a success. She offended by looking much more handsome and glamorous than Baudouin's Queen, and he attracted too much interest from continental royal ladies who had heard about his exciting bachelor life. Back home he did his own thing by deliberately under-dressing for the Dockland Settlement Ball, a function Margaret never missed. Instead of the traditional tails and white tie, he wore a dinner jacket, and the other men in the royal party were advised to follow suit. To revolt against outmoded formal men's wear was not a major blow for freedom but it was a beginning.

Sandringham for Christmas – and he was firmly back in the royal groove, Margaret carrying him with her into her ways rather than the other way round. There was a difficult time ahead for him. Soon she would be giving him a baby which would not only bring up the vexed question of his title again but also raise the awkward problem of their residence – there would simply not be enough room where they were. As to a job, Tony would not let them fob him off with a sine-cure.

A family Christmas was not the ideal occasion to discuss these contentious matters but Margaret raised them one by one without getting very far. She was in a bad temper and it was just as well that she and Tony were going to see the New Year in with his family. Cutting short their stay at Sandringham, they drove to London and caught a flight

(tourist class) to Dublin on the last day of 1960. The first
member of the royal family to set foot on Irish soil in thirty-
two years, Margaret, escorted by her husband, went straight to
Birr Castle.

Tony proudly showed his imposing boyhood home off as not
entirely unworthy of the royal residences to which Margaret
was accustomed. Birr Castle, a nineteenth-century house with
Gothic arches, baronial turrets and military crenellations, stands
on a hill in the heart of a wooded estate of some twenty-five
thousand acres. With the Messel flair for interior decoration,
Lady Rosse had created a white-gold-and-green, Irish country
house complemented by heavy native furniture. Tony had
planned to bring his royal bride home for a quiet weekend with
family and friends. He had invited Jeremy and Camilla Fry
(to show that Jeremy's replacement as best man had not
weakened their friendship) and Margaret had asked Billy
Wallace along (to show that she wanted him around even though
she had a husband). The Nevills joined the party and Tony's
sister came over from the de Vesci estate at Abbey Leix, a few
miles to the west.

On Sunday morning, the Rosses and their guests drove to
St Brendan's, the local church, turning it into an Irish 'Crathie'
for the day. It was crowded with fifty worshippers, ten times
the usual number, and hundreds stood outside in the rain to
get a glimpse of Annie Rosse's daughter-in-law. Later that
morning, Martin Parsons, the enterprising younger son of the
house, 'abducted' Billy Wallace and took him on a pub crawl
which did not please Margaret. On Monday, Billy and Tony
went out shooting with some aristocratic friends of the Rosses
who had drifted in. Even with local labour reinforcing the
regular staff at the castle (housekeeper, butler, two footmen,
two maids and cook), it was not much fun entertaining a royal
visitor as demanding as Margaret. Anne Rosse, locally known
as 'Annie O'' (for Annie-Get-Your-Gun Oakley) sighed audibly
with relief when it was all over.

Billy Wallace could also relax. On the return flight from
Dublin he unburdened himself to a mutual friend: 'I am so
glad Margaret has Tony. I could not have gone on much
longer covering up for her men friends.' Being Margaret's closest
friend and confidant had not been easy. In indifferent health

and tired of London high life, Billy sold his Mayfair home and bought a manor house, six-hundred-years-old Bagnor Manor, in Berkshire. The young man whose name had been linked with Margaret's for longer than either cared to remember was also looking for a wife . . .

Early in 1961, Margaret and Tony went to Oslo on royal business representing the Queen at the wedding of Princess Astrid of Norway who, like Margaret, had chosen a commoner, Johan Ferner, as her husband. The following week they were back in their old bohemian haunt in Rotherhithe where Margaret was at last formally introduced to Bill Glenton. Behind the outward appearance of marital bliss, both showed symptoms of an identity crisis. Time and again, like a married couple in a Pinter play, they acted out their loving in a different fantasy setting, using Tony's Room as a refuge from the reality of Palace mandarins and royal etiquette. Margaret got a kick out of washing the dishes after their *dîners à deux*. They seemed to be in search of something but neither knew exactly of what.

The Queen thought the bother about a job for Tony was at an end when he agreed to join the Council of Industrial Design in a capacity which was both unpaid and undefined. Although Margaret paid a highly publicised visit to her husband's office at the Design Centre in Panton Street, popular notions that he had taken on a nine-to-five job were quickly dispelled when it was explained that his main function would be to contribute ideas.

The Margaret and Tony show had lost none of its popular appeal but an examination of the newspaper coverage in this period shows Tony providing more and better copy for the disclosure merchants than Margaret. A former footman, David John Payne, who had worked at Clarence House for a few months, gossiped in print about his employers' courtship but had nothing more exciting to report than their occasional visits to the cinema to see sexy films. (He himself underwent a sex-change, as did, by coincidence, her biographer Gordon Langley Hall who married a black butler.) Even ex-stepmama Carol Lopez got into the act and told all about Tony for publication on both sides of the Atlantic. He was making news with such feats as wearing a plum-coloured waistcoat at the Palace reception for the King and Queen of Thailand, or spending a night with Margaret at the Central Station Hotel in Glasgow instead of putting up at the house of aristocratic friends.

In Kensington Palace, his carpenter's tools and materials spilled over from the workshop into the living quarters as he worked on a model for his wire-mesh and steel contraption for the Zoo. Conferences with architect Cedric Price and engineer Frank Newby who were helping to produce his huge aviary absorbed a good deal of his time. Margaret was puzzled but indulgent. By the end of March she knew that she was expecting a baby, confirmed by three physicians (Lord Evans, Sir John Weir and Sir John Peel) who had attended the Queen at Prince Andrew's birth. She told the family but as was customary an announcement was delayed for another month or so.

The forthcoming happy event did not disguise a growing difficulty in Margaret's relations with the Queen. Fond as Elizabeth was of her sister, she was perturbed by Margaret's swiftly changing moods and the element of unpredictability that attached to the Margaret-Tony combination. The Palace seemed unable to get rid of the notion that Tony might spout some unorthodox idea any day, that one could never be sure what the fellow would do next and whether he would carry Margaret with him – God knows where. He still did not belong.

It was a feeling to which Philip gave expression in his bluntly offensive sailor's manner when, at a Saints and Sinners lunch in the glare of television cameras and in the presence of sensitive microphones, he made a remark which seemed plain rude (although I, for one did not understand its full meaning): 'Unlike my brother-in-law,' he said at one stage, adding with a smirk, '. . . well, he isn't really, but you know the chap I mean.' It sounded like a gratuitous, pointless insult, and it angered the Queen who hated public displays of family disunity and told her husband to repair the damage. As incongruously as the original outburst, Philip made a clumsy attempt at flattery when, at the Zoological Society's annual meeting, he described Tony's Aviary as 'delightful'.

The week it was officially announced that Margaret was expecting a baby in the autumn, Tony was frantically trying to save his Rotherhithe hide-out which, with other buildings in the street, was scheduled for demolotion. (So, incidentally, was the late Baron's Brick Street Studio where Tony had learned his photographic abc). He did not succeed although he expertly beat the publicity drum. The press was more interested in Margaret's baby which experts discussed with greater elan than expertise : 'A Jones will be fifth in line of succession,' one explained while another, billed as 'a close friend of Tony's' predicted : 'No, he won't accept a title until he's earned it !'

In Margaret's eyes, he had already earned it. She had come round to the view that he should have a title, any title, as long as it saved her children the indignity of growing up as commoners. She could, of course, have asked the Queen to create her a Countess or a Duchess in her own right and handed down her secondary titles to her offspring. Once she ceased to demand a dukedom for Tony – to put him on a par with Philip – and the Queen renewed her offer of an earldom, Tony warmed to the idea. The prospect of a royal child without a title which agitated so many minds vanished when he agreed to become an earl.

With the principle established, he and Margaret spent hours discussing suitable titles. With his father's Welsh connection in mind, Tony favoured the name of Snowdon, and never mind Ramsay MacDonald's comrade who became Lord Snowdon in the early thirties. For his second peerage, he chose a title, Viscount Linley of Nymans, concocted from family associations – Linley after a branch which originated in Sheffield and cut quite a dash in London but died out in the early eighteenth century; Nymans after the original Messel residence which his grandmother had inhabited until it was destroyed by fire. What mattered was that his elevation should come before the birth of his son – 'Bound to be a son !' – who could then take the courtesy title of the second peerage.

The announcement that, owing to her pregnancy, Margaret would undertake no further official engagements after May 25th, 1961, came just in time to stifle noisy accusations that she was performing fewer public duties than ever and not earning her keep. Tony stepped into the breach reluctantly because public appearances and speeches were ordeals he sought to avoid. It was so bad that his hands shook violently when he read a speech and examined some delicate pieces of china at the Antique Dealers' Fair.

The problem of a bigger and more suitable house was solved when Tony cast a critical eye on Number 1A Kensington Palace in Clock Court which had been deserted for some time. Built by Christopher Wren, it comprised some twenty rooms, twice as many as Number Ten, but was pervaded by an odour of damp and decay. (One of the last inhabitants, curiously, had been the Duke of Edinburgh who had spent the night before his wedding there when floorboards creaked so badly that servants walked on tiptoe for fear of waking him too early.) The Queen assigned the property to Tony and Margaret who, rather than stay on at Clarence House until they found what they wanted had moved into Number Ten because it had been vacant. The Ministry of Works was instructed to make it habitable and it was estimated that the cost of renovation and adaptation would be in the neighbourhood of seventy thousand pounds, fifty thousand from public funds – well worth it, considering its noble architectural pedigree – and the other twenty thousand to be contributed from the Queen's private purse.

When these arrangements became known, they gave Willie Hamilton, M.P., professional scourge of the monarchy, another stick with which to beat royalty. He kicked up a fuss in the House of Commons, asked the Minister of Works (Lord John Hope) to stop the work (at Kensington Palace) and inveighed against 'a tiny, highly privileged, in the main useless minority' in contrast with ordinary people who were asked to make sacrifices. The contract for the work, when it was signed and sealed early in 1962 was for sixty-five thousand pounds which rising costs and extra work increased to eighty-five thousand. Lacing his attack on Margaret with insults, calling her 'idle' and 'a kept woman' (and later capitalising on his campaign against the monarchy with a book, *My Queen and I*) Hamilton revealed that Tony, stung by his criticism, had asked to meet him but, Hamilton assumed, had been warned off. Margaret shrugged off the insults with contempt which, since she is not supposed to answer back, was her usual reaction to public attacks.

So as not to risk being called 'a kept man', Tony intensified his search for a job. Whether the prospect of becoming a father had anything to do with it, whether he wanted to show that he could take care of his family without the help of his wealthy wife is difficult to say. His main motive was the wish, nay the need, to work. It so happened that one member of Jocelyn Stevens's circle with whom he had remained in close contact was the highly talented Mark Boxer, an excellent cartoonist and able journalist. Mark Boxer was involved with plans for a novel type of American-style weekly magazine to be published as a supplement and vehicle for colour advertising with an existing newspaper. The idea was quickly adopted by Roy (later Lord) Thomson, the Canadian owner of the *Sunday Times*, and Mark Boxer became the first editor of the trend-setting Sunday supplement.

Tony thought it was a splendid idea. It offered opportunities for ambitious photographers who had had virtually no outlet in Britain since the demise of the two picture magazines, *Illustrated* and *Picture Post*. Here, surely, was a chance for him to make a contribution. Mark Boxer and other Thomson executives res-ponded with alacrity. They could not overlook the advantages of associating the name of the Queen's brother-in-law with their new venture and acquiring the services of a top-class photog-rapher into the bargain. Both sides being enthusiastic, agreement was soon reached. Tony was engaged as 'artistic adviser', a high-faluting title which Margaret preferred to her husband being described as a photographer. He did not really mind as long as he could work with his camera. The Queen, in spite of sombre warnings about the hazards of the royal family becoming associated with one newspaper group, was swayed by the prestige of the *Sunday Times*. A salary of around ten thousand pounds a year plus expenses was agreed, and it was decided to announce the appointment at a later date.

While Margaret's condition condemned her to idleness, Tony was busier than ever. Designs for his new house, consultations with the Thomson people, preparations for the new baby – in his free moments he scoured stores for nursery furnishing (his first buy, thirty yards of chintz for curtains). He and Margaret had an anxious moment when news reached London from Brussels that Queen Fabiola had had a miscarriage. Margaret was taking no chances, resting and doing pre-natal exercises. Yet, friends wondered how she would adjust to motherhood which was not really her scene – to this day she does not like to be in the company of pregnant women.

The Scottish season was upon them and Tony went to stay with Margaret at Birkhall where Dr Middleton, the royal family's local doctor, kept an eye on her. As if seeking the company of children, Margaret saw a lot of Charles and Anne who came over from Balmoral. The Queen Mother's arrival brought up a most important topic – where Margaret's baby should be born. The Kensington Palace place was too small, a nursing home out of the question, and Buckingham Palace not to Margaret's liking. 'Clarence House, of course!' the Queen Mother insisted. Within a couple of weeks, medical equipment suitable for all contingencies was being installed in Margaret's old rooms. After her return from Scotland she was examined by three royal doctors and advised that her baby would probably arrive in the first week in November. She was fit and well, serene and very handsome.

October was an eventful month for the Joneses. It started with the announcement of Tony's elevation, and a week later Margaret moved to Clarence House. According to all accounts, she suffered the inevitable dicomforts of her condition with surprisingly good humour. Everything was going as planned but she chose Sister Annette Wilson of King's College Hospital as midwife in preference to the elderly Sister Helen Rowe, an old royal retainer. Presents for the unborn babe were arriving from all over the world, and on the first day of November people began to gather outside Clarence House. News on the grapevine suggested that they would not have to wait long.

The baby arrived at ten-forty-five a.m. on November 3rd. The crowd cheered when a notice was posted on the gate of Clarence House. Tony was the first to see mother and baby – yes, it was a boy (weighing six pounds four ounces), the spitten image of his father. The Queen came over from Buckingham Palace and Tony called staff and doctors together and toasted the baby ('My son, God bless him!') with champagne. Margaret was exhausted.

By the end of November it was back to Kensington Palace where a new nurse, Verona Sumner, took charge of the baby who started life in the cramped draughty house his parents were impatient to leave. The proud father's camera caught a young mother's love in Margaret's expression but the reality was not so felicitous. As so often, the upsurge of emotion for a new-born baby was mixed with apprehension and doubt. Would she be able to live up to her new responsibilities? What would married life be with a baby demanding her attention and affection? Margaret wanted time to think and plan, a new atmosphere, far from the pressures at home. She was dying to get away.

With the Christmas holidays so close, the christening ceremony was set for December 19th; by royal tradition it would be performed by the Archbishop in the Music Room at Buckingham Palace. The baby's names were already decided. With puckish delight, Margaret – with the Duke of Windsor in mind who, like her, was not one of the royal family's favourite relatives – had chosen David as the boy's first name and won over Tony who liked the Welsh connotation. Later, as if frightened by her own cheek, she meekly agreed to a semi-official explanation that the name was chosen in honour of her mother's brother, Sir David Bowes-Lyon. Nobody believed it for a moment. Albert, for the late King, and Charles, for great English kings of the past, were the baby's other names. His godparents were the Queen, Simon Phipps, Rupert Nevill, Patrick Plunkett and Lady Elizabeth Cavendish.

The water from the River Jordan used to baptize royal babies was hardly dry on little David Linley's head when his parents went off to Antigua for three weeks of sun, sea and solitude. They did not realise that their abrupt departure and apparent desertion of the baby would seriously damage their relations with the great British public. Departing from wintry Britain, they left behind a howl of criticism more ferocious than any Margaret had previously encountered. Her need for a holiday was not an unknown phenomenon, yet sycophants of yore turned their coats and rounded on 'perverse' Margaret who was said to be devoid of mother love. A lot of people thought she was 'a callous, selfish bitch' and said so. The baby was, of course, snug in the care of Nurse Sumner.

While they were out of harm's way, Tony's appointment as 'artistic adviser' to the *Sunday Times* was officially announced. It generated another outcry led by the rival *Observer* which denounced the arrangement. That the Queen's brother-in-law should allow himself to be drawn into a circulation battle might reflect adversely on the monarchy! Left-wing papers found fault because of the Thomson Organisation's Conservative bias and even *The Times* raised an eyebrow in disapproval – it would not be long before the old thunderer, like Snowdon, would end up in Roy Thomson's lap – but the late William Conner, the incomparable 'Cassandra' of the *Daily Mirror* put the matter in perspective when he wrote that his paper would gladly sign up Margaret as a woman's features editor. Snowdon's employer simply said that there was no other unemployed journalist with Snowdon's qualifications. Next there was a clamour for Tony to join the National Union of Journalists (which he did) and some of his Fleet Street colleagues seemed unduly bothered about his tax position because his ten thousand a year added to Margaret's fifteen thousand would give the Inland Revenue a considerable slice of the combined income. (However this was not really the case since most of Margaret's share was returned as expenses.)

With Tony's doings still attracting greater interest than Margaret's shenanigans, more than fifty photographers recorded his arrival at the *Sunday Times* offices where he was received by Editor Denis Hamilton. His royal connection was underlined when he went from his first editorial conference to a Buckingham Palace lunch to celebrate the tenth anniversary of the Queen's reign. His first job was to produce designs for the private offices of his boss (who soon followed his employee to the House of Lords) and his Editor. His first big assignment as a cameraman was to photograph Georges Braque on his eightieth birthday. (Soon there were angry Fleet Street protests whenever Snowdon scored over rival photographers suggesting that he was using his position to gain an advantage over them).

Margaret resumed her round of dreary official engagements

which were meticulously counted by her critics. Between her baby's birth and her Scottish summer holiday, she made sixty-six public appearances, one of them to watch her husband taking his seat in the House of Lords. On one of her frequent visits to the Frys at Widcombe Manor, she decorated the pillion of Tony's heavy motorbike by zipping on it through the landscape (no nun's habit, though).

At home there was more butler trouble when the third incumbent of the post gave in his notice. And there was more public discussion about the cost of 1A Ken Pal when it became known that a wall being built to protect the house cost about two-thousand two-hundred pounds. It did not look as if Margaret intended to settle down quietly behind that wall – on the contrary. When asked to go the Caribbean for Jamaica's opening of parliament she was, as someone remarked, 'off like a shot'. As used to be said of Mussolini and the Mediterranean, the Caribbean was fast becoming her private lake. As soon as she returned, Tony had another trip in mind which forced her to break with tradition and habit. Rather than celebrate her birthday with her family in Scotland as she had all her life, Tony wanted her to spend the day with his people. They went to stay with his sister at the de Vesci home at Abbey Leix. In a mellow mood Margaret posed for press photographers in the grounds.

The appointment of a young (thirty-four-old) Coldstream Guards officer, Major Michael Mitchell, as Margaret's equerry (official escort) indicated that Tony might not tag along behind his wife for much longer but for the time being anyway he retired to hospital – the National Hospital for Nervous Diseases – for what was described as a 'routine check-up'. The sad fact was that strain-induced pains no longer only affected his leg. He had developed a stomach ulcer. Yet he looked vigorous enough when he turned up at Kensington Palace to inspect progress at his new home where workmen were just putting in the sunken tub in the bathroom. When one of them asked whether the taps should be fitted at the top or the bottom, he was told – on Margaret's authority – to put them in the middle. Workmen were eloquent about Margaret's requirements: 'That thing she calls her loo', one of them explained, 'is one of those old-fashioned wicker commode whatsits handed down as a family heirloom. The wicker's a sort of natural dirty yellow colour, the legs mahogany-like . . .' They were also working on a lift big enough to take the pram from the basement to the second floor.

Not content with making his own fittings and pieces of furniture, Tony moved in some elaborate welding equipment and, his face covered with a visor, cut and welded metal slabs into a futuristic smell and smoke extractor which looked strikingly decorative. There was so much ironmongery about that Margaret reminded him they were making a home not a prison, a Freudian thought, but he proceeded to make an elaborate steel tube towel rack which did credit to his workmanship as did his restoration of the old fireplaces and the impressive mahogany doors he made with his own hands. His feeling for colour was reflected in coffee-brown tiles but some of his ideas were copied from designs at Birr Castle. Several major pieces of furniture came from antique shops in Bristol, discovered by him and Margaret during their weekends with the Frys. Blue was the colour motif which ran through the whole house. Tony's study, next door to the living room, was designed to give him total privacy while at the same time – as Margaret discovered only much later – enabling him to see through a spyhole in the door what went on in the living room.

Whenever Margaret visited the house, she wore an old skirt, Wellington boots and a headscarf, grist to the mill of the Americans who put her name high on the list of the world's worst dressed women and described her outfits as 'a schizophrenic mixture of chic and sheer disaster'. After a brief winter-sports holiday at Davos, Switzerland, with Tony and the Frys she became quite innocently involved in a diplomatic row when the government, angry about de Gaulle's opposition to Britain's entry into the Common Market, would not let her attend a charity gala film premiere in Paris. Margaret as a Councillor of State had to remain in Britain while the Queen was out of the country, they said.

With the move into 1A Kensington Palace, the pattern of her domestic environment was settled for years to come. The house, though spacious, was neither palatial nor regal; the living-room – apart from the dining-room, as far as even friends were allowed to go – furnished with two large sofas, low tables stacked with magazines, including some of the children's, a drink trolley, a desk which became rather untidy, and a grand piano which was Margaret's *pièce de résistance*. Family photographs and some of Tony's knick-knacks and travel trophies created a homely impression. The bedrooms, his and hers, on the first floor were separated by the bathroom. There was a nursery and one spare bedroom and in the basement the workroom, darkroom and secretary's office for which Tony paid his wife rent listing the amount for tax purposes among his expenses; he also paid the rates which were around one thousand pounds. Also in the basement were a staff sitting-room and dining-room – the staff sleeping quarters were on the top floor.

Behind the scenes, as if to confound Palace sceptics, Tony was discussing a new venture into an old tradition. The Queen offered him the prestigious but nebulous position of Constable of Caernarvon Castle which Lord Harlech (father of the current holder of the title), having performed his only duty – to receive foreign royalty – but once in his ten years' tenure, was about to vacate. It was a generous gesture to her sister on the part of the Queen, and Tony welcomed it as a means of improving relations with the royal family – and gaining some prestige for himself. The appointment was the first step towards a major royal function it would fall to Tony to perform – the organisation of the ceremonial investiture of the heir to the throne as Prince of Wales in Caernarvon Castle where the Duke of Windsor had been invested as Prince of Wales in 1911.

As if to balance the pull towards such solemn royal tasks, the Snowdons savoured the lighter side of life. They went water-skiing – Margaret no longer worried about photographers training their cameras on her legs (in private, she occasionally showed a hint of over-the-stocking bare thigh) – next appeared at an all-night party at Lionel Bart's Chelsea House (with its all-purpose sauna), mingling with artists, actors and pop stars, the foot-loose, free and fancy, the new world of entertainment with its East End accent about which the Queen and Philip knew next to nothing and probably did not want to know anything. At other parties, the mix was peppered with lesbians and homosexuals, and with men and women who lived together without the blessing of the church as was the fashion in the permissive society. For Tony there was, as with most things, a purpose behind these excursions; he was working on a book about London's artists and, combining work and pleasure, took his wife with him on his research.

It added spice to Margaret's kaleidoscopic existence which, considering the quickly changing scenes she moved in, required great adaptability. From Chelsea to Iserlohn, Germany, was further than the crow flies – or she flew in an aircraft of the Queen's Flight whose seats were specially adapted to her small size. Having visited one of her regiments she switched from the military world into the academic to be installed as Chancellor of Keele University. More contrast – she attended a party at Whitechapel Art Gallery and, after a Saturday at Ascot, moved on to Cambridge, not to visit Tony's old college but an electronics factory. At home, she and Tony enjoyed their romps with their spirited little boy who looked more like his father every day.

Yet another new departure – they went on a Greek holiday with the Marquess of Blandford and his Greek-born Marchioness, the former Tina Onassis, née Livanos. They made their base on Spetsopoula, the tragic private island of shipping magnate Stavros Niarchos and his wife Eugenie, Tina's sister, both of whom, while staunchly Greek, were very English in upbringing and manner; they were the same age group as Margaret and living like her in the stratosphere of international society. The island was stocked with Scottish grouse, good shooting for the men, while excursions in the fabulous Niarchos yacht to Delphi and other historical spots entertained and educated the women. For Margaret, the memory of a grand holiday was later spoilt by the Sophoclean tragedy which befell the Livanos sisters. Eugenie Niarchos died on Spetsopoula under mysterious circumstances, and Tina, having parted from Blandford and married her late sister's husband, ended as tragically shortly after.

Unburdened by any forebodings, Margaret, sun-tanned and refreshed, was thinking of life – not of death. Her second child was on the way, due to be born about the end of April 1964. Three royal relatives were expecting at the same time: the

Queen, Princess Alexandra (Mrs Angus Ogilvie) and the young Duchess of Kent. And – another entry in the baby records – for his thirty-fourth birthday, Tony took Margaret to Plas Dinas, near Caernarvon, to stay with his father and stepmother and their baby boy Peregrine.

CHAPTER THIRTEEN

While the birth of her little boy had caused Margaret a brief psychological upset, the arrival of baby Sarah – Lady Sarah Armstrong-Jones – on May 1st, 1964, posed few problems. Rigorous exercise helped the mother to restore her figure for the time being although soon afterwards her weight began to trouble her. There was probably, as we shall see, more behind it than met the eye but one feudal gentleman (quoted by Andrew Duncan in *The Reality of Monarchy*) remarked that she was, after all, a Hanoverian ... Her water-skiing on Sunninghill Lake was part of her slimming effort which received the Queen's sisterly encouragement. The sisters churned up the lake in a fast-moving speedboat. For a while it was like old times between them but it did not last. Margaret was eating and drinking too much, a symptom of deep underlying trouble.

Next on the Snowdons' list of foreign travel was a visit to the young Aga Khan's new holiday development on the Costa Smeralda in Sardinia into which he and his associates were sinking some thirty million pounds. 'K' (for Karim) to his friends, the Aga Khan installed his guests in one of his hotels, arranged parties for them at his villa in Porto Cervo, and ferried them around neighbouring islands in his little yacht, *Amaloun*. Karim's brother Amin and his English girlfriend and some London socialites were in the party but Tony was more interested in the view and in local types who made splendid pictures : 'He has brought enough equipment with him to make "The Ten Commandments",' one of his friends remarked.

All went well until Margaret, Tony and the rest went cruising without Karim. They were making for the little island of Sofia when *Amaloun* hit a rock, sprung a big lead and looked like sinking. As distress signals went out, Margaret and the others jumped into the water and kept afloat until they were picked up by fishing boats. Though badly mauled, the yacht did not sink and was towed into the harbour. Margaret was none the worse for her adventure and, to counter exaggerated reports of the accident, cabled the Queen that she was safe and well.

Summer holidays in Sardinia became a habit. It was during one of them that Margaret and Tony received an invitation to the yacht of Arndt von Bohlen, scion of the House of Krupp, who had renounced his share in the German steel, coal and armaments empire in exchange for an annual allowance of two million marks. Arndt, married to an Austrian princess, was famous for his flamboyant life-style and eccentricity which intrigued Margaret. She sent word that she was pleased to accept the invitation and, on the appointed day, walked with Tony to the spot where the Krupp yacht was moored. From the distance she could see Arndt standing on deck awaiting her arrival. Not until they were quite close did she notice what seemed to be his unusual appearance: it looked as if her host's cheeks were rouged, his eyelashes dark with mascara and his lips painted a bright red. Margaret was too shrewd not to realise that some people might draw the wrong conclusions. Quick-witted as usual, and before Tony was aware of anything untoward, she called out that she had forgotten something, apologised, turned smartly on her heels and was away. There was an abrupt change of plans.

If Margaret had side-stepped a scandal in Porto Cervo, she encountered a squall of criticism, much of it unfair, when she went on to Rome. Was it that she had another audience with the Pope which was too much for staunch Anglicans to take, or would her critics not stomach the wide range of her contacts? She spent some time with Judy Montagu and her American husband, Milton Gendel, and with Peter Sellers who was filming in the Holy City. Her friendship with the actor caused an Italian magazine to comment on what had long been the talk of London – the royal princess's interest in Goonery.

In spite of so much extramural activity, Margaret remained

loyal to many facets of her old routine. One of them was the Dockland Settlement Ball which she would not miss for anything. Tony, too, thought it fun, perhaps too much fun for Margaret's liking. They were both at the Ball dancing with different partners, Margaret changing hers with every dance, Tony seemingly stuck with one and the same, albeit very attractive girl for most of the evening without noticing that Margaret's eyes followed his and his partner's every twist and turn. During a brief interval between dances, Margaret walked over to the young lady and took her aside: 'Are you enjoying yourself?' she asked sweetly. 'Very much so, Ma'am,' was the reply. Margaret's eyes narrowed into her famous glare and her voice sharpened: 'That's enough, then, for one evening,' she hissed, 'run along home!' As she turned abruptly colour shot up into the hapless girl's cheeks. She disappeared from sight and Tony did not dance again that evening.

Just when Margaret began to think of her trips to Birr or Abbey Leix as happy family reunions, a jarring note was introduced on her 1965 New Year visit. The big car-load of police escorting her from the airport looked ominous enough but the situation became really fraught when she found the road blocked by tree trunks, a deliberate attempt to stop her. Crude posters demanding 'Maggie go home!' and 'Down with the Queen!' were an unpleasant reminder that this was I.R.A. country. Margaret was not told that leaflets drawing attention to her visit and asking people to 'Show your hostility!' were being pushed through letter-boxes. The climax of the campaign was an explosion at Abbey Leix where Margaret was staying with the de Vescis. There were demonstrations, intense police activity (and noisy court scenes the day some of the protesters were brought to justice) but royal training stood Margaret in good stead and she did not lose her nerve. She was in high spirits when – as she had been anxious to for a long time – she was taken on a pub crawl ending up at Paddy Burke's, the famous house in Clarinridge, County Galway, where the oysters and the stout were superb.

It was a far cry from Ireland to Uganda, the next station on the Snowdon's itinerary. At Kampala they were received by King Freddie, the Kabaka of Buganda, and his Prime Minister, Dr Milton Obote, but the only remarkable feature of the visit was the fate in store for their hosts. Obote deposed King Freddie who came to Britain where he died in penury; and, in the passage of time, Obote was himself ousted by the unspeakable Idi Amin.

There was a native flavour in the entertainment provided by Peter Sellers – who finds it easier to be someone else, preferably an African or an Asian, than to be himself – when in London a few weeks later he joined the party Margaret gave to celebrate the Queen's thirty-ninth birthday. They first went to see Sellers's fellow-Goon, Spike Milligan, in 'Son of Oblomov' and went back after the performance to Kensington Palace. Sellers and Milligan joined the Queen, Margaret, Philip and Tony and their entourage. It was, if anything, more hilarious than public goonery, Sellers and Milligan practising their pranks of spontaneous irreverence at the expense of their royal friends. They had brought their wives – Sellers was newly married to the Swedish actress Britt Ekland who was gorgeous but not, one would have thought, predestined to walk with royalty. Still, an intimate togetherness developed between the Snowdons and the Sellers, a gay period in their lives.

They all figured in a home-movie shot by Tony and directed by Jocelyn Stevens of which Margaret, Britt and Jane Stevens were the stars. Professionally, Tony recorded many of Peter's stage and film appearances – Peter and Britt parted even before Tony and Margaret went their separate ways. Margaret and Spike remained on good terms until she went to see him in cabaret when he astonished the audience – and her – with a ditty he delivered from the stage : 'Whoever you are, wherever you be, please take your hand off the Princess's knee.' Margaret smiled wearily but not even a Goon could do this sort of thing and count on her indulgence.

For her and Tony, private and professional trips alternated so rapidly it was difficult to draw a dividing line. They flew to Denmark for an export-boosting 'British Week' and to Amsterdam where Margaret toured the city in a jeep with Tony at the wheel. But it was a different story when he was off to Japan on his own on an assignment for the *Sunday Times* – his work was gaining wide recognition and his photographs were reprinted all over the world, *Paris Match*, for instance, paying him their top rate of one hundred pounds for a double page, or five hundred for his first feature. He was on friendly terms with the London men of American and French publications who were always happy to help their distinguished colleague.

Checking his camera on the Sunday he was due to leave for Japan, he found the shutter of the most important one not working properly. Impossible to repair but where to get a replacement? As a last resort he called a foreign photographer friend who rushed post-haste to Kensington Palace with an Ersatz-camera. The good Samaritan rang the basement bell, was admitted by Dorothy Everard, and joined Tony in her office. Tony was relieved and greatly appreciative. Upstairs, Margaret was packing his bags, as she often did; once or twice she came downstairs with shirts and pants to make sure they were the ones Tony wanted to take. There was some argument about the car in which she would take him to the airport, another of her regular chores. They were affectionate yet even in such situations the two highly-strung partners tended to clash in brief sharp rows.

It happened on one occasion when Margaret burst into Tony's study while he was discussing technical points with a colleague. Tony flew into a terrible rage: 'Never come in here without knocking!' he barked. Margaret went as white as a sheet – she was deeply shocked to be treated so rudely in front of a stranger. The visitor thought the real reason for Tony's outburst was anger with himself – he was embarrassed about his own lack of tact and sensitivity in allowing an outsider into his study where some photographs of Margaret which only a husband could have taken were prominently displayed on the wall.

His trip to Japan did not help the marriage which was going through some sticky passages but, for all the verbal combat, was still cemented by their mutual attraction. As one of Tony's friends explained, it was in Japan that he grew a beard which he brandished like a token of independence and – I quote – 'was up to all sorts of tricks'. That he spent much time photographing pin-table parlours, not the most savoury of premises, may have had something to do with it. He flew on to New York whence reports, more or less reliable, reached Margaret that – though he stayed with friends from *Vogue* magazine, arbiters of elegance – he had taken to wearing a cloth cap, another symbol of incipient rebellion, and was mixing with hippies considerably further way-out than the British variety, and drinking much more than at home.

'The news made Margaret ill,' one of her friends said. He did not exaggerate because within days she was in King Edward VII Hospital for what was routinely described as a check-up. Margaret's complaint was psychosomatic rather than organic, and rumours suggesting that she was pregnant could not have been more off-beam. Tony did not think there was any need for him to break off his trip and, I gather, communications between them were tenuous. What Margaret, suddenly confronted with another personal crisis, needed more than anything was peace of mind, a rest and a change of scene – her doctor, Sir Ronald Bodley Scott, suggested a holiday. Coming to the aid of his friends, Jocelyn Stevens asked her to spend a couple of weeks with him and his wife at his house in Lyford Cay, near Nassau, in the Bahamas, and, as concerned about her marriage as about her health and hoping to cure both closely linked ills with one stroke, called Tony and invited him along as well. It was arranged for him and Margaret to meet up in New York ('Perhaps we ought to meet in Reno . . .!' Tony quipped) and go on together to Nassau.

He promptly called a press conference to deny reports that his marriage was breaking up. Margaret flew to New York and showed herself briefly with her husband, both all smiles, at Kennedy Airport before flying on to Nassau where one of the Stevens's other house guests was Margaret's cousin Patrick, the Earl of Lichfield, another 'royal photographer'. In spite of Jocelyn and Jane Stevens's devoted efforts, the reunion was not a success; arguments and quarrels continued, some of them revolving around Patrick Lichfield who seemed to be comforting his royal cousin very solicitously.

Because Margaret and Tony circulated more freely than the other royals, more people came to know about their problem and it became a popular topic of conversation. The press soon cottoned on to the 'inside stories' but some of the accounts which appeared, particularly in foreign magazines, owed much to the imagination of the writers. Yet, however insignificant in themselves, a succession of minor contretemps added up to a formidable barrier between Margaret and Tony. Petty quarrels were the order of the day and best illustrated by an incident observed by one of Tony's associates who found him in Kensington Palace dressed in polo-neck sweater and slacks playing happily with the children when Margaret put her head around the door and reminded him rather forcefully that friends would be arriving presently to take them out and that it was time he went up and changed – his being late was a constant source of irritation.

He apologised, asked his visitor to wait while he went upstairs and changed. By the time he returned their friends were with Margaret in the living-room and Tony turned to his colleague: 'Come and have a drink with us,' he said.

'It was a hot night,' Tony's colleague recalled. 'Margaret was in a sleeveless dress and showing a podgy arm; she was wearing boots and too much bright lipstick. Tony made it fairly obvious that he did not like what he saw; the atmosphere was heavy with mutual resentment . . .' With an edge to her voice, Margaret asked Tony's friend what he would like to drink. 'A small whisky and water,' he replied. As if to punish the intruder, she poured whisky to the brim of the glass – no water. 'She did this sort of thing to Tony's friends,' her victim continued. 'I poured the whisky into a plant.' On a more convivial occasion, with Margaret nowhere in view, Tony asked his son to bring him a whisky and invited a visitor to watch through the spyhole as little David gravely and carefully prepared the correct drink. Intensely fond of the children, Margaret and Tony, each in their own fashion, fussed over them but theirs was a separate fondness rather than the same kind of love. For their sake they kept up appearances at home as they did for the public's sake when on view, and tried to shield the children from unpleasantness – not always successfully. Young David went through some crises of restlessness and, on one occasion, Margaret, anxious to amuse the boy, asked Jocelyn Stevens whether David could come and see a newspaper in production. In the event she went along too; they were shown over the machine room and Margaret was so delighted with the treat for the boy that she was charming as never before with compositors and executives alike.

A mutual friend insists that the couple decided at this stage – 1966, 1967 – to go their own ways as far as their private lives were concerned but I prefer other evidence which suggests that, as often in these cases, they slithered into this state of affairs, getting together briefly, parting again, travelling, homing, loving and hating each other in turn over a period of years. Outsiders only saw their smooth double-acts dictated by their crowded public schedule. They went to Scotland to look over a new skiing centre and test their skill on the snow, none too expertly. Tony scored a success of sorts on his own when he showed off his mammoth Aviary which was at last completed after four years of gestation. He was interviewed for the B.B.C. 'Tonight' programme by Derek Hart who became a close friend and associate in several television and film ventures, and also formed a relationship with Margaret which survived the end of her marriage.

Reconciliations after periods of feuding often came about because of the children. Tony and Margaret were equally concerned when their little boy developed ear trouble and had to go to the Ormond Street Hospital for Sick Children where cousin Anne had had tonsils and adenoids removed a few years earlier, and where Alexandra had recently completed a nursing course. Troubles rarely came singly – a few weeks later, David fell and cut his chin at Windsor, and had to have a couple of stitches.

Margaret's indignation about Tony's solo turn in New York was forgotten when she sniffed a chance for them to visit the United States together. She cleverly helped matters along until there were so many strands to the project, it was not surprising that they became tangled up. Once she had made up her mind, Margaret, wise to royal ways, organised two assignments which could make the tour at the very least semi-official. She arranged to attend a function of the English Speaking Union, and two export-orientated fashion shows staged by the Society of London Fashion Designers, both worthy of a royal princess's support and, incidentally, justifying charging the expense of the trip to public funds.

Margaret asked Sharman Douglas to issue a personal invitation – Margaret's old friend had since become a public relations officer. With all these factors in mind, an itinerary covering California, Arizona, Washington and New York was cobbled together and the Snowdons were on their way with an entourage of fourteen, a couple of Rolls Royces and an Andover of the Queen's Flight to ferry them around the States. That Tony's highly successful *Private View*, his book about London's art scene (which had sold some fifty thousand copies and earned him around thirty thousand pounds), would be coming out in the States while he and Margaret were there was convenient and augured well for the American sales.

The first stage of this 'fantastic tour' took them to Hollywood where they met the stars. With her grand allure, her poise and her spectacular coronet, Margaret looked every inch a super-star; curious that, while she was magnetically drawn to the movie capital's tinsel types with or without talent, her royal magic was so much more in evidence although she, like most of the actors, had star quality without qualifications. She 'did' San Francisco (cable-car rides, view of Alcatraz) and carried on gamely in spite of the sniffles and a touch of laryngitis. She turned rural for a few days on the Douglas's Arizona ranch, reverted to glamour in Washington for a White House dinner-dance with the Johnsons, and ended up in New York where exhaustion set in and made her irritable with reporters who had not treated her too kindly.

It was the organisers' fault that only a tiny elite came into contact with her, leaving many disappointed and offended. Ex-President Eisenhower's grave illness dominated interest at Margaret's expense although there were sometimes friendly shouts of 'Hiya Princess!' when she showed herself. Still, the 'most unusual royals' were scrutinised, their manners, clothes, sayings analysed yet, although Margaret was described as the most important British export after the Beatles and Scotch Whisky, the twenty-day royal tour did not strike a spark – it was difficult to say why.

A mix-up about seats on the return flight (the royal party's twenty-seat compartment cost six-thousand five-hundred pounds plus three-thousand pounds for excess baggage) compounded the adverse publicity. The brew was stirred by Willie Hamilton who asked some awkward questions about the 'Snowdon jaunt'. The headlines proclaimed 'Jet Set Parties and Private V.C.10 Complete with Own Hairdresser. "Who Pays?" Row over Snowdon Luxury Tour', and Margaret was called 'a very expensive young lady'. The trip cost over thirty-one thousand pounds for advance planning, air passages, the Andover aircraft, personal expenses, hotel accommodation, local transport, official receptions, communications and printing. The Beatles, it was said, did a much better job for Britain at much less cost to the public. Whatever others thought, Margaret hugely enjoyed her look at the American pop culture.

With Margaret-baiting a fashionable sport, the issue of her house on Mustique was bound to be raised. Her villa – Villa Jolie – on Colin Tennant's island was nearing completion and, if people thought it was another love-nest – William Glenton had just blotted his copybook by publishing his account of what had gone on in Tony's room in Rotherhithe – they were right in the long run. But by this time Margaret's partner would not be Tony. Before long she sold part of her plot on Mustique to cousin Patrick Lichfield, a pleasant young man to have around. While she looked westward, Tony flew east, to Prague, to attend an exhibition of industrial designs, his first 'royal' trip without Margaret – it was not practicable for a royal princess to travel behind the Iron Curtain. His mission – he impressed the Czechs with his expertise and his Aston Martin – was treated as a useful pacemaker for a possible visit of the Duke of Edinburgh to Soviet Russia. (A few years later Tony and Margaret made it to Yugoslavia but Margaret was not enamoured of life in the communist country and walked out of a Belgrade theatre in the middle of the performance.)

Through no fault of her own, Margaret was propelled into the headlines when she visited the R.A.F. in Germany and it was discovered that part of her speech – a sentence referring to the number of German aircraft shot down during the war – was cut to spare the Germans embarrassment. Since she had not written the speech in the first place and had no strong feelings on the subject, she was not pleased to become the centre of another row. 'Margaret censored' was the cry and, predictably, the item which the authorities had tried to suppress received much more publicity than if Margaret had uttered the controversial passage.

Controversy continued to follow her around with the public avidly picking up sticks with which to beat her. In a repeat performance of the aircraft seat trouble, she was blamed when a Saudi Arabian prince on a purchasing mission appeared to have lost his seat to her and it looked as if this 'insult' to an influential customer might cost Britain a hundred million pounds worth of export orders (it did not). Then, monotonously, more servant trouble – Chef Leo Groden left Kensington Palace with

Margaret's kitchen secrets to sell to foreign magazines but an injunction stopped him offering his story for publication at home. While this dispute occupied the courts, Margaret was in Cannes but arrived late for a performance of the British entry at the Film Festival and was angrily booed by the audience.

Back home, her mind was exercised by Billy Wallace's wedding to Elizabeth Hoyer-Millar, daughter of Lord Inchyra, a distinguished British diplomat. It was a nostalgic moment when Margaret entered the church (St Peter's at Lavington Park, Sussex) where she had often worshipped with the groom – a rash suggestion by a wedding guest that there, but for the grace of God, she might have gone, was slapped down with an angry hiss. The wedding was said to have marked the end of the Margaret Set which had been dead for years.

As the last of Margaret's Mohicans settled into married life (a short one, alas, for Billy died early in 1977), her own marriage was fizzling out. She saw less and less of Tony and when they did go out together their behaviour looked like a public extension of a domestic quarrel. Taking her out reluctantly to dinner at a Charlotte Street restaurant, Tony took along a portable television set and put it on the table. Instead of talking to her, he watched Harold Wilson expounding Britain's economic problems, a subject of great topical interest – but not to Margaret. She berated her husband in front of the waiters – not the first and not the last time. Waiters of several restaurants soon treated their friends to lively and often imaginatively embellished accounts of spats between the couple and the echoes of raised royal voices reverberated all over town.

Behind his back she referred to him no longer as 'Tony' but – with a curled lip and heavy satire – as 'My Lord Snowdon'. She criticised him as harshly to his face. Their arguments were about nothing and everything: 'No topic could be discussed without Margaret and Tony rearing up on opposite sides,' said one who had witnessed many. The bickering embarrassed others more than it seemed to worry them. Tony published another photographic essay about some Chinese beauties including one Mimi Chen, a greengrocer's daughter, who strongly resembled Jacqui Chan. It was a coincidence but mitigated against him.

No wonder Margaret was unsettled. She suffered from bouts of migraine and in her darker moods seemed to accept that it was all over – bar their public life. There followed a phase when she wanted to patch things up but something always intervened, as when Tony went to the London Clinic for an operation and missed the royal family's Christmas get-together (as he did often enough to justify suspicions that his absences were intentional). He was visited by Margaret but also by the very attractive young Lady Jacqueline Rufus Isaacs, daughter of the Marquis and Marchioness of Reading, who lived near Tony's cottage (Nyman) in Sussex where he often retired for thought and lonely motorbike rides and heart-to-heart talks with Jacqueline. Margaret could not hide her anger and would not even join her family on their traditional visit to church. The royal holiday was under the shadow of another Margaret crisis.

The day Tony left for Barbados with his sister to recuperate, Margaret, who would not go with him but agreed to follow later, went somewhat ostentatiously to the theatre with Patrick Lichfield. Seeing their picture in the newspapers Tony was not pleased and did not receive his wife with open arms when she arrived in Barbados. A day or so later, she and Susan de Vesci dined with Vivien Graves, the wealthy American widow of an English writer. Margaret had a few drinks, became maudlin and dropped her guard: 'Tony does not love me any more', she said tearfully. (Tony's comment: 'My life is not a bed of roses.')

Attempts by friends to repair the damage – and the Queen's concern to avoid a scandal – failed to bring about a real reconciliation. The situation deteriorated relentlessly and, as separations grew longer, times together, in public or in private, became more strained. New men and old cronies stepped in where Tony no longer cared to tread. At a fashion show in Paris, Margaret was in the company of her old admirer, Robin Douglas-Home whose marriage to a model had been dissolved. One of the young men about town forever running after famous women, Robin boasted of a much-publicised holiday with Jackie Kennedy (before her marriage to Onassis) but their relationship had not been what it seemed. He had been drinking and gambling heavily and, not long after appearing proudly at Margaret's side, took his own life. Stories to the effect that he had killed himself because of his unrequited love for her were fanciful, and the authenticity of love letters she was supposed to have written to him – they were later offered for auction in New York – was questioned.

Margaret looked rejuvenated when Patrick Lichfield, dressed like a peacock, took her out again and again. She spent a weekend with him at Shugborough, his big estate in Staffordshire, where she put in a few hours on a motorbike. It was no secret that Tony had no great love for his fellow earl and fellow photographer. Was it jealousy? Not so, Snowdon partisans contended. Tony would never assume that Margaret would go too far with a member of her own family. She continued to entertain Patrick at her discreet dinner parties at Kensington Palace and saw a lot of him in Mustique where he was her neighbour. They remained friends when, as she and Tony headed for separation, Patrick married the handsome daughter of the wealthy Duke of Westminster.

Many things turned sour for Margaret as, for instance, her friendship with the Aga Khan who had welcomed her to Paris in the autumn of 1968 as the star guest at his wedding to the delicious Lady Sarah Crichton-Stuart. The following year in Sardinia when Margaret was under great stress and Tony paying scant attention to her, she was all the more demanding of others, and there was some irritation when Prince Karim, the young leader of the Ismailis, who watches over fate and fortune of millions of followers (and works so hard that he keeps three secretaries busy even on holiday) was not always at her beck and call. When he failed to turn up for her birthday dinner, she took offence, left abruptly and there was a rift which was only thinly papered over. She never went back to Sardinia but by this time Villa Jolie on Mustique and the Caribbean ambience was already exerting the strange fascination on her which has endured to this day.

For a time, Margaret and Tony were mercifully out of the news but not for long. They flew to Japan where Margaret was photographed with a gin and tonic in her hand and embassy officials tried in vain to suppress the picture. (At home there was an unwritten rule not to photograph royalty drinking alcohol and her detective frequently asked photographers to 'lay off because she might want a drink'. At this point it was worth noting the strange osmosis – when they first met, her drink was gin and his whisky; when they parted it was the other way round. From Tokyo, Tony went on alone to New York where he startled people with his rather unconventional outfits – he and David Frost were refused admission to a posh restaurant because they both wore roll-neck pullovers and no ties – but there was method in Tony's flamboyance which helped to publicise his new venture into clothes design.

As the split widened, Margaret was caught up in some embarrassing situations. Richard Burton told the audience at a film premiere in Margaret's presence: 'My name is really Richard Jenkins and up there is a lady whose name is Maggie Jones.' Margaret would have preferred to forget her married name, neither did she appreciate a gushing remark about London dockland although she replied: 'Yes, there are some divine places down there.' It seemed a long time since she had enjoyed them.

CHAPTER FOURTEEN

However different the backgrounds, there was no escaping the similarities in the lives, loves and public personae of the world's three most publicised *femmes entre deux ages*, as the French used to call them – Jackie Onassis, Elizabeth Taylor and Margaret. Uneasy marriages for ever on the point of collapse, a succession of escorts – not to say lovers – restless wanderings around the world, pretences at useful work (though Elizabeth Taylor actually made films), all possessed a fading star quality threatened by advancing years. Ladies in this category tend to be credited with stronger personality, greater libido and more boyfriends than women on either side of the critical divide.

For the way they behave it is often impossible to give a rational explanation, nor do they themselves always know why they are behaving as they do. Domestic traumas rub off on public performances, and vice versa. Tensions are all the greater when their exposed position forces them to pretend that all is well all the time. They are not immune to mundane problems which harass lesser women. Margaret was gaining a lot of weight, had been eating and drinking too much ever since Sarah's birth and, while still looking sexy (in a Diana Dors sort of way), was no longer everybody's favourite glamour girl. Nor was it always easy for her to find the right escort – how could a royal princess call a man and ask him to take her out; how often could she give her little dinner parties for close friends among whom a favourite could be discreetly included? Elizabeth Taylor was never short of suitors, Jackie Kennedy-Onassis, an inveterate husband-borrower, boldly commandeered men to attend to her but Margaret, on the three or four nights when she had no public or private appointments, was sitting at home wondering how to fill the evening while Tony was God knows where: 'She was often terribly bored,' said one of the young men who came to her rescue now and then.

Loneliness, strangely, made her envious of Tony's busy life and even jealous long after they had opted for separate tables and separate beds. Her *bête noire* at the time was Pamela Colin, the handsome *Vogue* executive who had worked with Tony on some of his contributions to the magazine. Tony's friends hinted that he wanted a quick divorce so as to be able to marry Pamela but anyway she married Lord Harlech. By the same token, Tony might have been jealous of Colin Tennant who was and still is happily married but, as Tony saw it, was responsible for Margaret's Mustique behaviour.

There were rumours that she planned an orderly retreat into private life. Personal matters were becoming more and more important to her while public duties often seemed to be peripheral. The princess people saw had less and less resemblance to the real Margaret. Yet she continued to attend to her public duties meticulously – one hundred and seventy-seven functions in 1971, one hundred and fifty in the following year – if only to justify the increase in the royal family's Civil List allowances; hers went up to thirty-five thousand pounds a year (and under indexing to protect it against the ravages of inflation reached fifty thousand by 1976). From a public relations angle it was bad luck that delivery of her new Rolls Royce coincided with the 1972 rise. With no such automatic source of income, Tony worked harder than ever. His film on old age ('Don't Count the Candles!') in co-operation with Derek Hart earned him an award, his documentaries about pets ('Another Kind of Love') and midgets ('Born to be Small') reflected his preoccupation with the aged, handicapped, disadvantated and vulnerable, and told as much about him as about them.

The success of the Constable of Caernarvon Castle in presenting the young Prince of Wales to the people of the principality 'with pomp and splendour' (Tony's formula) endeared him to the Queen Mother who took his side in his running fight with Margaret. Some members of the royal family felt, not quite fairly, that he was taking a closer interest in his children than their mother – David graduated from kindergarten to prep school at Ashdown House. While Tony embraced ever more worthy causes (he had just been acclaimed by Quentin Crewe, a celebrated paraplegic, for his design of a novel wheel chair), Margaret was seen to embrace men like Nureyev. When Tony went to Italy to photograph the world's happiest married couple, Sophia Loren and Carlo Ponti, it threw his own unhappy marriage into stark relief.

One way or another, that marriage was moving from crisis to disaster. Parallel with Margaret's weight problem, Tony exhibited some stress symptoms. Pursued by Raymond Belisario, the tiresome specialist in candid royal photographs, he overreacted. His car hit Belisario's 'accidentally' and Tony was fined twenty pounds. He was in another car crash while in the company of 'a mysterious blonde' but Colonel Eric Penn, the Queen's equerry, spoiled a good story by revealing that the lady was his wife and, besides, Jocelyn Stevens' sister. Tony could not have been in more respectable company. Still, he and Margaret continued their embarrassing trips together – to Kentucky to watch the Derby, to the Seychelles (for the anniversary of the islands' separation from Mauritius) and Australia. Margaret lost a dear friend when Judy (Montagu) Gendel died in Rome but continued to take an interest in Judy's little girl and looked her up whenever she was in Italy.

Early in 1973, Mustique beckoned and a lot of things began to happen. As if to gird herself for the fray, Margaret replaced Lieutenant Colonel Frederick Barnaby-Atkins with a younger equerry, Lord Napier and Ettrick who helped to steer his emotional charge through the most difficult passage in her life. Straws in the wind – Tony no longer even took anniversary pictures of his wife and children, leaving the field to Patrick Lichfield who seemed to share honours with Colin Tennant as Margaret's closest associate. That autumn, Colin, son and heir of tax-exiled Lord Glenconner, played host to a gathering of friends on the family estate at Innerleithen near Peebles. Among the house guests was Margaret, more relaxed and convivial than in many a month but every inch a Scottish princess in her native Scotland.

She held the centre of the stage during pre-dinner drinks and, if her figure no longer resembled an hour glass, her alabaster skin glowed in the refracted light from the chandelier and her eyes were a quizzical blue with the sheen of velvet or steel. She looked voluptuous, sensuous, much more alert than on many occasions when television cameras or photographers' lenses projected smouldering emotion as sullen temper and stillness as apathy. Her expression was expectant, midway between her superior come-hither signals and her forbidding 'Keep off!' warnings.

One of her fellow guests was a young man, in appearance and manner the type which had appealed to her all her life: Roderick Llewellyn, looking even younger than his twenty-five years. Margaret surveyed him critically, as she assesses everybody and everything, and seemed to like what she saw. Colin Tennant had invited 'Roddy' to Scotland to partner Margaret and to keep the male-female balance of the party even. It was not true, as was later suggested, that Margaret had driven to the station to meet her 'blind date' from the overnight train, grabbed him by the arm and did not let go of him . . .

He did, however, before the evening was out find himself in a corner with Margaret and received the crisp command which she often addresses to a new face: 'Explain yourself!' From her lips it was a compliment but there was not really very much to tell. As one of Colin's guests, Roddy's background was fairly predictable – good grounding at Shrewsbury public school, elder brother Dai much at home in the gossip columns and the arms of nubile debutantes (something to live up to) and a famous father loyal to his peripatetic sons: brewer Lieutenant Colonel Harry ('Foxhunter') Llewellyn – Foxhunter was the show-jumper on which he won a gold medal for Britain in the 1952 Olympics.

There was no comparable distinction on Roddy's escutcheon, only a minor job as research assistant at the College of Heralds, and some previous experience as a male model in South Africa where an agency adertised his vital statistics, or some of them, as '5ft 10in tall, very slim, good teeth, fair hands, can ride a horse, waterski, drive a car or motorcycle.' Roddy was one of those deceptively effeminate, attractive, very English Englishmen much like some of the R.A.F. 'Few' of an earlier generation. Casual about his clothes and hair, he often wore a silver earring which added a studied eccentricity and gave him the aura of a well-bred gipsy.

In the overlapping world of society and entertainment, Roddy had acquired the reputation of one irresistibly drawn to the stars of society or show-business and able to get very close to them. Here, in Scotland, he was face to face with the superstar princess and felt the pull of her personality. This kind of situation is bound to trigger off in people the sort of admiration and infatuation which flatters and often produces a rewarding reciprocal aphrodisiac effect.

It was a portentous encounter – princess and gipsy – and the beginning of a romantic friendship across an age difference of seventeen years. It changed Margaret's life because Roddy Llewellyn became the catalyst who finally severed the taut and tattered bonds of her futile marriage. He and Margaret met again in London where, in Tony's absence, she included him in her small dinner parties at Kensington Palace. It may well have been the reason why tension-prone Tony was back in hospital while Margaret was once more in Mustique. The pattern of their lives was fairly obvious – as she returned to London, he flew to New York.

At this stage Margaret decided that the time had come to cut the Gordian knot of her emotional tangles. She wrote a note to her mother explaining her feelings about Tony and their marriage and asking for help. Elizabeth would have to be told ... The Queen Mother was aghast. Blaming Margaret rather than Tony for the shocking state of affairs, she told her daughter bluntly that she strongly disapproved of her attitude, thereby making it even more hazardous to approach the Queen who had always had a soft spot for Tony. Yet, the matter presently acquired even greater urgency when Margaret's new association was spotted. Her friends tried to shrug it off as another of her foibles but Fleet Street was apprised by the mavericks of the aristocratic milieu, mostly relatives and friends who, for a handsome reward, kept gossip writers informed about each other's romantic peccadillos – gossip columns could not survive without these rich sources from the horsey set's own mouths.

On March 7th, 1974, Tony's friends, including Derek Hart and Quentin Crewe were at Scott's, the Mayfair restaurant, to celebrate his forty-fourth birthday. They toasted him when he arrived but the mood of the party was strangely subdued. There was no Margaret. Her absence was the most striking feature of the occasion. Margaret was in Mustique – and not alone.

Mustique – mystique – had changed since Colin Tennant had awakened with a kiss the sparsely-populated, sleepy little island near St Vincent in the Grenadines, revived the derelict cotton and sugar plantations, and built a landing strip to bring the tiny dot on the Caribbean map within half an hour's airbus ride from Barbados. It had grown into a tourist centre on the lines of the Aga Khan's Sardinia, only smaller, more select and intimate, and frightfully, frightfully informal.

Villa Jolie, Margaret's Georgian-colonial-style house atop a cliff at South Point was worth every penny of the thirty thousand pounds it had cost even without Oliver Messel's tasteful contribution which had been a labour of love. The villa was staffed with a native West Indian cook and a maid and Fraser, the gardener. Between visits Margaret let it mostly to wealthy Americans though her latest tenants (at four hundred pounds a week) had been Mick and Bianca Jagger. They enjoyed the island but missed the highlights of the season which coincided with Margaret's ennobling presence. Mustique was her very own hiding place which, apart from her detective, only her closest friends were encouraged to share : Colin and Anne Tennant, naturally, Lord Napier and his wife Delia, Michael Tree, Patrick Lichfield ... But evermore frequently she cast her net to catch some attractive local fish.

'Margaret behaves quite differently on the island,' I was told by one of her regular companions. 'Liberated from the royal grind, she is much more easy-going. Yet, by sheer dint of personality, she becomes the queen of the island, holds court, knows all her subjects by name – inhabitants, staff, visitors. She gets up late, lies in the sun until she is a deep dark colour, wades into the sea in her old-fashioned, one-piece swimsuit, never a bikini.' They talk about her old-fashioned ways, how she has stuck to stockings (instead of tights), how she still drinks gin when everybody else drinks vodka. With little else to do on the island, these are the things that get noticed.

Tennant's staff of some twenty personable young men, dusky Grenadinians and Belgravians (by birth or adoption) who control the work force, supervise land and house transactions and do other chores flutter around Margaret like a male chorus around the ballet mistress. Disengaging herself and retreating to her villa at the end of another day, she often says: 'See you for lunch tomorrow!' It means a picnic lunch down at the beach and the invitation embraces all the young men within range of her eloquent eyes.

Next day, everything stops for lunch. Hampers of food prepared in the Cotton House kitchen are carted to the beach with bottles of wine in cooling buckets. The menu is no problem because Margaret's culinary tastes are conventional – the royal kitchens never catered for delicate palates. The conversation is not very deep but flows as freely as the wine. In the company of the animated princess, the young men have a marvellous time – but she does not allow them to forget to address her as 'Ma'am', and God help any of them who permits himself an unguarded 'Margaret'.

She never notices when the young men in her party anxiously glance at their wrist watches as fingers move towards three, three-thirty or four p.m. She is totally unaware when impatience turns into panic as duty rosters collapse, posts at the hotel or the booking offices remain unmanned and telephones unanswered. She is in her element: 'It never occurs to her that we have jobs to do,' one of the young men sighed. 'She has a lack of awareness of other people's need to work.'

The occasional dislocations were a small price to pay for Margaret's stimulating presence. While the young men were back at work, she rested to emerge refreshed for a leisurely evening in the grounds of her villa or at Colin Tennant's house. The atmosphere was that of a tropical Somerset Maugham setting, smooth on the surface but pregnant with possibilities and a deep-down feeling that something, anything, might happen tonight, tomorrow, any time. A hint of excitement filled the air, the top people's version of holiday fever. So much to gossip about: perhaps a middle-aged American lady's getting over-enthusiastic about a booking clerk, or Basil, the Cotton House barman from St Vincent, paying court to a ravishing widow.

Before setting out on this latest trip to Mustique early in 1974, it occurred to Margaret that the young man she had first met at Colin Tennant's Scottish seat and had come to like would be a splendid companion on the island. She asked Roddy Llewellyn whether he would care to join her – she had already arranged for a couple of friends to stay with her at 'Jolie' but there was another spare room ... This is how Roddy came to be grappling with the problem of the expensive trip. He knew the Caribbean well – his father owned a house in Barbados – but some of his friends worried lest, not being very gainfully employed, he might find it difficult to raise the five hundred pounds fare. They underestimated either his resources or his resourcefulness, his determination and the magnetism of his hostess. Within a few days Roddy was in Mustique and installed in Villa Jolie. He fitted in well with the set-up : Colin Tennant and his crew, Margaret and her friends, swimming, sailing, lazing, drinking, talking, sleeping. Life in Mustique.

Even before Margaret had returned to London, reports of her house guest on the island had reached Clarence House and the Palace : 'The Queen Mother's dominant concern was still to save Margaret's marriage,' said one courtier, 'but the Queen was angrier than ever when Roddy seemed to become a permanent fixture in Margaret's life, visiting her regularly at Kensington Palace – where Tony hardly set foot outside his working area – or meeting her in the houses of mutual friends.' Parting from Tony which looked inevitable was one thing, but a scandal could become a threat to the Monarchy. The Palace watched apprehensively to see how much further Margaret would go with complete disregard for the repercussions. The answer seemed to be – very far. Friends defended her by reminding the starchy set that she had been in the vanguard of the swinging sixties and become the most popular member of the royal family – perhaps she was more in tune with the people of the permissive age than the ladies and gentlemen in the Buckingham Palace ivory tower.

Yet, her friendship was not running as smoothly as official and unofficial observers assumed. There was a hitch when she was in Mustique again in the autumn while Roddy was in Barbados waiting for an invitation to join her. Losing patience when it did not come, taking, perhaps, too much for granted and flying across the narrow stretch of blue sea off his own bat, he arrived at Mustique just in time to see Margaret leaving. She waved him goodbye and flew home.

Over the grapevine which links the London residences, country houses and night clubs of the livelier aristocrats came news that Roddy Llewellyn was suffering from deep depression. Fallen from grace! Dropped by the Princess! The discarded young man was said to be pining and hiding away with his father in Wales. Brother Dai commented: 'Poor Roddy!' It was not as grim as it looked and it certainly did not last. In a trice, Roddy was back in royal favour. New dinner invitations, hours behind closed doors. This, some initiates whispered, was not a passing infatuation after all. It seems that this person in Margaret's life had somehow inspired the colourful, mysterious collage she made with her own hands, a wooden board adorned with an old Dinky car, a moth, a scrap of tapestry, a pen nib, a pheasant feather, a piece of burnt parchment, a child's fan. A puzzle wrapped in an enigma – what was the meaning of it? 'A private message,' was all Roddy would say.

His message to her was that he had found a new interest which he shared with a number of friends, mostly fringe aristocrats with proud names yet remote from the regular pastures of their famous families. In partnership with seven others, he had acquired Surrendell Farm in Wiltshire, some three hundred acres of land and a near-derelict house which only just qualified as a 'manor'. Having restored the house, they tended the land living as a commune – 'Drop-outs!' they were called locally. Among Roddy's companions on the farm were painter-sculptor Sarah Ponsonby, daughter of the Earl of Bessborough's heir presumptive; the Earl of Caithness's half-sister; a Courtauld, and more of that ilk, with the odd film couple thrown in; a free and easy lot who had turned their backs on the beautiful people and lived together, worked together, played together. Roddy's chief contribution was his knack of growing vegetables which earned him the nickname 'Green Fingers'.

He spoke so glowingly about the simple life close to the soil and far from social pressures, that Margaret was infected by his enthusiasm and decided to see for herself, an opportunity for Roddy to return her hospitality. Their association was over a year old when she first took the road in the direction of Bath, best known outpost of civilisation, before reaching a cluster of small villages and – Surrendell Farm.

The commune made Margaret feel at home. After a very informal lunch she was shown over the farm and poked around in Roddy's vegetable patch – weeding, she said. New people dropped in and it was difficult to know who belonged and who did not. In the evening, with Roddy pounding the piano, Margaret joined the others singing such ancient favourites of hers as 'Chatanooga Choo Choo' and 'Blue Moon'. She promised to come again and, though accommodation and facilities were not up to the standard of the well-appointed residences she normally frequented, returned to Surrendell Farm for a week-end away from it all, almost as good as Mustique; the remote, simple life as, she imagined, ordinary people lived it. As with Tony in Rotherhithe, she felt transported into another world. She was also followed by watchful eyes and careful note was taken of her doings and associates for further reference, if necessary.

Although matters were obviously coming to a head, it was a tortuous business with many baffling interludes. At one stage, Roddy Llewellyn disappeared from his regular haunts and turned up in Istanbul, of all places, followed by frantic in-quiries from Kensington Palace. Soon he was back in London where Margaret was helping him to decorate his new flat in Fulham. Then – with her taking an active interest – Roddy and his friends from the Surrendell commune launched a restaurant, Parsenn Sally, in Bath as an outlet for their 'organic' farm produce. One of Roddy's chores was to deliver the vegetables in his battered blue Bedford van. Margaret dined at the restau-rant at a time when the promoters were still their own best customers.

Presently the incongruous couple were off together on a cheap flight via Luxembourg to the Caribbean, a fateful trip. Was Margaret heading for a place in the history books as the guilty party in a constitutional crisis? Not for years had she given her-self over to the good life with less inhibition. In retrospect, one of those present thought there might have been a hint of bravura – or was it despair? Margaret danced the nights away with a succession of partners including Basil, newly promoted deputy general manager of the Cotton House. No, she had not deserted Roddy who was never far from sight. A photograper roaming the island soon caught in his lens what he had come to catch – Roddy and Margaret in their swimming gear in sweet harmony at a seaside sundeck. His photographs, the first of the couple together, soon reached Europe. They were published by

German magazines (which are obsessed with the peccadilloes of British royalty) and were reproduced in Britain by the burgeoning newspapers of Rupert Murdoch, the Australian press tycoon. It was the end of the worst-kept royal secret in the realm – that Margaret and her husband were no longer living together as man and wife.

Although it has been said that the royal family welcomed the publication and the forays of *Private Eye* into Margaret's private life as a means of preparing the public for a shocking situation, it is a highly questionable theory. The truth is that the Queen and the Queen Mother were angry about the untimely revelation because it made the scandal public just when they were busy discussing with Margaret how to avoid it. These discussions were said to have been heated. The Queen Mother took a stronger line than the Queen, but sisterly love was strained to breaking point. Margaret who could not anyway plead concern about 'the church's teaching' again wanted a divorce. The Queen who did not have the power to stop her pleaded for a compromise – a separation.

Neither the Queen nor her faint-hearted advisers appreciated that a marriage problem, even a royal one, was no longer the emotional issue it had been in Edward VIII's time. A separation, while it might disturb a small minority, would at worst raise a short rumpus which would soon subside. They should have known that in spite of sporadic sniping from the extreme left the monarchy and the Queen were too soundly based in the lives of the people to be shaken by such a little local difficulty. Once Margaret was persuaded to agree to a separation, the Queen discussed the matter with the Archbishop of Canterbury (shades of Townsend).

It was likely that there would be a divorce once Margaret and Tony had lived apart for two years by which time even diehards would accept it. All that was heard from the Archbishop was an expression of concern for the well-being of the children. In a climate of growing bitterness a rumour spread that Tony had asked his wife to give up Roddy for the sake of the children, about to enter public school. But the real truth was that a parting of their ways, separation or divorce, which had been in their minds before Margaret had met Roddy, had been postponed again and again until the children were old enough to cope. It was decided to send David and Sarah to Bedales, the co-educational boarding school in Hampshire which (when my own daughter joined it a generation earlier) was already progressive and liberal and made life easier for youngsters from broken homes before separation and divorce became widespread.

Little else could be saved from the ruins of this inauspicious marriage. The Queen had no option but to accept Margaret's decision. To obstruct her, had it been possible, would only have made matters worse. In official language: Her Majesty gave her consent for Princess Margaret and the Earl of Snowdon to separate. Lawyers quickly settled all points at issue. Tony was to receive an amount to compensate him for the loss of his grace and favour residence (assumed to be around the eighty thousand pounds which he eventually paid for a house of his own in Kensington) since Margaret was staying on at 1A Kensington Palace. Margaret was to have custody of the children and Tony reasonable access; he also undertook to make a contribution to their upkeep.

A weightier consideration was the official statement which would shape public reaction to the bombshell about to be detonated at Kensington Palace. It had to be phrased so as to serve not only the interests of both parties but take account of the Queen's Crown and Church. At this stage, Jocelyn Stevens, man of the world, experienced newspaper executive and friend of the couple was called in for advice. After discussing the problem with Margaret and Tony who each had a lot to say for themselves and each wanted their side of the story to be publicly stated, he went to see the Queen and the Queen Mother who were hoping for a quiet, dignified end of the affair. Stevens hammered out a draft statement which owed much to his suggestion to keep it short and to the point: 'I helped,' he said modestly.

That his newspaper had a head start with the news of the impending split ('Margaret and Tony set to part,' said the *Daily Express* banner headline on Wednesday, March 17th, 1976) was a by-product of his efforts. The press, in fact, played a bigger rôle in the final phase than was generally appreciated. Pending an official statement which was expected within a day or so, other papers could only copy the news for their later editions, some using a question mark as an escape hatch just in case. No need for such caution. A Palace spokesman told *The Times* that Princess Margaret's marriage had been discussed by the royal family which was as good as confirming the facts. That evening, by an uncanny coincidence, Group Captain Peter Townsend talked on the B.B.C. radio about his former chief King George VI, but did not mention the Princess who seemed, with another leading man, to be engaged in a repeat performance of their experience twenty years earlier.

As behoves royal persons, the chief protagonists in the drama played it cool. Margaret in a long white gown looking more svelte than of late went to the National Theatre while Tony drove to Heathrow Airport to catch a flight to Australia to supervise an exhibition of his photographs. Two days later, on Friday, March 19th, at two-thirty p.m., the last shred of uncertainty was removed when a brisk, simple statement was released from Kensington Palace: 'H.R.H. the Princess Margaret, the Countess of Snowdon, and the Earl of Snowdon', it said, 'have mutually agreed to live apart. The Princess will carry out her public duties and functions unaccompanied by Lord Snowdon. There are no plans for divorce proceedings.'

At this precise moment, Margaret and the children were on their way to join the Queen Mother at Royal Lodge, Windsor. She looked wistful, thoughtful, but whatever was deduced from her appearance was deceptive because, as with most people concerned when such matters come into public view, she had long assimilated the situation. Some ten thousand miles away in Sydney, Tony seemed less in control of his emotions when he talked to reporters. 'Desperately sad ... pray for the understanding of the children ... every happiness for Princess Margaret ... love, admiration, respect for her sister, her mother, her entire family ...' The Queen was 'naturally very sad' and Margaret's press secretary, Major Griffin, said that separation had been a possibility for some time and, bearing the interest of the children in mind, was the best course. Someone close to Margaret agreed that it had been 'a rough marriage' which was putting it mildly.

The other party in the tangle, Roddy Llewellyn left the commune and was last seen by his fellow communards running across the fields ... He, too, had drawn up a statement but Lord Napier to whom he read it over the telephone told him to hold his horses. Colonel Llewellyn (might he have been in line for a knighthood?) said angrily that neither he, his wife nor anyone else had anything to say. He had not reckoned with his son and his son's friends being 'captured' by the *Daily Express*. The picture of Margaret and Roddy at Surrendell Farm which heralded the beginning of the end was reproduced with a neat double-entendre caption: 'The picture a husband could not take.' Somewhere along the line, one of Roddy's girlfriends on the farm was photographed topless tilling the soil.

Acres of copy about Roddy and the commune, echoed all over the world, created the impression that, by her association with him, Margaret, and Margaret alone, was to blame for the sad end to the marriage. If 'dear Jocelyn's' newspaper presented her in this manner what sympathy could she expect? As her rapidly swelling collection of press cuttings showed, she did not altogether lack supporters. Among those rallying to her side was, surprisingly, Nigel Dempster who had been the first to publicise stories about her and Roddy. Margaret, disregarding dire warnings from friends ('What if Dempster turns?'), had been on typically erratic on-and-off terms with the gossip columnist. 'She just likes him,' one of her friends said despairingly.

People assumed that the noisy reaction to the separation would put a stop to Margaret's association with Roddy Llewellyn, and that, surely, no more would be heard of the man. They were wrong. 'They never stopped seeing each other,' I was told. Roddy was reunited with Margaret at a friend's house and, again, at Kensington Palace. A secret tryst? Yes and no. He was staying at the London house of Lady (Virginia) Royston who was as infatuated with Mustique as Margaret. 'Virginia and I are old friends,' Roddy told a reporter adding with a chuckle: 'Wouldn't everyone like to know that I am in London!'

It was tantamount to advertising his presence. Naturally he was observed turning up in his old van at Kensington Palace that evening at eight p.m. and, again, leaving five hours later. The incident, particularly his remark to the reporter, provoked a devastating reply from John Junor, the ascorbic Editor of the *Sunday Express*; 'I can tell him someone who does not give a damn where he is,' J. J. fulminated, 'or whether I see or hear of him again.' The paragraph's nasty sting was in its tail: 'And that goes for his lady love too.'

As an epilogue to a royal episode of considerable social

significance, it sounded like a modern version of Ludwig Uhland's poetic 'Troubadour's Curse', invoked against an offending monarch:

> Your name shall be forgotten,
> Clothed in eternal night,
> Shall, like a final gasp, be
> Hissed into empty void!

Far from it. The events would be referred to time and again because they marked a long step forward from traditional hypocrisy (beyond the Earl of Harewood's divorce and re-marriage, sanctioned by the cabinet to relieve the Queen of any ecclesiastical responsibility; and several matrimonial complications among the Bowes-Lyons) which had condemned royals to continue desperately unhappy marriages rather than face the scandal of separation or divorce; they also marked a throw-back to a less strait-laced period when royals could discard or decapitate wives, take lovers, remarry and generally do as they pleased.

The Wiltshire commune dispersed, the restaurant in Bath passed into other hands, Roddy Llewellyn disappeared briefly but was in Margaret's company again as late as 1977. On the threshold of a dangerous age, Margaret herself kept a lower profile and appeared to her friends to behave less impulsively because, they thought, she no longer strained against intolerable marriage shackles. Having proved to herself that nobody, not even the Queen, could prevent her from doing exactly as she liked; having realised that, conversely, nothing she did could detract from the Queen's personal authority and prestige, she began to mend her fences with the royal family; and, though she was neither asked for nor would have given, a promise of good behaviour in the future, she was welcomed back into the fold.

Another kind of honeymoon came into being and, like all honeymoons, it will not last for ever. If behaviour patterns in similar, if less exalted quarters, are a guide, the odds are that Margaret will shock again or at least extend the narrow frontiers of royal tolerance a little further. She will, of course, continue along the never-ending path of royal 'duties' and functions, trip from gala premieres in the cinema to first nights in the theatre, go backstage to greet old stars and meet new ones; she will fly off to Mustique while the fascination lasts to shed the royal garb and put it on again for Balmoral, Sandringham and Windsor.

In whatever guise she appears, she will remain the younger sister, never reconciled to her status. Second-best, even to a queen, is no place an alert mind inhabits gladly; yet royal eminence is not conducive to the new relationships that people with old hang-ups desperately need. It does not look likely that she will ever be really happy, or much happier than she has been – except at brief phases in her life; she will be consumed by the same passions that have agitated her in the past. The Townsend trauma may still haunt her in one form or another although, while the unhappy outcome left a tremendous impact, I do not subscribe to the view that her happiness was destroyed for ever when she could not marry the first man she loved. Neither do I accept that the Queen really thought or said, as a royal author (Robert Lacey) suggests, that Margaret would have been better off married to Townsend. The Queen, like everybody at court, knew all along that Townsend, however heroic he was in the war, was not a strong-willed he-man but, on the contrary, hesitant and indecisive, a far weaker character than Margaret.

Rubbing shoulders with *la vie de bohème* was another experience that has left an indelible mark on Margaret and made her dissatisfied and bored with conventional companions, male or female, such as were available to her. It is at the root of her constant search for better or, anyway, more stimulating company. Her sexuality will for some time manoeuvre her into unorthodox situations and she will continue to provoke fantasies and keep the rumour factories churning out stories about her. That they are so persistently proffered at home and abroad goes to show how much excitement Margaret generates, how many people think her capable of extraordinary behaviour, how uneasy lies the head the wears the coronet. A royal princess by vocation, sometimes exuberant, often frustrated but always obstinately doing her own thing and sticking her neck out, she resembles a trapeze artist whom people watch with fascination but expect to fall and end up with a broken neck. Few wish her ill but many perversely hope that she will provide the ultimate thrill – or scandal. Her programme may be dull, but Margaret herself rarely is. Whether on duty or on holiday, alone or in company, separated, divorced or remarried (as she may be sooner than many think) she remains a colourful character actress on the royal stage. And liable, at any time, to steal the show.

INDEX

Laszlo, John de, 79
Laszlo, Rosemary de, *see* Townsend, Rosemary
Legge, Mrs Gerald (later Lady Lewisham, Dartmouth and Spencer), 95
Legh, Major Francis, 137, 157
'Les Ambassadeurs', 56
'Les Girls' (film), 132
Lichfield, Patrick, Earl of, 11–12, 14, 69, 187, 191, 193, 194, 198, 201
Limburg-Stirus, Countess van, 124
Linley, David, Viscount, 171, 175, 188, 189, 198, 207
Lipton, Marcus, M.P. 90, 157
Llewellyn, Dai, 199, 204
Llewellyn, Lt.-Col. Harry, 199, 208–9
Llewellyn, Roderick, 13, 30, 199 200, 202–3, 204, 205, 206, 208, 209, 210
Logue, Sheila, 152
Longest Day, The, (Cornelius Ryan), 163
Lopez, Mrs Giuseppe, *see* Coombe, Carol
Lopez, President, of Portugal, 115–16, 118
Loren, Sophia, 198
Lorentzen, Erling, 80
Loss, Joe, 159
Lovat, Lord, 59
Lowther, Jennifer, *see* Bevan, Jennifer
Lowther, John, 113
Lyford Cay, 187

MacDonald, Bobo, 51
MacDonald, Ruby, 73, 100, 157, 166
McEwen, James, 67
McEwen, Robin, 67, 93, 94
McNeill, Jane, *see* Dalkeith, Countess of,
Macmillan, Harold, 142
Mafalda, Princess, 143
Manchester Guardian, 116
Margaret, Princess, Countess of Snowdon; birth at Glamis Castle, 18; relationship with Elizabeth, 20–4, 27–8, 30, 131–4, 142, 170; introduction to Philip, 25; introduction to Peter Townsend, 29; importance of Philip's relationship with Townsend, 34–8; visit to South Africa, 39–46; and the Margaret Set, 56–8, 59, 73, 95, 122, 192; visit to Italy and France, 63–5; and death of George VI, 77–9; and the Townsend affair, 88–94, 103–20, 133–4, 138–9; tour of Caribbean, 100–3; tour of East Africa, 123–4; introduction to Antony Armstrong-Jones, 126; further visit to Caribbean, 137–8; visit to Canada, 140–1; to Rome, 142–3; to Portugal, 143–4; engagement to Antony Armstrong-Jones, 149–51; wedding, 159–61; birth of son David, 174; birth of daughter Sarah, 182; marital problems, 186–90, 192–5; visit to USA, 189–90; and Roddy Llewellyn, 199–200, 202–5, 209–10; separation from husband, 206–8; *et passim.*
Margaretha, Princess of Sweden, 141
Marina, Duchess of Kent, 24, 63
Marks, Derek, 85
Marlborough, Duchess of, 98
Marlborough House, 92, 145–6
Mary, Princess, Duchess of Teck, 69
Mary, Princess Royal, 53, 63, 74
Mary, Queen, 18, 29, 53, 75, 78, 86
Matapan, Battle of, 35
Mathieson, Isobel, 166
Maugham, Somerset, 129
Messel, Maud, 156
Messel, Oliver, 85, 125, 129, 201
Michael of Rumania, 51
Middleton, Dr, 174
Milford Haven, David, Marquess of, 50
Milligan, Spike, 13, 129, 185
Milroy Club, 56
Mills, John, 56
Mitchell, Major Michael, 177
'Monseigneur' (night-club), 65
Montagu, Judy, 62–3, 94, 95, 122, 142, 183, 198
Montagu-Douglas-Scott, Lady Alice, 50
Montagu-Douglas-Scott, Lady Caroline, 53, 55, 60
Montague-Smith, Mr, 152

217